DENS.]

BVDA
VNGARIAE CAPVT
...les. vulgo OFEN.

C

D

E

F

...æ Virginis nunc Meskita. D. Colles viniferi. E. Bassa Budensis.
...x facinus perpetrandum paratum: Dellij vulgo appellantur:
...us lege plura in descriptionibus Turcicis Ioannis Lewenclauij.
...aglius Anno 1617.

S.]

An Illustrated History
of Budapest

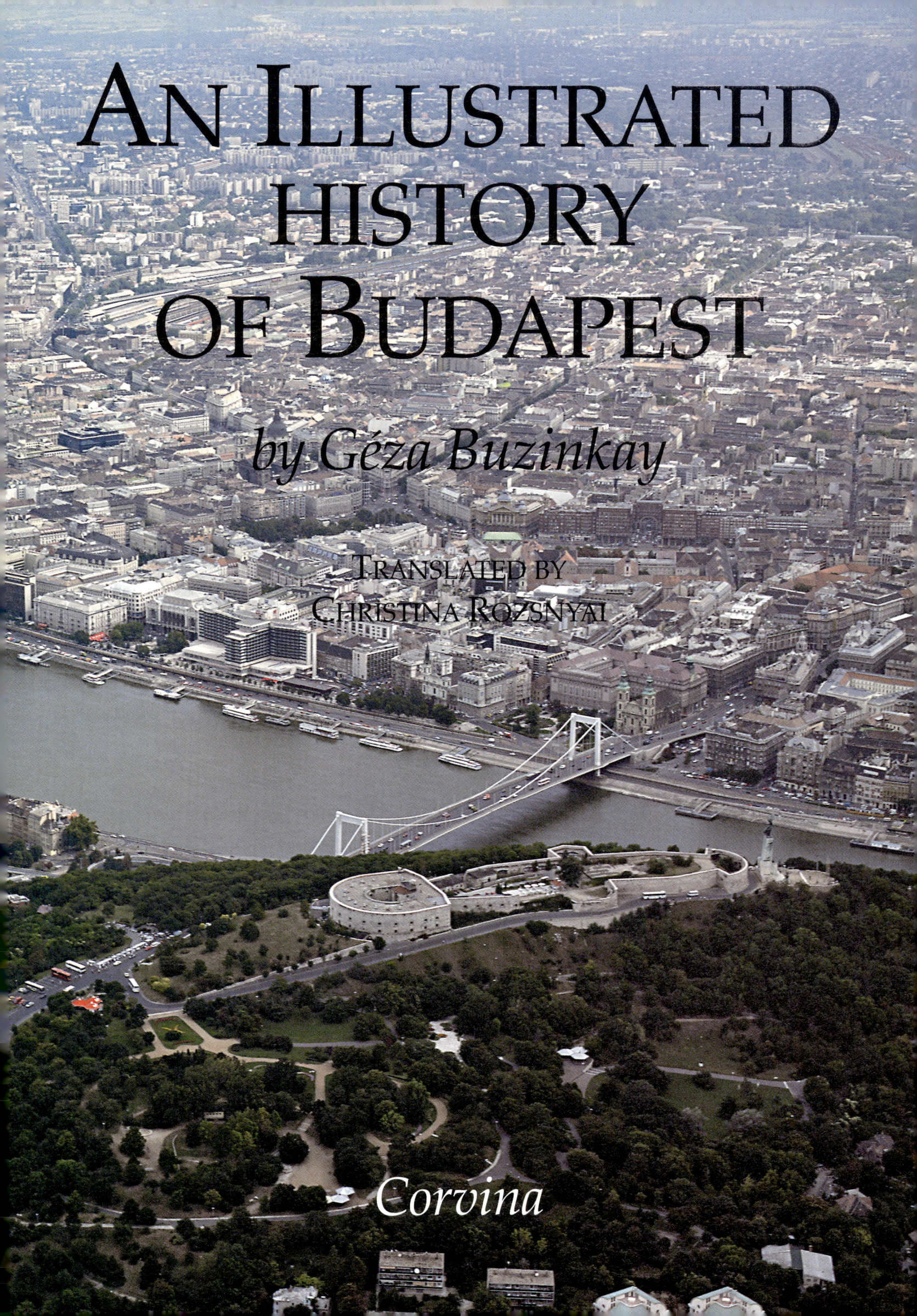

An Illustrated history of Budapest

by Géza Buzinkay

Translated by Christina Rozsnyai

Corvina

Contents

*To the memory
of my mentor and friend
Péter Hanák*

Introduction

However visitors come to Budapest, they promptly regret not having been born a bird. They realise that they have not the advantage of grasping the complete terrain. Nature has provided the pedestrian a recompense: Gellért Hill. Hovering above the Danube, the steep rock makes a splendid viewpoint from which to survey the changing landscape below: the hills of Buda, the barely rising amphitheatre that is Pest, and between them the imposing river, segmented by islands and bends. There below is the metropolis with its vast expanse of buildings that appear so close that one can make out the separate houses within a given block (provided there is no smog – for which there is a fairly good chance).

Visitors to Gellért Hill, whether foreign or local, are overwhelmed by the sight time and again. Budapest is frequently described as a city of unmatched beauty, second only – say those eager to appear objective – to, say, Lisbon, or Rio de Janeiro – depending on one's tastes and experience. A romantically inclined patriot may put it in something like the way Imre Áldor did in 1866, "[...] The eye proudly scans the vast terrain that is the Hungarian capital. [...] All the beauty that God has bestowed on the earth is reconstituted here in utter brilliance. [...] Thus I pose the question, [...] Could a more fitting site have been chosen for the capital?"

Why, in fact, was this particular place selected to become the capital of Hungary? Was it simply the natural beauty that our forefathers, those "men of such noble constitution", perceived? Was it selected at all? By whom, and when? Perhaps it just developed into a capital? Was it made, or did it make itself?

A profusion of questions not easily answered.

Especially if one considers the environmental shortcomings of the place, most notably the dust clouds that on occasion used to settle into mud, long acknowledged by otherwise enthusiastic visitors, locals and city planners. Count István Széchenyi, the man who conceived modern Budapest, in the mid 1830s wrote an entire book on the subject. In it he remarked, "Given a choice I should suffer anything more willingly than to live forever deprived of the lovely colours of nature, as in Buda-Pest; [...] an ashen shroud extends as far as the eye can see, the charming hues of nature are absent, and there is always the vexing sand to contend with." The claim of this being a Paradise on Earth has just as often been challenged.

To put it succinctly, Budapest became a capital, and in many respects the centre of the Danube region, because of its favourable location along a convenient traffic route. It grew into a metropolis following set – albeit repeatedly disputed and modified – plans. It is a city that was designed and built according to a scheme, and yet its most distinctive marks were left by involuntary forces. To resolve this paradox is to tell the story of Budapest. And one more point: Budapest's is not the history of Hungary. This fine and often barely sustainable distinction is a matter of careful consideration: the stories of capital and country must not blend. This book is about how the city – cities – functioned, about the lives of its inhabitants over the centuries and millennia. National matters come into play only in as far as they affected the life of the town, the city, the capital.

Where Prehistoric Peoples and Cultures Met

One look at the map immediately shows why Budapest has always been an important place. It is close to Europe's geometric centre, it is at the cross-roads of geographic regions and of civilisations, at the intersection of ancient trade routes. Mountains that gradually slope into gentle hills converge on a great river and a vast plain. Mediterranean Latin, Alpine German and, from the east, Slavic civilisations meet here: this is the focal point of Roman Catholic, North-European Protestant, and Greek Orthodox/Byzantine cultures.

Budapest is a young city. This is generally understood to mean that the city's centre is barely more than a hundred years old, or that the city has the sprightliness of youth and dynamic development. Indeed its youth is even more basic, because the land itself is young geologically.

The region began to take shape some 200 million years ago. It was then covered by ocean, whose dolomite and limestone sediments shaped the Buda hills that now slope onto the Danube. For 90 million years all this area was dry land. Geologically this was an uneventful period. Then, some 70 million years ago, the upheavals began that moulded the landscape into what it is today. Once again it was covered by ocean, from which what were to be the Buda hills emerged as islands. The areas under water had marl coated onto the limestone. Some 40 million years ago the forebears of today's hills, János-hegy which with its 529 meters is the tallest of the Buda hills, and Hármashatárhegy, rose while their basins sank and the terrain became fragmented. Some of the caves that are a feature of the area today were formed at this time, eventually and much later producing hot springs, which in turn created natural landmarks such as the Pálvölgy dripstone caves. At the edge of the range, protrusions rose which have now become the fashionable residential area of the Buda Hills, Márton-hegy, Orbán-hegy, Nap-hegy, Ferenc-hegy, and the more appropriately named Rozsadomb, or Rose Hill.

From that time on the Buda Hills have always been above water, which only reached into ravines. The ocean sediment, called "Kiscell clay", covered the entire Buda terrain. In the period around 11 million years ago, volcanic activity was the shaping force, leaving behind the Visegrád and the Börzsöny Hills. At the time the Mediterranean covered the plain of Pest, extending to the southern edge of the Buda mountains. The water receded only three to four million years ago, after being landlocked for some time. Two million years ago the Buda range took on its present shape, and a million years later, in the Pleistocene period, the early Danube deposited gravel and sand on the Pest side. On the Buda side thermal waters formed springs which, as they grew into lakes, created limestone deposits. (Lime condensed as the water, rich in calcium and hydro-

carbonate, was evaporating.) As the lime petrified, it trapped countless plants and marine animals, turning them into fossils. The loose layers of tuffaceous limestone formed a vast cave system, including the present ten-kilometre network that runs under today's Castle Hill. In these caves Neanderthal man found shelter and protection, because of their many escape routes. Much later the caves became multilevel cellars for the houses built above them, as well as military facilities.

The Danube shaped its environs less than one million years ago, cutting ever more deeply into the land. It created five levels, like the Kiscell plateau in Óbuda or the Budafok Hill. The lowest level, in Pest, extending all the way to Kelenföld, would still be a flood area today if it were not for the dams and embankments now in place. The sand deposits of the Danube make up the terrain on which Pest was built, and the lower level areas of Buda.

Near Budapest's city limits, in the valley cutting through the Érd plateau, archaeologists have uncovered one of the earliest human settlements here. Some 50 thousand years ago Neanderthal man sited a hunting camp here, since it intersected an animal migration route. A group of 30-35 people hunting within a radius of about 30 kilometres hoarded their prey, or at least as much of it they were able to carry, to the encampment. Beside the great number of smaller animals found here – bears, wolves, cave lions and hyenas, wild horses, wild donkeys, and reindeer – there were also mammoth, buffalo, woolly rhinoceros, and giant red deer. The latter's antlers had a spread of some 3.5 meters.

The hunting camp, situated in a gorge shielded by steep cliffs, consisted of two parts. One was used as a workshop and dwelling; for this we have the testimony of the remains of a fireplace, along with tools, cutters, drawing-knives, scrapers and drills fabricated from local stones, for which there are chippings indicating that these were manufactured on the site. The other pit contained animal bones, most of them of bears, and was used as a "larder" for meat – some 7 tons of it. In this cold period before and during the last Ice Age, when even average July temperatures rarely topped 16 °C, they covered the pit with soil, a practice primitive tribes have followed well into the twentieth century.

The source for the flint used to make the tools was discovered above Denevér Street in the community of Farkasrét in the Buda Hills. Hard stone used for striking, and mining tools made from antlers have also been found here. The excellent hunting grounds and sheltered camp were used for some 15 thousand years. The tools are from the same culture that originated in the south of France and spread from the Mediterranean all the way to this most distant north-eastern frontier.

It was much later, between 4600 and 3900 BC, that the first permanent settlements were established on the Buda side near the Danube. The inhabitants belonged to the widespread Central European Culture, as indicated by their linear-pattern pottery. They polished their stone implements and produced numerous bone utensils, and nets for fishing. They practised agriculture and grew grain, built their houses of wattle and daub; archaeologists have even been able to reconstruct a loom. They made vessels

1. *Inside the Pálvölgy Caves*

bearing the faces of animals or humans for cultic purposes, and buried their dead in a reclining position with wares and implements placed into the pits for use in the afterlife. Remains from this culture were unearthed as far north of today's Budapest as Békásmegyer and as far south as Nagytétény.

From this period on the territory, with the river and its fords offering excellent trading routes, has been continuously inhabited. The population was by no means stable, however, with a great variety of peoples and tribes from the south, south-east, and south-west making their home here at various times. Around 2000 BC a fierce group, that knew the use of the bow and arrow and domesticated animals, arrived from the west, probably from the Iberian peninsula. Relics of that Bell-Beaker Culture, as it was named after its red-burned, bell-shaped vessels, have been found everywhere from Northern and Southern Europe to Northern Africa. In Central Europe the culture reached as far as the Danube. Several settlements have been uncovered on Budapest's Csepel Island, including the remains of a large, pillar-supported structure.

Aquincum, a Town Established by Celts and Romans

Among the various tribes competing for the occupation and settlement of the region, the people arriving from the Alpine Rhine area after 14 BC, who buried their dead in mortuary mounds, or *tumuli*, were those who conclusively determined Hungary's attachment to that part of Central Europe that looked to the West for its cultural orientation. The territory along the middle reaches of the Danube was their frontier. The nomadic Scythians, of Iranian origin, settled near the Danube fords; later the Illyrians populated the whole Transdanubian territory. A tribe of theirs, the Pannon, settled here, and gave their name to the region, Pannonia. The Illyrians were conquered in the early third century BC by another Indo-European group, the Celts. They made this territory a part of the first extensive European civilisation, since their culture spanned the whole of the continent, from the British Isles to Spain, from Transylvania to the Black Sea and on to Anatolia in Asia Minor.

The Celts that occupied the area of Hungary brought with them the La Tène culture, named after the town on Lake Neuchâtel in Switzerland. Its art is characterized by geometric ornamentation blending with stylised, images abstracted from nature. In what is today's Békásmegyer, the northernmost district of Budapest on the Buda side of the Danube, they established a settlement; here they engaged in agriculture, manufactured iron implements, and used the pottery wheel to fashion their earthenware.

After 60 BC the Eraviscans, one of the few Celtic tribes whose name has come down to us, populated much of the area of modern Budapest. In addition to Békásmegyer they had major settlements around the ford in Tabán, north of Gellért Hill, and a fortification, their centre of power, on Gellért Hill from which they could overlook the Danube crossing, the place where Erzsébet Bridge stands today. Lofty fortresses, called *oppida* in Latin, were the feature of the settlements the dominant Celts built all over Europe; these were at one and the same time used for defence and as religious and economic centres where coins were minted. The Budapest *oppidum*, discovered as late as the 1990s, is the earliest forerunner of a town here.

The Celtic *oppidum* gave rise to a separate stratum of society which built its houses apart from those of the agrarian population, and the widespread use of money testifies to the existence of merchants also. Celtic society was advanced enough to allow individuals to amass considerable fortunes, as seen, for example, in the magnificent women's clothing found in many tombs. Their houses were built in a regular rectangular layout from wood, or wattle and daub, with a pole in the centre supporting the gable roof. The houses were recessed in the ground or else carved into caves. No ritual sites have been discovered, though well-developed cultic practices can be deduced from the countless finds from Roman times of mother and fertility goddesses, of gods of war and death that they had adopted. In Aquincum – itself a Latinised Celtic name – the remains of a circular temple surrounded by columns for a mother goddess has been unearthed.

The Celtic settlements were finally subjugated by the army of Augustus Caesar around the time of the birth of Christ. With this commenced the Roman presence in the area, which lasted for more than four centuries. In the fourth decade of the first century the defences along the Danube were set up. This line of defence, known as limes, took on special importance at the end of that century. The camps – one of them, Aquincum, can be seen in today's Óbuda – of the four legions established in the Province of Pannonia were completed around this time. Between the camps, auxiliary camps were set up at a distance of some twenty to thirty kilometres. The ruins of two of these have been discovered in Albertfalva and Nagytétény. As a consequence of a military and administrative reorganisation in AD 106, East Transdanubia became in independent province, Pannonia Inferior, with Aquincum as its seat. Its significance as a frontier against bar-

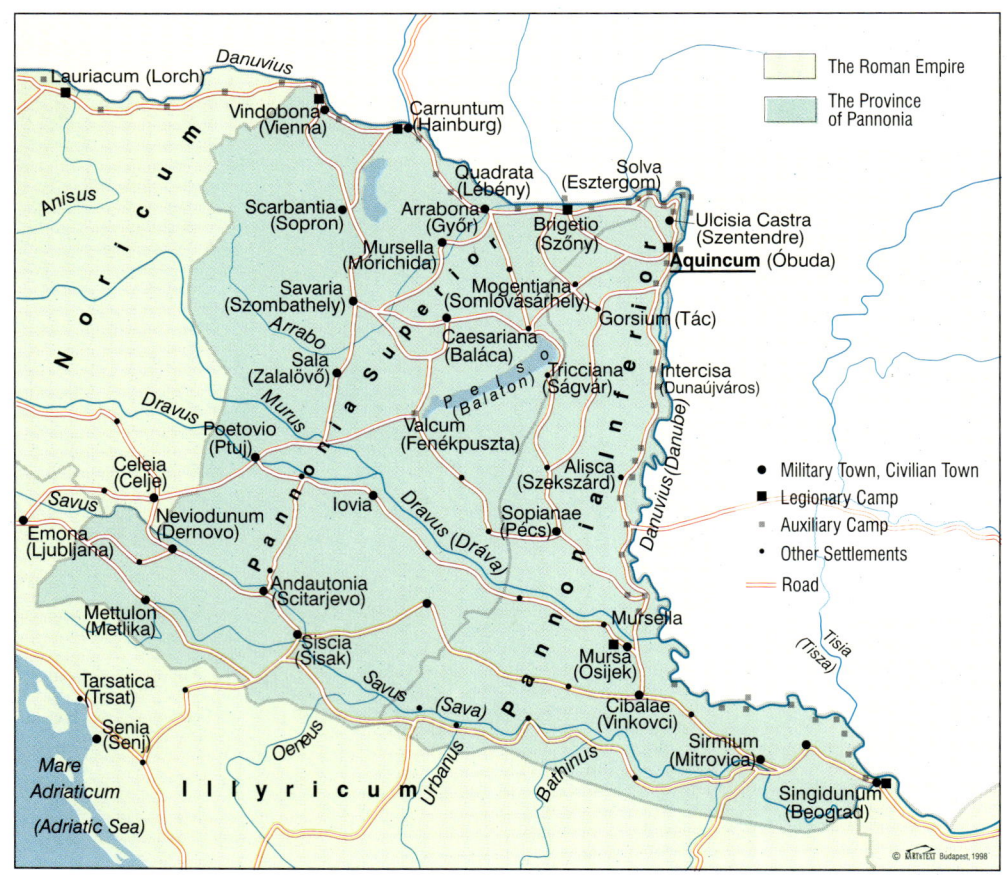

2. *Camps and settlements in Roman times in the Province of Pannonia*

3. *Roman settlements and camps within present-day Budapest*

barian attacks was considerable. Several of the governors were to become emperors. The first was Hadrian, who ruled the province between 106 and 108, when he raised the governor's palace on the Danube island near Óbuda. Later, in 124, he conferred municipal status to the civilian town of Aquincum. This affected more than simply the town's administrative ranking. While its inhabitants had hitherto been considered vanquished Celtic subjects, those among them who were elected into the leading municipal body, the *magistratus*, now became Roman citizens. Aquincum was ruled by the governor, who was responsible both for the army and public administration. His residence on the Danube island was a magnificent two-story palace laid out on 120 metres by 120 metres. (It can no longer be seen, since after World War II the deep, concrete foundations of a large assembly plant of a Soviet-administered shipyard were constructed over it.) However, the inscribed, votive altar stones each governor placed into the palace shrine at the time of his inauguration, are in the

Museum of Aquincum, along with the remains of the palace murals and sculptures, and the surviving fragments of the mosaic floors from the rooms used for official functions and from the bath wing.

In the central courtyard of the Governor's Palace stood the official sanctuary of the imperial cult, and in front of the main entrance the larger-than-life-size sculpture of the reigning emperor. Ingeniously, the head of the toga-clad figure was fastened to the neck by dowels to facilitate replacement.

The names and more or less detailed biographies of the 48 governors of the province of Pannonia Inferior are known. The career of Caius Iulius Septimius Castinus, for example, was typical for Rome. He was a relative of the Syrian-born wife of the emperor Septimius Severus, and alternately held numerous civilian and military offices during his lifetime. He began as a military tribune in Rome, went on to become financial officer or *questor*, and later still tribune of the plebs, and trusteeship judge. He then went on to take several positions as judge or praetor for different cities in Italy. After that he was named governor of Crete, followed by the position of commander-in-chief of the

9

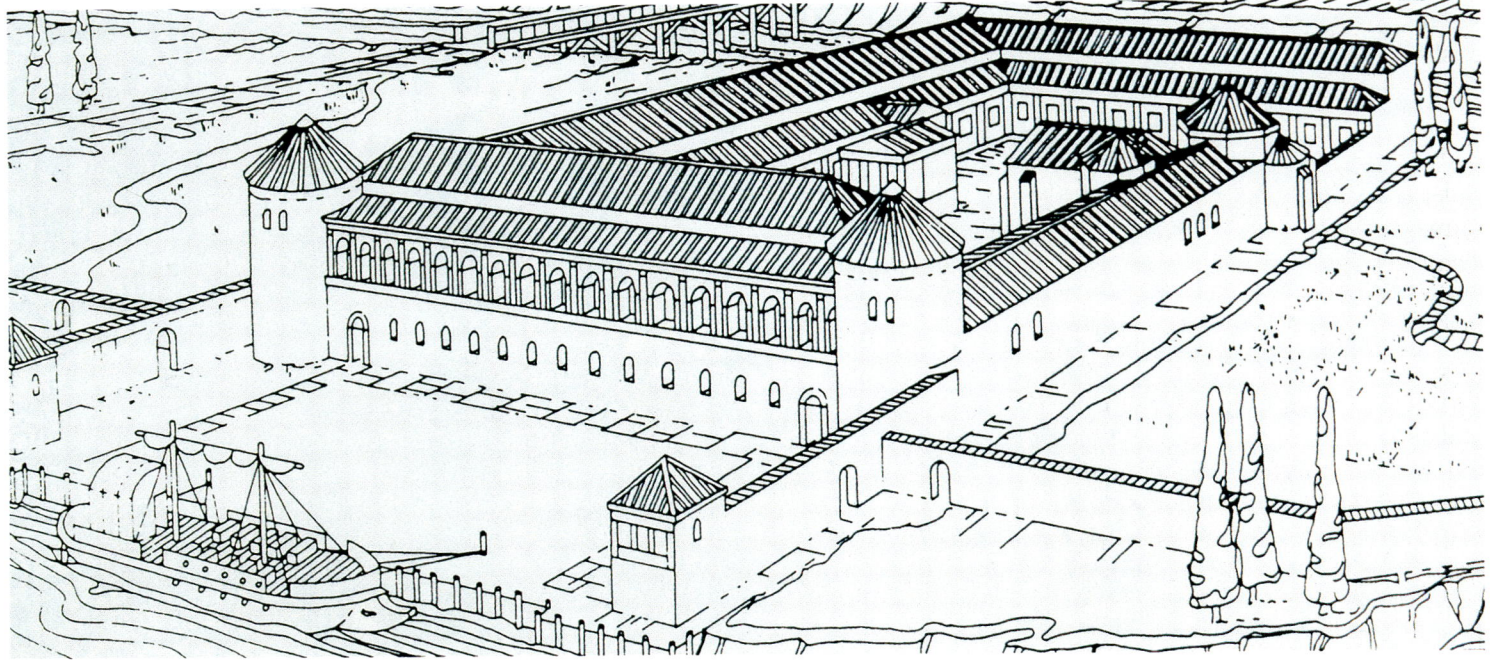

4. *A reconstruction of the Governor's Palace*

legion in Germania, then sat on the governor's throne of Pannonia between 209 and 211, and finally returned to Rome to become consul.

The centre, or *castrum*, of the legionary camp stood near today's Flórián Square in Óbuda, at the foot of the Árpád Bridge. It housed a garrison of some six thousand men in addition to auxiliary troops.

5. *A mosaic floor depicting the story of Hercules and Deianeira, excavated in a Roman villa in Megyfa Street*

6. *A Mithras shrine in Aquincum*

The Aquincum legion, or *legio II adiutrix*, stationed previously in Britain and Germania, was mustered from citizens in northern Italy and western European provinces, with some north Africans. They had received some schooling and knew something about literature, mythology, and jurisprudence, thus bringing with them and disseminating Roman culture and civilisation. The function of the Roman army was not only to conquer, but to spread culture and bring civilisation to the peoples it came into contact with. It installed Roman law and public administration, architecture and civil engineering, including the building of roads and bridges, and town infrastructure, including aqueducts and sewage systems, street networks and baths. Wherever the Roman army stayed and set to building – its main mission in times of peace – it erected cities after a common plan and with facilities which citizens could live and feel at home in, whether they happened to be in northern or southern Europe, Asia Minor, or the Iberian Peninsula.

Remains of the legionary camp are displayed in the pedestrian underpass at Flórián Square. At the centre of this extensive camp surrounded by high and thick walls, bastions, and a double moat, were the headquarters of the commander, which also housed the camp shrine. Surrounding it, following a set layout, were barracks, assembly halls, officers' quarters, stores, arsenals, workshops, the baths, gymnasium and infirmary, along with aqueducts and sewage systems and a network of streets. The governor's suite, around five hundred, was headed by one of the century commanders. He was in charge of the guard and of the messenger service, as well as of the intelligence service, of the judges for public administration and criminal cases, and of treasurers. The office also oversaw the scribes, archivists and librarians, and the officials in charge of all areas of public administration and foreign affairs.

Like other civilian and manufacturing settlements surrounding military camps or fortifications, Aquincum was known for its lively commerce. In contrast to the disciplined and transparent set-up of the camp itself, the military town, home to over 20 thousand inhabitants, had winding streets, some unpretentious barracks, shops, and an always busy street life. Its heart was the town's most important establishment, the large, enclosed forum.

On the southern edge of the town was the larger of the two amphitheatres of Aquincum. With a capacity of over ten-thousand, the monumental structure with its tiered seating testifies to the fondness of the Roman populace for bloody animal and human contests.

7. The civilian town of Aquincum and its amphitheatre

Two kilometres north of the legionary camp was the civilian town, containing some 15 thousand inhabitants. Its administration was conducted by a municipal council of one hundred members. The town officials, two mayors, the supervisors of public buildings and public works, and the financial counsels, were chosen from among them. The public officers had to have private fortunes – the minimum of which was set – since they received no remuneration for their function. When Aquincum was conferred municipal status, the local Eraviscan aristocracy, wealthy landowners, rose to acquire significant influence in town government. The interiors of the villas unearthed in the area show the splendid lifestyle of this section of the population.

It was freed slaves who had managed to acquire a fortune of their own who made up the class of those engaged in trade and finance and the order of priests. The lowest municipal order was that of the artisans, who formed corporations, or collegia, to protect their interests and carry out public duties. One such corporation was responsible for fighting fires. From the ruins of their headquarters a singular archaeological find, a portable water organ, has been discovered.

The civilian town also had its amphitheatre, though it held a mere three to four thousand spectators. Adjacent to it are the foundations of the quarters of those who had the chief role in the contests – the gladiators.

ALT OFEN.

population, the local inhabitants were joined by newly arriving Germans, Sarmatians and, sometime later, the Avars. Houses were shared by several families, the large rooms were subdivided, and the altar slabs were plastered with mud to be used as fireplaces. While the Roman lifestyle disintegrated, the new settlers found themselves in a vastly more civilised way of life with the buildings and equipment they were in possession of. The workshops of the Roman town were still in operation during the Hun occupation, and it was in these that they manufactured their daily implements and women's jewellery.

Villages close by with a Celtic population were considered suburbs, and their inhabitants were without Roman citizenship. The administration of these was assigned to the civilian town. Such outlying settlements were Vindonianus (Békásmegyer) and Vicus Basoretensis (Kiscell).

From the late second century on the composition of the civilian town, and its leadership, changed. To joining the original Celtic and Eraviscan population and subsequent settlers, mostly from Italy, Gaul, and Germania, came immigrants from the east, Syrians and Jews from Asia Minor. Later they even were even to become the majority in the government of the town.

This same change also led to the spread of eastern cults and mystery religions, such as the cult of Mithras. The remains of seven shrines have been uncovered. Behind the altars are sculptures of Mithras with one knee on the bull as he sacrifices it. He is surrounded by numerous symbolic images, including the Sun, Moon, a Snake and a Scorpion. Not much is known about the cult, apart from its popularity with the army and the fact that there were two grades of initiation its followers had to pass through.

From the beginning of the third century Christianity spread in Aquincum, with an early Christian basilica erected around the middle of the century. Its spread affected the lifestyle. The bloody contests in the amphitheatre were discontinued, and valuable artistic objects connected to the earlier cults, such as sculptures of the gods, fell prey to the new religious enthusiasm.

For more than four centuries, the region had flourished as part of the world's most developed and organised civilisation. Now not even the Empire, much less its cities, were able to withstand the new waves of invasions from the east and the repeated onslaughts of barbarians. Aquincum had to be destroyed to survive.

By the beginning of the fifth century the civilian town had been deserted, only a garrison of Huns and Germans remained in the fortress on the Danube shore. In the fortified military town, which offered protection to the civilian

The Huns, the mounted tribe of nomads tribe led by Attila, the subject of so many subsequent legends, could not adapt themselves to living in stone dwellings. They refused to settle in Aquincum for quite some time. Yet the name of Buda (originally designating what later became Óbuda) purportedly stems from Attila's younger brother who, while Attila was busy campaigning in the West, renamed Aquincum after himself. When he learned about it on his return, Attila was furious. He killed Buda and decreed that the town take on his own name. Another form of Attila was Etele, known to the Germans as Etzel (the name he went by in their Niebelung legends) and Aquincum's successor supposedly was known for some time as Etzelburg. The dull truth is, however, that the name stems from a much later period. Buda was the name of the King's legate, a judge of the royal court here, in the eleventh century. It was a commonly used name during the time of Árpád dynasty (tenth to thirteenth centuries), and it is from him that the settlement most likely took its name.

In the late 430s the first wave of Hun invaders destroyed everything in the town that could have been used in its defence. For a good century afterwards Pannonia and the area Budapest occupies today were not unlike the battle scenes seen on the cinema screen. A succession of bloody skirmishes were fought on horseback, with one band barely distinguishable from the next. If they paused to recuperate they were soon driven on by the next mounted horde following on their heels. One such people were the Lombards; on their way to northern Italy they stopped to rest here. After the Easter of 568, they concluded a pact with the Avars whereby they quit the territory.

The Avars, whose origins are mysterious, ruled here from the last third of the 6th century, and under them the region recovered some of its former importance. Initially they settled only on the Pest plains, their chieftains making their seat on the north of Csepel Island. Later arrivals established their main settlement on the Buda side.

A Provostship in Óbuda and Kiln Settlements in Pest

The Avars were overcome by Charlemagne in the early ninth century; Transdanubia, along with the area around the Danube Bend, was annexed to the Frankish Empire. It was at the end of that century that the Magyar tribes arrived, and there are indications that they, too, recognised the significance of the central location of the Budapest area. Five of the seven tribes settled around here, and both the principal chieftains established camp at this site. One of them was Árpád, the chief warrior. According to Anonymus, the first Hungarian chronicler whose name is not known, Árpád and his warriors "... proceeded along the Danube to the large island. They set up camp near the large island, whereupon Chief Árpád and his noblemen marched onto it. When they saw the bounty and richness of the place, and the advantage of the water of the Danube, they exceedingly rejoiced in it. They decided that it was to be hence and for ever more the island of the chief, and that all noble persons should be given a court and manor there. Directly Chief Árpád hired artisans and had them build splendid houses for the chieftains. Then he decreed that all horses, exhausted over many days, be brought there to graze. He assigned a clever Cumanian, who was called Csepel, to oversee his grooms. As it was the home of the Master of the Horse, the island is named Csepel until this very day. Chief Árpád and his noblemen and their man and woman servants sojourned there in peace and power from the month of April until the month of October."

The other principle chieftain, who was in charge of sacral matters, was Kurszán, and he established himself in Óbuda. He thought the former military amphitheatre was a palace and used it as such; it was known for centuries thereafter as Kurszán's Castle. After his death Árpád appropriated all powers to himself, including the estates of his co-chieftain, and transferred his seat to Óbuda. It is here that the chronicler Anonymus believes him to have died in the year 907. A "white church" was erected over his tomb. The site has never been found, but once or twice each generation of professional and amateur archaeologists makes attempts to find it, with fresh zeal.

In every difficult period of Hungarian history, and especially in the light of the recurring foreign occupations – of which there have been plenty – distraught pundits and popular jokes charge their Magyar forebears with having chosen a place of transit to make their home in, rather than moving on to the more secure territories further west. But in fact, they did try. In over half a century of forays into much of western Europe, the Magyar hordes pillaged wherever they went, while congregations trembled as they prayed, "Save us, Our Lord, from the arrows of the Magyars." That their pleas were heard, however, was only a matter of time. In 955 the Magyars suffered a devastating defeat near Augsburg.

The grandson of Árpád, Taksony, became the survivors'

new chieftain. He established his seat on the left bank of the Danube across from Csepel Island. The community of Taksony still bears the memory of this Magyar leader. Surrounding the camp, close to the fords, Islamic merchants settled for an extended period. They played an important part in the establishment and early development of Pest.

During the of Magyar raids on the West, Óbuda remained the princely seat. However, it lost this status when Géza, who became leader of all Magyar tribes (972-997), changed the nation's political orientation toward the West and established his seat in Esztergom (Gran). Perhaps his decision to move was inspired not only by his desire to be closer to the West but by a lingering aversion to the town of stone. The prominent twelfth-century poet and chronicler, Otto von Freising, stemming from the medieval Austrian Babenberg dynasty, noted that "their quarters are quite shoddy, as the houses are made of reed, rarely wood, and even more rarely of stone, and therefore they live in tents throughout summer and autumn." The Hungarian queen gave a tent as a present to Holy Roman Emperor Frederick Barbarossa in 1189, when he passed through Hungary en route to the Third Crusade. During the visit the king took him hunting to Csepel Island and the environs of "Buda," i.e. Óbuda.

Hungary's first king, Stephen I (997-1038), who established the kingdom as a Christian state and was canonised before the end of the eleventh century, did not regard the area or the remnants of the town and civilisation here as a suitable location with respect to administration, religion or economics. Nonetheless he established a consequential institution in Óbuda, the Religious Chapter of Saint Peter, which in the Middle Ages became the town core. The cluster of outbuildings, stores, residential buildings and the church probably stood near today's Fő (or Main) Square. This set of buildings, devoted to administrative and church functions, was later expanded to accommodate the King on occasion. A Danube ferry was adjacent. Along incoming roads artisans and merchants settled, and a typical medieval European town, with its double centre began to evolve.

Erected and expanded by kings, Óbuda – or Buda, as it was then called – had by the twelfth century evolved into a town of major importance. By royal charter it had been given sole fishing rights in the Danube for the entire stretch between Szentendre and Csepel islands, and it grew wealthy on the customs levied on Danube shipping and through other levies. Its provost ranked as one of the kingdom's highest dignitaries, one of them even holding the office of royal chancellor also. The man who signed the Gesta Hungarorum, the first Hungarian chronicle, as "P dictus magister," and was consequently assigned the "name" Anonymus, is thought to have been Péter, Provost of Buda under Béla III (1172-1196).

Not much later, from the reign of Andrew II (1205-1235) on, (Ó-)Buda gradually grew from a centrally located town into a capital and royal seat. With increasing frequency, the king would hold the spring legislative and juridicial sessions, falling around Lent, in the town. The region covering today's metropolitan Budapest was by now filled with settlements, and there were many legends promoting its high standing.

Around the year 1000 settlements were established at the Danube crossing to the south, near today's Erzsébet Bridge.

Initially Pest was raised on the ruins of a Roman fortress called Contra-Aquincum, and facing it on the Buda side was Little Pest, which in modern times became the Tabán neighbourhood. On September 24, 1046 this was the scene of a tragedy. The spread of Christianity that had begun barely a generation earlier was met by ferocious pagan revolts. Bishop Gerard (Gellért to Hungarians) of a noble Venetian family, had come to Hungary on Stephen I's bidding, as a tutor to the king's son Emeric (he too was later canonised). Gerard subsequently became the Bishop of Csanád, wrote Hungary's first theological treatise, and was a compelling disseminator of the faith. On that fateful day in September, he was 66 years of age, an old man. The medieval Illuminated Chronicle describes the scene as follows. "As Saint Gerard the Bishop was of small stature and all his strength had been depleted in the service of God, he was travelling by carriage. On reaching the [...] ford the villains, that is Vata and his satanic lot – they offered their souls to the devil – assailed the Bishop and all his companions, and showered them with stones. Saint Gerard persistently cast the sign of the cross on those who stoned him; seeing this their fury grew further, they attacked him, and overturned his carriage at the Danube bank, put him onto a cart, and rolled him off Kelenföld Mountain. And as he was still breathing they pierced his chest with lances, then shattered his brain on a stone." In commemoration of this episode the hill was renamed Gellért Hill. Soon a chapel was erected on it, which survived for five hundred years, until the Turkish occupation. In 1904 the Saint Gellért monument was raised on it, whose giant figure overlooks Erzsébet Bridge.

The heart of Pest took on was is generally considered its "original" appearance in the fifteenth century. An "original" of this sort must, of course, have its precedents. It was already in the fifth century that areas around the fords began to be developed. Szenterzsébetfalva, later shortened to Szentfalva (around the present Egyetem Square) was established at this time, soon followed by Bécs, or Újbécs, around today's Martinelli Square. The three settlements existed side by side for some time, had independent legislatory bodies and developed individually. Towards the end of the eleventh century the ancient highways running to the Danube were turned into streets. On the plots along these stone buildings were raised, and with these constructions the Roman remains gradually disappeared. In a corner of the former camp, a splendid parish church, a basilica with two towers and a nave with two aisles was erected. The Church of Our Lady, still on this site, though in reconstructed form and now known as the Belvárosi ("Inner City") Church, has imposed a twist in the road leading off the modern Erzsébet Bridge. The roads converging on the church were broadened here to make up Pest's main square. Facing the south portal stood the town hall, west of it a large complex containing a huge oven. Structures such as this, usually sunk into the ground, were facilities for preparing, baking, and preserving food. Cave-like, they were originally used as lime kilns; without any need for remodelling, they also made excellent wine cellars. The kilns became the feature of Pest settlements in this period, and gave Pest (and Bécs, one of the neighbouring settlements – both meaning "oven") its name. The still-used German name for Buda, "Ofen," can likewise be traced back to these kilns. The "quite large and wealthy German town", as a contemporary chronicle had it, was of course protected by a stone wall, built to be impenetrable.

Neighbouring Szenterzsébetfalva – literally "Saint Elizabeth Village" – was once a settlement of tents and wooden houses that was torn down in the latter part of the 1100s. A unique chapel of pink stone, surrounded by a graveyard, was built on the site. The village took its name from Elisabeth (Erzsébet in Hungarian) of the House of Árpád. Sister of Béla IV, she married the margrave of Thuringia, and was canonised soon after her death for her good deeds and selflessness in caring for the sick.

Beyond the town wall to the north was Bécs, with its own array of kilns and a spacious stone palace that must have been a royal court. The area was of some importance for the inspection of traffic on the busy Danube crossing and harbour where today's Vigadó Square is located. For the purpose of securing the considerable revenue from customs, a harbour was constructed at the Danube bank, with stone pillars for a pontoon bridge and wooden, stone-reinforced docks. Set between the Pest walls and Szenterzsébetfalva, a cluster of monastery buildings for the Dominican order was erected in the 1220s or '30s. It was an enormous structure, permitting refuge for ten thousand people.

In the memory of Hungarians, the "Mongolian invasion" is synonymous with utter devastation. It occurred in the thirteenth century when Mongolian hordes stormed into Europe from Asia. Their manner of attack, by invading en masse on horseback while releasing a shower of arrows, did not much differ from that of the Magyars who had terrified the west of Europe three hundred years earlier.

In early spring 1241 King Béla IV convened the leaders of the realm in (Ó-)Buda, and crossed over into Pest in mid March in anticipation of his troops. For a month battles raged around Pest before the main Mongolian force readied for the final attack on April 16th. The Dalmatian prelate Thomas, Archdeacon of Spalato (now Split, Croatia), chronicled the event as follows. "The Tatar army, after setting up camp all around, began to attack the town from every direction, shooting arrows relentlessly, and showering it with spears. On the other side the hapless Hungarians took up the fight against them and tried to resist them with all their might. They strained their catapults and crossbows, hurled innumerable spears and arrows into enemy ranks, and propelled many rocks with their ballistae. But the Tatars' deadly arrows struck their targets with exactitude, and thus caused certain death. No cuirass, shield or armour could resist an arrow launched by a Tatar hand. [...] So great was the blight befalling the town of Pest as God's vengeful sword wallowed most profusely in Christian blood. [...] Over a hundred thousand men died a terrible death in a single day and within an area not at all large. [...] The water of the Danube was red with human blood. When barbaric death had raged to satisfaction and they withdrew from town, they set fires of every sort, and before the enemies' eyes the greedy flames devoured all."

To this day archaeologists encounter a thirty-centimetre layer of ash and charred wood where the Pest settlements had stood. Only the crumbled town wall of stone remained.

The Danube, quite broad and deep at Pest, was able to check the Mongol warriors – but only until it froze over. In late January their main force was able to cross the ice. The Mongols burned (Ó-)Buda to the ground, along with countless other towns on this side of the Danube, and failed only where they encountered stone fortresses. Having discovered the Mongol weakness, King Béla initiated extensive reconstruction as soon as the horde had withdrawn. Their withdrawal was quite sudden and unexpected: it turned out their Khan had died and they had been summoned to assist in the struggle for the suc-

10. *The coat of arms of the university in Óbuda, 1483*

cession. The destruction they left in their wake was not confined to buildings: the royal seat, that had begun to emerge in (Ó-)Buda, was shattered. Its new development would take a different turn.

Immediately after the Mongols' departure the king commanded the fortification of the towns and castles in the realm. Apart from this physical reinforcement, his plan called for granting the towns privileges to strengthen them economically too. Very soon came the news, however, that the Mongols were returning, and the reconstruction was interrupted. In 1247, Béla IV ordered the population of Pest and (Ó-)Buda to remove themselves to Buda's Castle Hill, and to immediately begin the construction of a modern, fortified town. When the Pest population resettled on Castle Hill they brought along their town charter (re-issued in 1244 after the original had fallen victim to the Mongols) making the town of Pest legally a suburb of Buda. Though Pest was quickly reconstructed and its commercial significance restored, it retained its subordinate position for a good one and a half centuries. Even the town's highest official, the chief magistrate, was nominated from the Buda magistracy.

In Pest, meanwhile, as the thirteenth century drew to a close, a new town was taking shape, upon and within the old one; the people that settled it were conscious of living in a town with a history. Pest's civic pride was bolstered also by another factor. From 1286 on, and with increasing regularity, the king convened the representatives of the medieval Hungarian nation, the country's ecclesiastic and secular dignitaries, on the field adjacent to Rákos Creek, on the outskirts of Pest. These were memorable times: for centuries afterwards the Hungarian nobility referred to the Rákos-Field "Diets" as the occasions when it had been capable of challenging its king.

The reconstruction following the devastation retained the urban structure of old Pest and integrated the new buildings into this. One such new construction was the Franciscan monastery on today's Ferenciek, i.e. Franciscan, Square. It was a noted edifice, as it was the venue of the celebratory masses attended by the Diet in the 1280s and '90s. The church on the site today was raised in the eighteenth century.

The town grew, gradually expanding to areas beyond the ruined walls. To the north, touching on the Franciscan monastery gardens, was the square where livestock markets were held. The Dominican monastery was reconstructed. In Szenterzsébetfalva, whose name was soon abridged to Szentfalva, the church was rebuilt, though in a coarser version; the main square of the settlement took shape, and finally, for a century and a half, it was raised to the rank of a market town. It became a centre of Pest county, at least to the extent that county meetings were held there.

11. *A relief fragment carved by an Italian master in Óbuda in the mid 12th century*

Pest, a Thriving Medieval Commercial Town

The development of Pest accelerated during the reign of Sigismund of Luxemburg, King of Hungary (1387-1437) and Holy Roman Emperor. Sigismund contributed considerably to the town's progress, most notably when in 1406 he awarded it its own royal charter and thus restored its independence from Buda. The parish church was rebuilt in the Gothic style, its chancel is still extant in that form. The houses of the increasingly wealthy and independent burghers were clustered in the town core, while the king acquired Újbécs to erect a fortified castle in place of the palace that earlier stood there. The gate tower stood where today's Váci Street runs into Vörösmarty Square; its layout is marked by stone tiles on the modern pavement. The large tower of the castle stood at the intersection of Váci and Régiposta Streets. The castle, raised by French master builders, remained unfinished; even the completed parts were demolished at the end of the century.

During the reign of King Matthias (1458-1490) the burghers had attained such affluence that they launched on a wave of construction. There was hardly a house that was not rebuilt or at least remodelled, refurbished and modernised. They again reconstructed the Parish Church, completely demolished the Franciscan church and monastery to erect new edifices in their place, of a size that

12. Hatvan Gate as it stood in the late 18th century, shown on a painted trade sign from 1836

13. Layout of Pest in the late Middle Ages

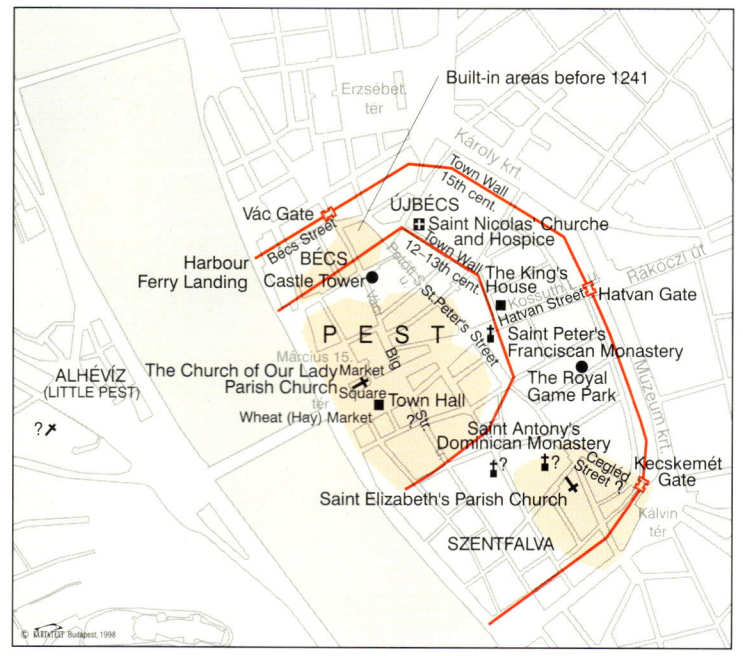

could, and did, house the king, his entourage, and the members of the Diet all at once when the house was in session. The Pest residence of King Matthias probably stood nearby. Pest by now looked much like Buda, differing only in scale, with fewer mansions and the somewhat less pompous houses for its burghers, contrasts only natural between a capital and its precinct. In fact Pest's status as a precinct of Buda was by this time a mere formality and outdated. In 1469 Pest had obtained the right to elect its independent, twelve-member magistracy and, after securing several additional privileges, it came to be regarded as the country's second town before the century was over. Now the town wall was raised, largely along today's Small Ring. Sections of it can still be seen in courts of buildings and

bastions. One of them later housed the first theatre in Pest for half a century, before it was razed in 1815.

The main street of medieval Pest was Váci Street, then going by the name of Nagy, that is Large. It was lined with splendid houses owned by wealthy burghers, and near the main square by Hungarian-owned butcheries. Another main thoroughfare was Kecskemét, then Cegléd, Street where landed lords and patricians holding high functions had their mansions.

The process which Pest underwent as it discovered its potential as a commercial town, and developed as an urban centre after the mid-thirteenth century, was just the reverse of Óbuda's, which had held administrative significance up until that time. By the mid 1400s the royal palace in Buda Castle had clearly taken over as the seat of power, gradually attracting officials and merchants from Óbuda to join the burghers who had relocated there earlier. In 1343 King Louis the Great (1342-1382) bestowed the castle of Óbuda onto his mother, Queen Elizabeth; from this time on it was always the property of the queen consort. On the site of the destroyed Chapter House of Saint Peter's the queen had a new parish church, Saint Mary's, erected, and established a convent of the Order of the Poor Clares, securing its income from the

14. *The town seal of Pest, 1481*

integrated into some of their walls. Finally, in the early 1500s, the large, fortified municipality received its charter as a free royal town.

The area within the walls was now over twice the size of the old fortified town, it included, in addition to Pest itself, Újbécs, Szentfalva, the Dominican monastery, and the municipal hospice., Szent Miklós Hospice, built around this time. This common town wall manifested the expansion of Pest and the inevitable integration of the other settlements. The town could be entered through three gates, Bécs, later Vác Gate (at Váci Street); Hatvan Gate (on today's Kossuth Lajos Street not far from Múzeum Ring); and Kecskemét, or Cegléd, Gate (on Kálvin Square at Kecskeméti Street). On the Danube side were raised round

levies on the Danube ferries. Some years later, in 1355, the king divided the town between the queen and the Chapter. With that Óbuda enjoyed fewer privileges than both Pest and Buda, because the Chapter's property became a market town. The southern section was the queen's, and contained the market and ferry landing; the northern part was the Chapter's, and known for its fine ecclesiastic buildings, it evolved into a settlement with a strong ecclesiastic character. In the Chapter's school instruction was excellent. In fact the quality of teaching was so high that in 1395 King Sigismund established a university with four separate faculties attached to the school. However there were no fortifications raised around Óbuda. Left without defences the Turkish army devastated it in 1526.

Buda as a Medieval Royal Seat and a Free Royal Town

Before the Mongolian invasions there had been a village known as Little Pest (subsequently Tabán) which expanded along the slope of the future Castle Hill to the north-west. Compared to Pest and (Ó-)Buda, this was a community of minor significance, and was burned down by the Mongolian hordes along with the rest. Yet the Mongolian invasion drew the king's and court's attention to the advantages the location offered. The physical features of Castle Hill made it ideal as the place for a town that, in time of need, could also offer shelter to the population surrounding it. When news spread of another impending Mongolian attack, the fortification of the hill was stepped up and the king commanded the inhabitants of Pest to move there. This same strategy was followed in several

other of the major towns in the kingdom, a comprehensive scheme that enjoyed the financial support of the Pope as well.

In Buda it was easy to use stone for construction since much of it could be excavated locally, eliminating the necessity of bringing it in from distant quarries. Castle Hill possessed natural caves from which limestone could be extracted, and which could also be used as cellars - or for shelter when danger threatened.

Within a relatively short time, a new town of considerable size was erected. Construction proceeded according to a plan, which was not a custom in that age. Initially the houses of the civilian population were raised, from the north all the way to the royal residence at the southern tip of the Hill. By the middle of the thirteenth century a wall, one and a half metres thick and six to eight metres in height, embraced both the royal palace and the civilian quarters. The wall had bastions and turreted gates, and ran along the edge of the plateau. The gates had four different means of defence: before them ran a dry ditch; over this a drawbridge could be lowered; each stone gateway had a portcullis; and there were additional iron doors with iron fittings. The four town gates were also customs points. From the north two gates led into the town. One was Szombat (Saturday) Gate, at the bend of today's Táncsics Mihály Street, which had a series of shops beneath its arcades. The other was near today's Bécsi (Vienna) Gate. Two southern gates were between Dísz Square and Szent György Square, the one further east, closer to the Danube, was Szent János (Saint John's) Gate, also known as Vizi (Water) Gate, while the western one, at the edge of the Jewish quarter, was called Zsidó (Jewish) Gate, later renamed Fehérvár Gate. There were a number of additional, smaller, gates for pedestrian use.

From the mid thirteenth century Hungary enjoyed an extended period of peace; Buda was able to thrive and complete its fortifications. Gunpowder was not to be known for quite some time, and only at the turn of the fourteenth to the fifteenth centuries, when the Turks using cannon inflicted defeats on the country, did the king begin to reconstruct Buda's walls and bastions the better for them to withstand the new technology of war. During this period, the walls were moved outwards, which increased the area available for residence. A second line of walls was built and the space in between filled with earth, at some places four to five metres across. No canon ball of the time could possibly have penetrated fortification works like this.

From the northern gates the streets led into the Hungarian part of town and to the large royal residence known as the *Kammerhof* or *Magna Curia*. The royal court, with its functions of public administration and court of justice, combined with favourable geographic and economic aspects, had turned Buda into a royal seat and the capital of Hungary. It was unusual for a town and a royal court to exist side by side; in Buda this produced both positive and negative effects. While, for example, the royal charter gave the burghers the right to elect their chief mag-

15. *A map of medieval Buda*

ænfæs ercommunicatur.

Otem tempe fr Nicolaus de or

burghers of Buda signified peace and order, a condition that prevailed for half a century.

The establishment of the royal court in Buda spurred the development of the town and secured its burghers both wealth and a way of life in keeping with their station. The stronger the court grew and the more pronounced Buda's function as a capital became, the more the citizenry was able to expand its own administration and economic independence. In 1347, when King Louis the Great (1342-1382) permanently removed his court from Visegrád to Buda, he once again awarded the town its privilege of electing its own chief magistrate. Thus the

istrate – a position of absolute authority over the inhabitants – Buda's economic and military significance – where money was minted – entailed that a military commander was very soon placed above him. The office of the commander, referred to as rector, existed for a hundred years. Similarly Buda's right to hold national fairs was revoked by the king. Buda reciprocated, and for years would not allow the king to enter his own house, which stood within the town. Once during a struggle for the succession in 1302, Charles Robert of the house of Anjou, a pretender to the throne with the backing of the pope, was driven off from Buda along with his army. It took him five years to conquer the town, to 1307 when two Buda aristocrats changed over to the king's side. The contemporary *Illuminated Chronicle* related the events. "In the still of night, on Thursday following the Virgin Saint Petronella's Day [May 31], he entered Buda through the gate near the Jewish synagogue. Immediately he attacked and slayed the burghers of Buda who were his enemies and traitors. Chief magistrate Petermann ran off naked, and barely escaped thus. Showing no mercy he had two of the burghers, [...] from amongst the twelve burghers [of the town magistracy], bound to the tails of horses and drawn through the town squares and streets, and their bones thrown into fire, and he confiscated their goods and chattels and took them into his possession."

It took two full years before order was restored to the extent that on July 15, 1309 the king was crowned in Buda, and the Diet convened here. The king's victory over the

royal court and national functions did not act to suppress the town's rights as a borough, on the contrary the two became clearly distinct. One tangible outcome of the distinction was the building of a royal palace to replace the king's house within the town proper.

Louis the Great began building his residence at the southern tip of Castle Hill, on a slope slightly below the plateau. Initially it comprised István (Stephen) Tower, named after his brother, and the palace attached to this. Soon a two-level chapel was completed as well. His successor, Sigismund of Luxemburg (1387-1437), engaged in even more extensive construction, involving builders from the workshop of Peter Parler, who was the master builder of the Cathedral in Prague. To the north he erected the Friss (New) Palace over the castle courtyard. This was a large two-story structure, whose spacious great hall, seventy by eighteen-metres, extended to both stories. In the course of this reconstruction, a set of wonderful gothic statues were discarded; these were unearthed on the Palace grounds in the 1970s and have since been exhibited as testimony to the splendour of Sigismund's time.

The market at the castle was established on the site of some thirty houses – part of which was the first Jewish quarter – acquired from the town. From this time on the tournaments were held here; aristocrats condemned to death, were executed here. (Decades later the brother of the future King Matthias, László Hunyadi, was beheaded at this spot.) Sigismund built the huge "Csonkatorony," or Unfinished Tower, which in spite of its height of four or

19

five stories and its four-metre-thick walls, was never fully completed. The fortified tower was intended as the quarters of the castle guard, but soon came to be used as a keep, by Hungarian kings and, later, by the Ottoman Turkish conquerors. Various wings of the building were raised at this time, including the section containing what is today called Knight Hall, one of the gothic rooms which now forms part of the Budapest History Museum.

Sigismund had the palace surrounded by fortified walls, gates, and a moat, typical of medieval castles in the west of Europe. Buda boasted a unique installation not found elsewhere, however. On both banks of the Danube huge "water bastions" were erected, connected by thick chains. These were set up for military and security purposes; the intention was to check the Turkish fleet. In addition, in the bastion that stood on the site of the present Ybl Miklós Square, and in the adjacent castle wall that runs up to the Palace, an engineer from Nuremberg built a water pump that siphoned filtered water from the river up into the Castle. Over two hundred years later the Turks admired the invention, as testified in this account: "It is in a large tower on the shore of the Danube. In the tower a variety of wheels revolve and their bails dive successively into the Danube water and the Danube, through this force, spills into jugs and is driven ever higher like a fountain, until it reaches a spout in the middle castle, where the filtered water pours out. It is so wondrous a work that one must see it."

Apart from smaller wells driven into the caves underneath Castle Hill, there was only one other possibility of drawing water, this was the a system of pipes established to conduct water from a spring on near-by Svábhegy Hill.

The German citizenry of Buda had received a coat-of arms and charter when they were in Pest, before its inhabitants were relocated after the Mongolian invasion. As the original charter, which was modelled on that of the Saxon town of Magdeburg, was destroyed in the devastation, the king reissued it in 1244. The charter regulated the administration and judiciary, the procedures for electing its parish priest, and established the tithe for the parish. Towns never attained all their economic and trading privileges all at the same time; it was a step by step procedure over time, and it was their franchises that largely determined their significance. Among Buda's privileges were its Staple rights, whereby merchants passing the town had to enter it and offer their goods for sale. These rights enabled Buda to link into long-distance trade, and constituted one of the town's major sources of income.

It took some towns up to two hundred years to attain all these major economic privileges. Acquiring and maintaining them generally involved a determined struggle and considerable confrontation, since these privileges always encroached on the prerogatives previously held by another entity. It was usually the church whose rights were infringed on. For Buda, the confrontation involved three ecclesiastic bodies at once. The archdiocese of the former royal seat of Esztergom had vast fiefs; the provostship of Óbuda had a long tradition of local economic domination, which extended to the foot of Gellért Hill; they were joined in the mid thirteenth century by the Dominican nuns on Nyulak, or Hares' (later Margaret), Island.

The island itself was a royal hunting domain, where in 1247 King Béla IV established a nunnery, in fulfilment of an oath he had sworn on his escape from the Mongols. He had vowed to offer his daughter Margaret into God's service as a nun, if the Tatars would abandon the country and enable him to return home. Margaret, whose aunt Elizabeth had already been canonised by this time, took her vow of poverty seriously; her ascetic life soon made her into a legend. A few years after her death she was beatified, and six and a half centuries later canonised. It is in her honour that the Island of Hares, where her convent was sited, was already being named after her in the fourteenth century.

The convent which the king had established for his daughter was bestowed many royal and aristocratic endowments, vast fiefs and privileges, including Staple rights. In the second half of the thirteenth century the Dominican convent was the wealthiest seignior in the region.

As Buda was establishing itself as a new economic factor, it had to compete with existing interests. The ensuing clashes brought down a succession of reprisals on the town of Buda in the form of interdicts, sometimes from a bishop, sometimes from the Pope himself. A church interdict counted as one of the most devastating sanctions in medieval times, since it entailed that the members of the religious community could not administer the sacraments, Holy Communion or confession, neither could marriages or baptism or burials be solemnised. But Buda stood fast, so much so that in the early 1300s, under the first alderman known by name, the same chief magistrate Petermann who also opposed King Charles Robert (and whose name was until recently commemorated with a street near the Vienna Gate), responded to a papal interdict by excommunicating the Pope himself!

A great deal is known about the town's privileges and functioning, since in the early 1400s a codex, the *Buda Book of Law (Budai Jogkönyv)*, compiled the privileges, laws and regulations relating to the borough. There was some urgency behind the preparation of this collection since for a good half century Buda had clearly been emerging as the leading town in Hungary. Subsequent town charters came to be modelled after the "Buda Law."

Following the appearance of the *Buda Book of Law* the king was prevented from interfering in the affairs of the borough; he was left with only one office, namely to approve the chief magistrate. Buda's town council, or magistracy, was in close contact with the Master of the Mint, and some of the chief magistrates or town council members even advanced to head the treasury.

Only a burgher of Buda, a man holding real property, could be elected to the magistracy or to the position of chief magistrate. Regulations excluded criminals, the sick, heathens and the poor, as well as those who acted as spies or who would nod approval in all matters, from election to the leading body. For chief magistrates, there was the additional provision that prior to their election they had to have held a public function in the magistracy for at least six years.

There was one other important provision: only those German patricians could become chief magistrates whose four grandparents had been German, and in the magistra-

proprietor at the door of his house, who then joined the procession which finally conducted the new chief magistrate to his own house. Buda's Town Hall stood for many centuries on Main Square facing Matthias Church.

Some of the magistrates had additional functions apart from sitting in council meetings, passing laws and participating in court proceedings. One was responsible for guarding the great and small seals of the borough, another kept the key to the chest in which the seals were stored and also served as the town notary, charged with writing the minutes of the council meetings and composing official documents. There was a magistrate in charge of lesser fiscal matters, two others who made up the magistracy of Pest, and two elected officials to represent the two other townships of Viziváros (literally Water Town) and Tótfalu. These latter two, together with elected guild officials, were in charge of the town constabulary. The magistracy oversaw the work of the town officials: the damage assessor, tax-collector, night-watchmen, constables, henchman, catchpoles serving also as prison guards with the turnkey at their head, the collector of rubbish, dubbed "refuse count", and the rest. Important functions were those of the market judge, who oversaw order at markets and fairs as well as the cleanliness of the town, and the keepers of the town scales, weights and measures.

cy only one third could be Hungarian, alongside the two thirds who were German. After 1439, the ratio became 6:6, and the chief magistrate was chosen alternately from one or the other party.

On Saint George's Day, April 24, elections were held amid grand festivities, whereby the outgoing chief magistrate placed the insignia of his office, a green branch and a white staff, on the ground before the town council. (On pronouncing judgement in the court of law he had sworn an oath upon the white staff, and by breaking the branch he had proclaimed guilt.)

Immediately after he was sworn in, the new chief magistrate was faced with an array of duties. First of all he had to present himself at the royal palace, after which he had to return to fetch his magistrates to present them to the king. On the Sunday following his election, he progressed through the town, where he was greeted by each single

Safeguarding the weights and measures was especially important at a time when no general standards of measurement existed. The *Buda Book of Law* describes the strict supervision of what in 1405 King Sigismund proclaimed the national standards of measurement. The unit of weight for precious metals, including money that was minted in Buda, in the mid-thirteenth century became the "Buda mark". The standard of weight became the Buda pound (490 grams), the liquid measurement the Buda icce (0.88 litres), the linear measure the Buda ell (58.3 cm). The reference standards displayed the town's coat-of-arms, and the use of false measures entailed extremely harsh punishment: the confiscation of all property for the very first offence.

It must be noted, however, that while King Sigismund set the national standards, the local communities in various

18. *A memento of the refined lifestyle of a burgher family of Buda from the late 14th century: a fresco fragment showing a dancing couple and a clown, discovered on the second floor of a house from what was Jew Street in the late Middle Ages, on today's 24 Táncsics Mihály Street*

parts of the country never relinquished use of their own, accustomed measurements.

Medieval towns possessing a royal charter functioned according to a strict hierarchy, where everyone had his fixed place. Birth and wealth were crucial, but not rigid, categories; in times of peace an individual could attain great fortunes, and contribute to the towns development and culture. In the late Middle Ages Buda and Pest each had two schools in which the seven liberal arts *(septem artes liberales)* were taught by teachers, "lectors" and "correpetitors", all clergy, over a period of eight years. There were three lower-level subjects – dialectics, rhetoric and grammar – while the other four – mathematics, geometry, astronomy and music – constituted the upper level. In addition students were expected to become proficient in Latin, Greek and Hebrew, while teachers had to be proficient in Hungarian and German. In the final decade of the fifteenth century, astronomy may have been taught following the German scholar Regiomontanus, a recognised mathematician of his time, who had spent three years here as King Matthias' court astronomer. To pursue higher education students could attend colleges and universities, mostly abroad. For a brief period in 1389 a university operated in Óbuda, counting among its professors many known scholars.

The population of Buda consisted of various groups of people. Hungarians coming from Óbuda settled in the northern section of the Castle, while Germans from Pest lived in the central area. The burghers of the town had three distinct levels. The most affluent were the merchants and owners of real property, the patricians who were the town leadership. From their ranks came the chief magistrates and magistrates. The second order were the guild members and less wealthy merchants, while the third comprised those without property of their own, day labourers, craftsmen, artisans without certificates of mastership, the poorest burghers and the poor without citizenship.

There was a second kind of division as well, according to which the German burghers held the highest rank. Until 1439 two-thirds of the twelve-member town council were German patricians. In 1251, as servants of the royal treasury Jews were granted prerogatives comparable to citizenship. Until the mid fourteenth century they had their own quarter around Jew, later Szent György (Saint George), Street, by today's Szent György Square. Presumably the royal mint stood here, supervised by a Jew named Henuk, who acted as the head of the treasury. That explains why on the coins of Béla IV and Stephen V the mint marks are in Hebrew.

Buda's Churches and Their Congregations in the Middle Ages

Congregations embraced communities in the vicinity of individual churches. Buda's main church, Saint Mary's or the Church of Our Lady, popularly known as the Matthias Church, was the main church for the Germans. The Hungarians raised their own parish church, Mary Magdalene, whose tower still stands on today's Kapisztrán Square. The old Jewish quarter had a synagogue of its own and when, after twice being driven out, Jews were finally permitted to return to Buda in 1364, the king allowed them to settle in the vicinity of the former royal residence, the *Kammerhof*. This became the Jewish quarter of medieval Buda, and it had two synagogues.

The first church to be built, between 1255 and 1269, was the Matthias Church, with a nave and two aisles, and two steeples on the west façade – though one was never completed and stands half-finished to this day. As Buda's main church it performed a multitude of functions. When kings were crowned it took on national prominence; it also exercised patronage over its own large holdings. The festival mass celebrating elections to the magistracy on Saint George's Day was held in it, and the town seal was kept here in times of necessity. Here they buried the patricians, chief magistrates, prelates, some members of the royal court and a few aristocrats and dignitaries of the realm. The tomb of János Frangepán, the Ban of Croatia, was here, and the exquisitely carved tombstone of one of the fifteenth century's wealthiest aristocrats, Stibor, the Transylvanian Voivode, has also been discovered. Adjacent is the sepulchral chapel for the family of the Palatine Miklós Gara, and another belonging to János Ernust, a Jewish banker from Vienna who converted to Christianity and became Treasurer of the Household to King Matthias. The tombstones from the church (most held today at the Budapest History Museum) present a cross section of Buda society in the late Middle Ages, and also reveals its international character. There was a bishop from Zagreb, a burgher who owned properties in both Vienna and Buda, and burgher families from northern Hungarian and countless German cities, from Breslau (now Wrocław, Poland), Regensburg, Nuremberg, Bamberg, and many others.

Nearby there was a Dominican church, where mostly the Italians and Spanish were buried. They included burghers and artists from Florence, Milan, and Padua, from Como and Modena. The prestigious Humanist scholar of the Italian renaissance, Pietro Paolo Vergerio, who died on July 8, 1444, was laid to rest in this church.

The Hungarian church on what was then Szombat piac (Saturday Market Square) already stood in 1279, as documents reveal. For a hundred years it was involved in legal dispute with the Matthias Church to attain its own parish rights. Finally, in 1390, the city government demarcated the bounds for both churches, whereby the section north of today's Hess András Square became the Hungarian parish. Initially built with only a nave, the church was given two aisles in 1350, while the tall steeple (the only part of the building still standing) was raised in the late fifteenth century. Only a few, artistically pleasing but archaeologically immaterial, tomb fragments have been discovered, the rest have been lost because of the number of times the church had been damaged and rebuilt before its ultimate demolition after the Second World War.

Within what today may seem a small area there were, in addition to the two parish churches, numerous other churches and monasteries built in the Middle Ages. The Dominicans built their Saint Michael's Church and monastery a few years before the adjacent Matthias Church. Its tower, parts of its cloister and the walls of the chancel still remain standing within the Hilton Hotel complex. It was significant not just as a church and burial place for the Italians and Spaniards of Buda, but because it housed the city's most important school, the Dominican College, where theology and philosophy were taught.

The other great medieval mendicant order, the Franciscans, had its Church of Saint John the Evangelist on the site of today's Castle Theatre, with a large monastery attached. Here they ran a theological college whose teachers at the turn of the fifteenth and sixteenth centuries included Pelbart of Temesvár and Osvát of Laska, prominent Latin scholars and professors of rhetoric.

Almost directly across from Saint John's and facing west on Castle Hill stood Saint Sigismund's Collegiate Church. Founded by King Sigismund in the early 1400s, it was the newest church in Buda, but because of its proximity to the Royal Palace it performed some of the functions of a royal

19. The portrait of Jakob Mendel, Jewish prefect of Buda, on the seal he used in 1496

chapel. King Matthias' first wife, Catherine of Podebrady, was buried here; it was here that in 1514 the Bishop of Esztergom Tamás Bakócz proclaimed the crusade against the Turks, which ultimately led to the largest peasant uprising in Hungarian history under the leadership of György Dózsa. Rising amid the grass, the foundations of the twin-aisle church can be seen on Szent György Square.

After the middle of the fifteenth century, King Louis the Great had several chapels built in Buda. Saint George's stood on the market square, today's Dísz Square, and another in his own palace. The remains of a medieval sepulchral chapel, All Saint's, lie underneath the southern arm of Fishermen's Bastion.

Within the Hungarian parish, between the Anjou kings' town house, the *Kammerhof*, and today's Vienna Gate, was the "new" Jewish quarter, with its two synagogues. The smaller one can be visited today as a museum in Táncsics Mihály Street, where there are several medieval tombstones with Hebrew inscriptions. The Jewish community of some five hundred, the centre of Hungarian Jewry in the Middle Ages, lived just like other privileged groups at this time. They joined in holiday parades with their own cavalcade, swords, shields, and banners depicting the *Judenhut*, the Jew's hat, framed by gilded flames on a red background. Thus the sign that had formerly stood for the segregation of Jews had advanced to become a proud symbol of "chivalry".

Initially a Jewish chief magistrate, a position filled by high dignitaries at court, oversaw the Jewish community of the whole realm. A 1470 ordinance by King Matthias changed the position to a Jewish prefect, retaining his national rank. The first prefect was Jákob Mendel, a wealthy banker from Nuremberg who was highly respected in the community. The function was carried on by his descendants and family up until the Turkish occupation. The Mendel family was very affluent, owning three two-story stone houses on Zsidó (Jewish) Street, the part of today's Táncsics Mihály street near the Vienna Gate. The larger synagogue was built in the courtyard of one of the houses. In the pogroms that were to follow, with greater frequency after the late fifteenth century, these houses were never spared.

The chief instigator of the greatest pogrom of all was, however, of an uncommon sort. Having escaped from Spain, a man by the name of Selomo Szeneor had arrived in Buda in the 1490s to visit a relative. He amassed a fortune, settled down in Zsidó Street and took on the utterly Magyar name of Attila. His wealth was so considerable that King Louis made him his vice-treasurer. When it became known that he had a relationship with a Christian woman he converted to Christianity to avoid a scandal. He had himself baptised by the archbishop, with the country's palatine as his godfather, taking the name of Emeric Fortunatus. He abandoned his former wife and children in Zsidó Street, and moved with his new spouse to elegant Szent György Street. Entrusted with order amid the shaky financial situation of the king and court, he was not entirely successful. He launched into a series of adventurous undertakings, and when the king realised that money was being minted at half under par he had him imprisoned in Csonka Tower to avoid further embarrassment. His term

20. *The head of a man wearing a* chaperon, *from a limestone statuary made around 1420*

21. *The gentleman and the herald with the helmet may have been members of the Buda court around 1420. The statuary was carved from limestone in the court stone-cutter's workshop*

lasted only two weeks, but when he was released, an army of servants to the nobility (they being away at the Diet on Rákos Field) broke into his house and plundered it, taking away his gold by the bagful. Fortunatus himself escaped, but the pogrom raged on for three days, extending to Zsidó Street as well. The military had to be called in to establish order. With the remuneration he was awarded Fortunatus undertook a series of financial transactions which were so successful that in the summer of 1526, a few weeks prior to the catastrophe of the Battle of Mohács, he was able to donate a considerable sum of money to the king for warfare. He died shortly afterwards – but not before he returned to the old faith. A life that is the stuff of fiction!

Alongside stories and legends and tomb inscriptions, a wonderful archaeological find evokes the life and times of Buda in the Middle Ages. In 1974 were discovered over sixty sculptures and fragments of statues from around 1420, the late reign of King Sigismund of Luxemburg. The statues had been made in the king's stone-cuttery, which employed masters who had arrived to Buda via Vienna. The sculptures seem to be faithful portraits of living figures, with expressive faces, contemporary clothing and hairstyles. When seen together, they provide an impression of what life at court must have been like. There is the knight grasping the hilt of his sword, wearing a breastplate under his cape; the page holding his lord's helmet; the man with the head-dress in turban fashion; men wearing *chaperons*, hats that hang down to the side below their

NVS·PHI·IPPVS·HISPANVS·DESCOLARIS   RELATOR·VICTORIE·TH

Úri Street, that has retained its bridge spanning the alley (now Balta köz) below. It was built around 1430, and some of its original vaulting is still intact. What has not survived are the murals by Masolino, the fine early-renaissance master from Italy. He lived in Buda for several years on the invitation of the builder of the house, the Florentine Filippo Scolari, Treasurer of the Household to King Sigismund, successful military commander in the Turkish wars, builder of Hungary's south-eastern border fortresses, and the wealthy owner of large holdings.

On reaching Balta köz (Hatchet Alley) with its thick medieval ambience, tourist guides like to tell a story about King Matthias' brother László Hunyadi, who was attacked by the hired killers of a rival noble family lurking in this dark alley but put up an heroic – and successful – resistance. (He fell prey to his enemies at another location.) The event may just as well have taken place, but the name of the street surely does not stem from it. In the mid nineteenth century there stood on its corner at Tárnok Street, a popular inn owned by a man named Hackl, the German word for hatchet.

Another Italian mansion is still an impressive edifice. Standing on Országház (Parliament) Street – Olaszok utcája, or Italian Street in medieval times – its neighbours are countless smaller burghers' houses that were originally built in the Middle Ages. In the court of number 2, which now houses the Alabárdos Restaurant, a two-story arcade with large arches speaks of the splendour of a building of times gone by. Here, as in many other medieval gateways in the Castle District, are a series of ornately carved niches. There is disagreement over the original purpose of these architectural motifs that are specific to Buda; they may have been seats for the guards of these houses, or – and this seems more likely – they were used as counters for measuring out wine. In favour of the latter view is the fact that the houses of patricians had niches too, and many of the inhabitants of the Castle District had vineyards in the Buda Hills, and sold their wine from their homes.

Though the Germans were the dominant population in Buda, the borough differed in some significant respects from cities in Germany. The single-story houses, to which in the late Middle Ages a second story was usually added, were commonly made of stone, and the half-timbered or wooden structures that characterise German towns in Buda were confined to outbuildings. The overall look of streets and squares differed as well. While in the cities of Western Europe the ridges of the house roofs are at a right angle to the street and the gables face the street, the roof ridges of the Buda houses are parallel to the street. In this manner wings extending into the courts could be established for stables and coach houses. The best, most ostentatious rooms were on the floor above and facing the street. Called *palatium* they were used as great halls and dining rooms, and had wooden ceilings, ornately carved stone window frames and frescoes on their walls. In the early fifteenth century there were 322 houses in Buda; in them

shoulders; beards and moustaches; short and almost shoulder-length hairdos, but always with thick, wavy hair; courtly figures in richly folded capes gathered in belts with metal mountings; the round head with thick jaws; the longish face with a slightly cross-eyed, contemplative look; or the women's heads draped with scarves; and the ladies in capes; the girl and the child's head; apostles and saints in the clerical dress of the time, with hoods, and clasping a book kept in a leather bag. Paint remnants indicate the array of colours, the bright reds and blues, greens and browns and gold, that they once wore.

The proximity of the royal court with the thriving economic and cultural activities that went with it, the presence of aristocrats and dignitaries, had a considerable effect on the life of the borough. The wealthy German patricians built their houses (like the three-story Gothic house still extant on 31 Úri Street), just as the aristocrats raised their palaces. One building in the Castle District remains, on 19

were 679 rooms, 1416 pantries and closets, 460 cellars, and quarters for 2707 horses.

At this time 69 craftsmen were active in Buda; a quarter of them worked with iron and metals or manufactured weapons. According to the *Buda Book of Law* it was the artisans in particular who formed guilds: the goldsmiths, bell founders, blacksmiths, spurriers, wire drawers, pinmakers, joiners, butchers and other master craftsmen. Some of the streets were once named after their trades. The merchants established one joint guild, although commerce was significant in Buda. In fact, in the fourteenth century, merchants were the town leaders.

Buda had two market days each week; the one on Wednesdays was held in front of Matthias Church while the Friday markets took place on the square before Mary Magdalene. The bi-annual national fairs lasted two weeks: around Whitsun was the spring fair, held in Felhévíz to the north outside the town walls, while the autumn fair on September 8th was inside the city.

With Buda having staple rights, foreign merchants regularly participated at the markets and fairs. Luxury items such as silk and jewellery were imported mostly by Italian traders, basic goods were usually sold by merchants from southern Germany. Broadcloth was the most important commodity, and the street it was sold in was soon renamed Nyirő (Shearer) Street. The cloth merchants became the wealthiest burghers. In the early 1400s 49 different kinds of cloth from all parts of Europe were sold in Buda. There were also spices from Asia and Africa; the most expensive "Zendal" silk from Tripoli; and even Chinese porcelain was known here. Many foreign merchants, Austrians, Germans and Italians, bought first storages, then shops, and finally houses in Buda; many became influential Buda patricians, a few even attaining positions of national rank, like the Florentine merchant Filippo Scolari.

24. *Balta köz, or Hatchet Alley, as seen from Tárnok Street, with a corner of the "Hatchet" Inn in the foreground, in a photograph from around 1900*

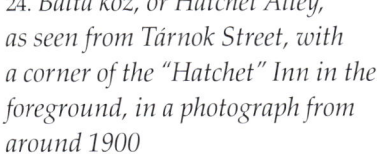

A Ray of Light At Dusk: King Matthias' Buda

Declared king by unanimous voice on the ice of the Danube, Matthias Hunyadi reigned between 1458 and 1490. One of his first undertakings was to enlarge and remodel the Gothic Palace in Buda Castle, and to establish a system of fortifications with the Mace Tower and Round Bastion. After the king's marriage in 1476 to Beatrice of Naples, who brought to Hungary Italian humanism and sophistication, a splendid entourage, and contacts with the prominent scholars and artists of the age, the palace was rebuilt in the Renaissance style. For almost fifteen years, Chimenti Camicia, a Florentine, was the king's master builder, and established the Renaissance style in Buda. Initially five Florentine inlay makers were contracted, then Camicia set up a workshop employing some twenty Italian and Dalmatian stone-cutters, while Hungarian masons were trained to erect the walls. First the Danube wing, closing off the main courtyard, and the South Wing were reconstructed, then the three-story palace chapel and library were built. Hanging gardens modelled after those in the palace in Urbino were laid out on the hillside facing north-west. Next, the wing west of the main courtyard was given a Renaissance façade, and a second story added. The wing housed the spacious throne room, a splendid staircase with eighty steps leading up to it. Finally, a three-story loggia was added to make up the main courtyard's ornate façade. Its columns and arches were of red marble, while the balusters were of white Buda marl. In the centre of the court stood a well with a statue of Pallas Athena, the Greek goddess of wisdom and knowledge. Sculptures of the Hunyadis – János, the father, military commander and governor; Matthias' murdered brother János; and the king's – were placed in the top story of the East Wing. The column capitals displayed various coats-of-arms and heraldic animals.

Matthias bought and commissioned art works from the best Italian, especially Florentine, masters of the time. Mantegna, Filippino Lippi, Pollaiuolo, and perhaps even Boticelli provided paintings, while Verocchio sculptured two bronze reliefs for him. The greatest master of all, Leonardo da Vinci, painted a Madonna to Matthias' commission. In addition, the king acquired the finest library of his time. The Corvina Library was second in the world only to the Vatican's, containing over two thousand codices, illuminated with splendid miniatures. Most were manuscripts in Greek or Latin, dealing with a variety of subjects: philosophy, theology, history, philology, poetry and rhetoric, geography and astronomy, architecture, medicine and military science. The Corvina served as a model for the Florentine ruler Lorenzo de Medici for establishing his own library. The codices' miniatures were created by Italian artists, foremost by Attavante degli Attavanti of Florence, a favourite also of the Medicis and the duke of Urbino; in addition to his Italian commissions he was also able to establish a workshop with over thirty masters in Buda. Headed by Felix Ragusanus from Dalmatia, it employed known Italian illuminators, and its bookbinders manufactured the painted silk and leather bindings with ornate metal mountings. Barely a tenth of the codices are extant, 208 volumes now in 43 different cities all over the world.

Although the great majority of the volumes were hand-written manuscripts, there were also a handful of incunabula, the earliest printed books produced with Johann Gutenberg's movable type. Buda's first printing press was set up in these years by the German Andreas Hess, brought in from Rome by the vice-chancellor. The square in Buda Castle where the press operated has been named Hess András Square in his honour; here at Easter 1473 he produced the first book printed in Hungary, the *Budaer Chronik*.

The members of Matthias' court and its highest officials included excellent humanist scholars. Most prominent was Chancellor and Bishop of Esztergom János Vitéz, who founded Pozsony University and gathered excellent scholars, poets and astrologers in his own court; he also corresponded with many humanists in various parts of Europe. His nephew Janus Pannonius became Bishop of Pécs and served as a diplomat to Matthias, but is considered also as the first Hungarian – though still Latin-language – poet of consequence. He, too, was a member of Matthias' human-

ist circle. The king hosted a great many foreign artists and scientists at court, some of whom he also employed for given lengths of time. Because of them a few first-hand accounts survive of the palace, which a mere half a century later was stripped bare and devastated.

One Italian humanist scholar, the queen's reader Antonio Bonfini, Matthias commissioned to compile a comprehensive history of Hungary and his reign. In his *Rerum Hungaricarum Decades* Bonfini described Matthias' capital. "In Buda Castle there was, beyond Sigismund's splendid buildings, not much to be seen. He [King Matthias] undertook to adorn it. He graced the inner palace splendidly. In the section overlooking the Danube he raised a chapel, furnished it with a water organ and a baptismal basin of marble and silver. To it he attached a proper Chapter. Above he built a library, abundant with Latin and Greek books; the books are lavishly executed. Before it, facing south, is a vaulted room where the entire firmament can be seen. He raised palaces that are in no way inferior in splendour to Roman palaces. There are spacious dining halls and finely executed bedrooms; the rooms are distinguished by their variously decorated, gilded ceilings. The door frames are inlaid. On the mantels of the ornate fireplaces are placed quadrigas and other Roman-style decorations. Below is the treasury, the other storages and the armoury.

"In the building's eastern wing there are also all sorts of bedrooms and dining palaces. These can be reached by a high staircase over covered corridors. The council and assembly room is also here. Proceeding further we come

25. *Buda and the Royal Palace in the late Middle Ages, in a coloured woodcut by Michael Wolgemut, from Hartman Schedel's* Weltchronik *of 1493*

upon high, vaulted rooms: they serve winter and summer use. They allow the sun to shine in. There are also richly gilded reception rooms with hidden, deep niches here and there. The appliances are silver, as are the chairs.

"[...] The floors are inlaid like mosaics, in some places of burned stone joined by wax. In several parts, at proper places, cold and warm bathrooms can be found. The tiles of the fireplaces in the dining rooms display protruding eyes in their centres, and are beautiful not only in colour but for their illustrations of imaginary figures.

"[...] The water for the well of the Royal Palace comes in from some seven miles hence; through tarred pipes and leaden taps.

"Sigismund's corridor nearly surrounded the castle. Matthias extended it, although at not excessive expense. – He built a long, broad terrace adjacent, with many glass windows. On top of the castle wall he had a small wooden structure erected, containing a dining room, bedroom and bathroom, and in the back a living room and study. It extended directly to the Danube.

"In the near-by valley below the Castle are pleasant grounds. Here he had a marble villa constructed. – On the

29

26. *"King Matthias the Triumphant," returning to the Royal Palace in Buda. Oil painting by Gyula Benczúr, 1919*

garden side it has a covered porch. In the garden densely planted trees constitute a maze. Cages contain an assortment of foreign and domestic birds. The garden contains shrubbery, groves, orchards, and arbours, and all sorts of trees. There are pillared corridors, halls, lawns, gravel paths and fish ponds. Above the upper story and the attic rise turrets, one wall of the dining room has mirrors, and one cannot imagine anything pleasanter and more beautiful. The roof of the villa is covered with silver plates."

In 1490 King Matthias died. He was succeeded by kings from the Polish house of Jagiello, who ruled for over three decades, without affecting significant change or any construction in Buda. The fame and the humanist spirit of the renaissance king's seat continued to attract many scholars and artists, from Central and Northern Europe in addition to Italy. Still, the quick and spectacular development Buda experienced in the fifteenth century had waned, as if by augury, to a weary lull. Yet the life of the citizens continued as before, with many boisterous and spectacular feasts. In his report to his Prince the envoy from the Italian city of Modena wrote in 1501, "In Buda at the Corpus Christi procession – which His Majesty attended before a huge crowd – I witnessed an interesting spectacle. A prophecy has it that the Moslem creed shall die out if Mohammed's coffin is shattered. Following the prophecy they erected before our house Mohammed's mosque containing a coffin surrounded by dummies of the sultan and many of his pashas. As His Majesty and the procession reached the mosque, they hurled a flare onto the mosque and the coffin, and it caught fire along with the 'Turks' around it. Anything that the fire did not consume, throngs of Hungarians assaulted with sticks and stones, smashing it to pieces, even tearing it up with their bare teeth."

After his victory a quarter century later the imperial Turkish army commander, the Sultan Suleiman I (the Magnificent), looked in awe at the abandoned rooms of Buda's Royal Palace, mumbling, "Oh, if this palace stood in our Istanbul it should be our seraglio." Instead he chose to pursue a more attainable solution.

On August 29, 1526 on the field of Mohács a 25 thousand-strong Hungarian army suffered a devastating defeat. The Turks, under Suleiman's command, outnumbered the Hungarians three to one. Nearly all the religious and secular leaders of Hungary fell in the battle, including the young King Louis II, who drowned as he attempted to flee across a swollen stream. The news reached Buda the following evening. The queen packed up immediately and, together with the Lord Chief Treasurer, the Bishop of Veszprém, the papal legate, and the castellan, she fled to Pozsony the same night. The Royal Palace remained unguarded, but it was only a week later that the first Turkish forces arrived near the town. They proceeded first to plunder and burn the monasteries around Buda, then aggregated into small bands to pillage the whole of Transdanubia. Meanwhile the Turks built a pontoon bridge between Buda and Pest. As the famous Turkish traveller and chronicler Evliya Chelebi noted, "Suleiman [...] had the treasures of King Louis packed into seven leather chests, and the many military supplies, objects of rare beauty, thrones laid out with precious stones, hundreds of window shutters and doors containing precious stones, bronze and gilded shining angel figures, the bronze statues of old kings, and the splendid candlesticks presently standing at the right and left of the *mihrab* of Istanbul's Hagia Sophia Jami, and several similar objects, he had carried away from their places and hauled to Istanbul by ship." He also confiscated the gold and silver objects found in churches, then passed over into Pest with his army, looting and burning it. Finally he proceeded south-east to complete his conquest before the onset of winter, when he was obliged to return to Istanbul. Turkish guards remained behind only in the castles along Hungary's southern borders. Despoiled and devastated, yet without the presence of the invaders, Buda and Pest began to recover.

Budun, a Provincial Seat of the Ottoman Empire

Buda's German patricians and wealthy burghers fled, carting all their movable possessions with them. The poor, including the Jews, stayed behind to face the conquerors. The Turks treated the Jews with the impassiveness of a subjugator; they massacred the elderly, and while they transported the young off to Istanbul, they did not sell them off as slaves, but allowed them to live free as merchants. Just a few hapless souls of Buda's original population remained.

Pillaged and abandoned, the town nonetheless retained its eminence as a once splendid royal seat and capital. As the country collapsed into anarchy, competing groups were busy trying to establish a king of their choice on the throne. Two succeeded, and they took turns ruling and laying siege to Buda. King John I (1526-1540) was hand-picked and placed on the throne by those of the nobles who rallied for the national cause. This was the same nobility that, after it had quelled the peasant uprising in 1514 and punished the peasantry by enacting into law that they were to be serfs forever, regarded themselves as invincible. Their chosen king was John Szapolyai, Voivode of Transylvania, who had defeated the peasant armies and had their leader, György Dózsa, tortured and killed in a manner that was considered cruel even by medieval standards. As a deterrent, Dózsa was placed on a hot throne and adorned with a red-hot crown, while the remains of his collaborators, partially burned and quartered, were displayed on the town walls of Buda and Pest. Moreover, Szapolyai was in part to blame for the catastrophic defeat of the Hungarians at Mohács, when he had set up his camp with his Transylvanian troops and simply waited until he had "missed" the battle. Following the country's utter defeat, his army alone, not inconsiderable at that, remained unscathed. Once he took the throne there was hardly a single agreement or contract he honoured. To secure Hungarian "independence", he turned to the Turks for support against his rival, Ferdinand of Habsburg (1526-1564), who himself claimed the throne through a marriage contract of a former member of the dynasty. Ferdinand was the younger brother of Charles V, the Holy Roman Emperor whose contemporaries justly claimed that the sun never set over his dominions, which spanned much of Europe as well as America.

In the years of fighting that followed Buda declined in significance. Mostly King John dominated it, while Ferdinand was laying siege to it. In 1529 Sultan Suleiman's army of two

hundred thousand secured it for King John, purportedly after the two had concluded a treaty. In truth John had already kissed the hand of the Sultan as his vassal on the battlefield of Mohács. Everyone who could fled Buda, and those who could not faced almost certain death. Pozsony (now Bratislava, Slovakia), at the centre of the north-western part of the country that was retained by Ferdinand, became the coronation town, and was to remain the Hungarian capital for over three hundred years.

King John died in 1540, and at the last assembly at Rákos Field the Hungarian Estates proclaimed his one-year-old son king. The supporters of Ferdinand again laid siege to Buda. Pest was already under their control, and the defenders of Buda negotiated with the besiegers, when the sultan's army, in alliance with Hungarians, drove off Ferdinand's force. By now, however, the Turks had had enough of the constant bickering and decided that it was time to establish the area as the westernmost province of the Ottoman Empire.

On August 29, 1541, on the fifteenth anniversary of the Battle of Mohács, they occupied Buda by deceit. From his camp in Óbuda Suleiman dispatched envoys to the widowed Queen Isabella, residing in the Castle, to convey his gratitude for the resolute defence of Buda, at the same time expressing most obsequiously his wish to see John Sigismund, her orphan son. In the company of the child's

27. The capture of Buda in 1541 – from a Turkish perspective. Sultan Suleiman the Magnificent acknowledges the surrender of John Sigismund, and introduces the Muslim faith in the occupied territories. An illustration to Seyid Lokman's chronicle titled Hünername

31

28. *The Mausoleum of Gül Baba on Rose Hill in Buda, built between 1543 and 1548*

The Turkish chronicler Evliya Chelebi related how, after seizing the city, "they held victory celebrations lasting seven days and seven nights" – just as in fairy tales. Matthias Church was hastily converted into an Islamic house of worship. As the Buyuk Jami (Great Mosque) or Eski Jami (Old Mosque), it welcomed Sultan Suleiman on September 2nd when, after a triumphal march into Buda, he attended a thanksgiving service there. It was at this service that the Islamic monk Gül Baba died, who has remained known to posterity because of his mausoleum on Rózsadomb in Buda. To this day the cupolaed building is honoured by Moslems as a holy shrine. One of the many legends surrounding Gül Baba has it that Rózsadomb, meaning "Rose Hill", received its name from the roses he was fond of growing here. Actually he oversaw the Bektashi order of monks entrusted with the spiritual care of the janissaries. While not free from sectarian zeal and directed to inculcate fanaticism in the janissaries, the order exhibited tolerance toward Christians.

For nearly a century and a half Buda was a Turkish town. The Turkish garrison stationed here consisted not only of infantry, cavalry and artillery, but also the Danube fleet. One division of the permanently posted army of around four thousand, the Tatar cavalry, was stationed in Pest.

As the highest lord of the province, the pasha of Buda resided for some time in a palace on the Danube bank under the Castle. A Bohemian aristocrat on a diplomatic mission in Buda recounted how on Fridays – the Islamic holidays – "[...] the pasha would conduct processions to the mosque. [...]

guardians, Treasurer György Fráter, Noble Lord Bálint Török, and Chancellor István Werbőczi – a staunch champion of pro-Turkish policy – she permitted the boy to leave. They received a warm welcome in the Turkish camp, and while the Hungarian guests were being given a splendid feast, the janissaries, the dreaded elite corps of the Turkish army, entered the Castle in small groups, each group feigning interest in the splendid surroundings. Once enough of them had entered, they seized all weapons and declared Buda captured. If that were not enough the plague, the gruesome peril of medieval Europe that devastated much of the urban population, broke out. Two days after the sack of Buda, the Sultan announced to Isabella and György Fráter that the central section of Hungary was hence a part of the Ottoman Empire, with Budun as the provincial seat, and a pasha to rule it. With that the half century of the political disintegration of Hungary was complete.

The town itself naturally lost all its privileges and independence, and a *cadi* of the Islamic order was appointed as chief magistrate. Officials, ranked according to a strict hierarchy, administered its affairs. The Sultan made Werbőczi the chief justice of Hungary – an election or any other European convention were not even attempted. The 83-year-old former chancellor survived the distinction by just a few months. Although the plague is an explanation for his demise, it was said that the Buda pasha had expedited it by a drink he had offered. Be that as it may, the Turkish authorities forbade his burial within the Castle walls. As a twist of fate he, who had expressed a dislike for Jews and had introduced various discriminatory passages from the Middle Ages into the Hungarian legal code, was interred in the Jewish cemetery in Krisztinaváros (Christina Town) below the Castle Hill.

29. *The Pasha of Buda receives the envoy of the Habsburg Emperor in 1628*

Leading the train were three hundred janissaries followed by several hundred *spahis,* or Turkish cavalrymen, and finally the pasha himself followed, garbed in splendid gilded attire. He remained in the temple for some two hours, when the procession would return in the same order."

On the site of the present-day Capuchin church in Víziváros (Water Town) on Fő, or Main, Street stood a complex of buildings that included a *jami,* a bath, and a religious school, or *madrasah,* built by Toygun Pasha in the mid sixteenth century. Not far away a dervish monastery was established. The Mustapha Pasha Jami, the predecessor of today's parish church in Tabán, south-west of Castle Hill, was built by the most prominent Turkish architect, Mimar Sinan, who also designed the Great Suleiman Mosque in Istanbul.

After the turn of the sixteenth to the seventeenth centuries the pashas established their residence in the former Franciscan monastery of Saint John in the Castle. With the exception of a handful of public buildings and jamis, however, the town presented a sorry sight. Described by an emissary of the German emperor, "In Hungary's capital, the royal seat, many houses and mansions stood that are now fallen to ruin, in most places propped up by poles, because the Turks care for nothing only to have a place for their horses, and aside from that the rain may leak in wherever it will. [...] They do not mind that mice, lizards, weasels, snakes, or scorpions install themselves in the houses, they use houses only in the way a pilgrim uses shelter, merely to protect them from frost, heat, wind and snow. If the emperor so commands, they must move on directly. The noble lords surround their houses with fine gardens, and in the gardens they have baths. [...] Otherwise they build nothing at all, but allow the houses to fall utterly to decay."

With its surrounding hills and mountains giving rise to numerous spas and hot springs, Buda was especially suited for establishing baths, whose use was prescribed by Islam. The availability of medicinal waters was a long-known fact,

as the names of two outlying districts, Felhéviz and Alhéviz (Upper and Lower Thermal Spring), indicated. In both localities the Turks raised several complexes containing spas, particularly under Sokollu Mustapha, Pasha of Buda in the 1560s and '70s. Four of these baths still operate today: Császárfürdő (Emperor's Bath) in what was once Felhéviz; Királyfürdő (King's Bath), with its cupola still a noted landmark on Fő Street in Víziváros (Water Town) between the Danube and Castle Hill; and two in Alhéviz, now Tabán: Rácfürdő (Serb Bath); and Rudasfürdő (Pole Bath) with its octagonal central pool and a cupola. The Turks undertook their most significant constructions in Water Town.

Apart from religious buildings and baths, the Turks raised mostly military structures, such as the round bastions still seen along the Castle wall overlooking Krisztinaváros (Christina Town) to the west. Not only the Castle District itself was enclosed by a wall, the "suburb" of Water Town had its own walls and towers, also on the Danube bank. The fortress and its gates became part of the oriental way of life in Buda, always ready for battle even in peacetime. As Evliya Chelebi described it, "Vienna Gate, [...] has several iron gates. The spaces between these gates are vaulted and the sky cannot be seen hence. In July they are refreshing places. The gates are fifty paces apart. Here thousands of weapons of all sorts adorn the walls, and the soldiers of the castle stand armed and ready at any moment. Over each gate on the vaults are iron grids, ingeniously set, with halberds and spears below them, and the iron grids are suspended on chains in such a manner that they may be released over the enemy in times of battle, and the spears are capable of piercing several of them and obstructing the entrance."

The magnificent heart of the royal castle, Friss (New) Palace from King Sigismund's time, was now a magazine.

30. *The interior of Rudas Baths as depicted in 1845*

33

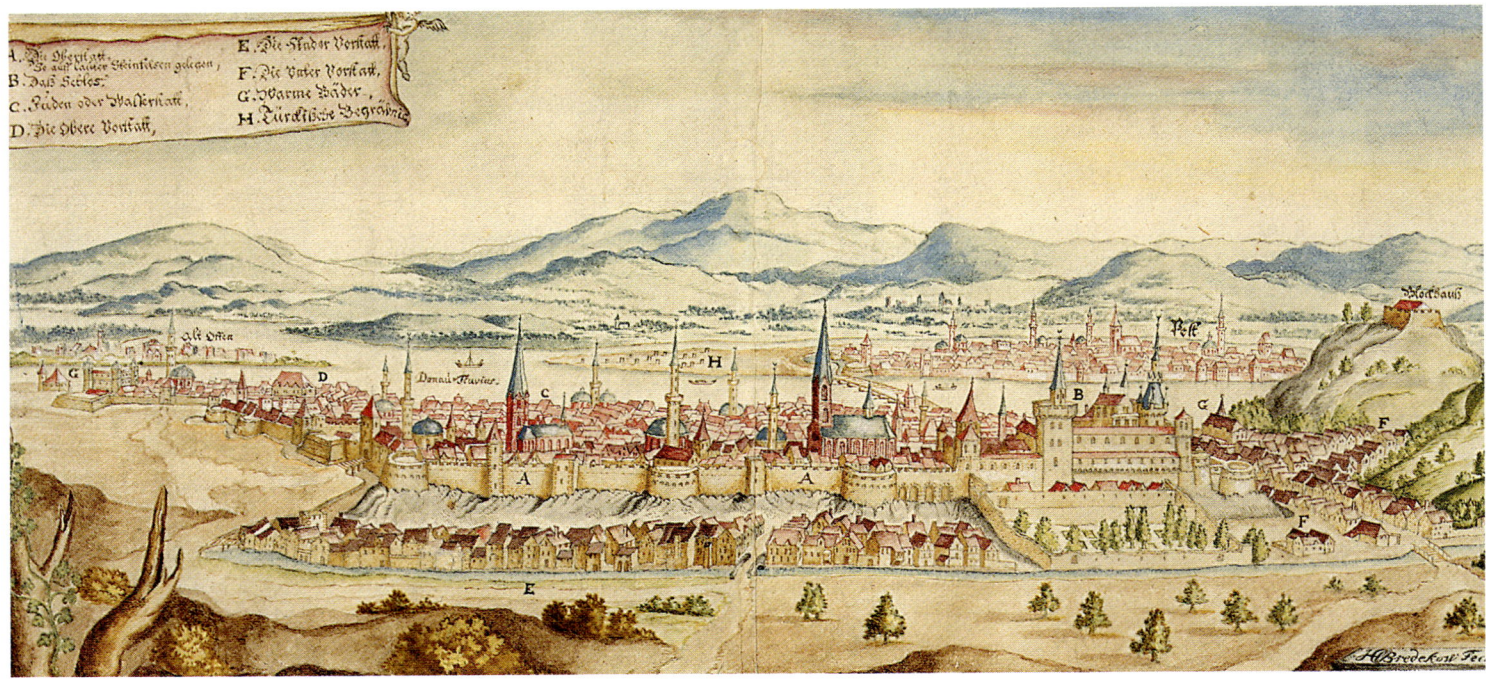

31. *Buda and Pest as Turkish towns in a painting from 1684*

During a spring storm in 1578, lightning struck, and the ensuing explosion was so great that the stones thrown up ruptured the pontoon bridge, some even hitting the Pest bank. The explosion and fire that followed destroyed much of the Danube wing of the palace. "Csonkatorony", the half-finished tower, remained unscathed, however, and retained its function as a dungeon for countless Hungarian prisoners. The room housing King Matthias' Corvina library escaped damage as well.

What had been a Central European town was now a Balkan one; the traditional commerce of Buda and Pest with the West was largely interrupted, and directed toward other Turkish provinces. Artisans and merchants from Balkan cities were offering their wares; on the markets they sold oriental clothing and peculiarly decorated ceramic wares along with hoards of copper ware and leather goods. Three hundred artisans set up shop here. Across from the main mosque was Kasandzhilar Yolu, today's Szentháromság Street, lined with copper-ware shops. Evliya Chelebi praised the splendour and size of the grocers most of all. The Turkish artisans established something akin to guilds as organisations to protect their interests. Unmarried journeymen, who had their separate lodgings, bequeathed the word *betyár* to the Hungarian language, which it means "highwayman" or "scamp" and its distinctly negative connotation indicates their notoriety.

The inhabitants of Budun were mostly Turkish, or more precisely Bosnians of the Greek Orthodox faith, resettled from their native land, a part of the Ottoman Empire. A sprinkling of Hungarians, moving in from outlying areas or perhaps returning to the town, resided here. For half a century their church, Catholic and Protestant together, remained Mary Magdalene's. In 1596, however, it met the fate of all the other churches: the Turks converted it into a mosque. In commemoration of their capture of Eger Castle (whose fate is lamented in several ways, including, in a major Hungarian novel) it became the Fethiye Jami, or "Victory Mosque".

The Jews continued to live in the old Jewish quarter, and were regarded by the Turkish administration as an independent, autonomous community. Only a fraction of the former Jewish population, some thirty families, were left, though by the time Buda was recaptured from the Turks they had multiplied to around a thousand people. The majority were Ashkenazim who had arrived from German lands and spoke German as their mother tongue. They were now joined by originally Spanish, or Sephardic, Jews coming from the Balkans. Ongoing tensions persisted between the two communities who, though forced to live side-by-side, maintained separate synagogues. That of the Sephardim can still be seen on Táncsics Mihály Street.

The judge of the Buda Jews (*kethüda*) was lower in the Turkish hierarchy than the Hungarian official had been in his. At the same time, the Jews were granted the right of freedom of worship and trade. Their main pursuits were foreign commerce and money-lending. Some were able to accrue considerable fortunes, to the extent that they could buy Christian prisoners as slaves. Living in houses of stone, they all owned books and codices.

The Jewish communities in Turkish Buda also played host to rabbis travelling from German towns to the Holy Land; those who stayed here for an extended time stimulated local religious and intellectual life.

Under these circumstances, with the Jews enjoying relative tranquillity and prosperity as well as tolerance on the part of the Turks, they integrated into the Turkish town; During the sieges they fought on the Turkish side. On some occasions, the successful resistance to a siege was attributed to their courage alone. As a consequence the Jews experienced the liberation of Buda quite differently to the Christian population and the liberating armies.

Though equally protected by a wall, Pest was a much smaller town, and a deputy of the chief magistrate of Buda was in charge of its affairs. The two towns were connected by a bridge of seventy pontoons linked by chains and overlaid with planks. In the centre were larger boats that could be drawn aside to open the bridge. Three hundred guards watched over the bridge, with a separate division for the boats themselves. Tolls were collected at both ends.

1683: A Christian Alliance to Liberate Buda

The control of Buda involved much more than its tangible consequences: it involved a symbolic significance to which both the Ottoman Empire and Europe were sensible. The European reaction – articulated by the Pope – demanded the expulsion of the "pagans" in the name of Christianity. Of course the unity of Christendom was precarious at a time when the Protestant faiths were challenging the Catholic and gaining ground, and especially with the Inquisition advancing. Even more ambiguous were the policies of the individual countries. After Spain, the Habsburg Empire was the major power in Europe. It had gained considerable strength in Central Europe, and had more than once ventured into alliance with the Ottoman Empire to counter France. There were several attempts to liberate Buda, they all failed. The siege of 1602 gave the most cause for hope, when the armies of the Holy Roman Emperor briefly freed Pest.

The year 1683 finally brought a breakthrough in the changing tides of military successes and failures. The Turkish siege of Vienna was raised, and the defeat so severe that their Grand Vizier was only able to collect his hastily retreating troops a hundred kilometres away. It was the beginning of the end of the hitherto unimpeded expansion of the Ottoman Empire and the prelude to its long decline. Now the Imperial War Council established as its mission the liberation of Buda. The imperial forces set off to clear the line of the Danube to preclude an attack from their rear. In 1684, the imperial army laid siege to Buda. But what had seemed an imminent victory turned into a defeat. This brought home the lesson that only a much larger army rallied with the concerted efforts of the Holy Roman Empire could hope to overcome the superbly fortified Turkish provincial capital.

Two years later curious events seemed to augur a forthcoming victory, expediting the renewal of war. An eye witness described some of them. "At that time a wondrous thing happened in the town of Buda, something we saw with our very eyes. On that day came thousands upon thousands of peculiar birds cheeping in a ominous manner, and flew all at once over the fortifications of the town, and drove out all the birds that had long made their nests in the castle. They struck or attacked not one of the native birds, yet these were seized by fear of the strange birds and their calls – they were such odd birds that no one had ever heard about or seen in this country. The indigenous birds then soared and flew away in concert. The folk wondered at the sight and cheeping. As for the strange birds, they made their nests in those of the native birds and took their place. [...] But even before that happened [...] we witnessed an even stranger event: for a day and a half all rivers, all springs, even the Danube stream, were stricken with snakes and scorpions, and whenever a person went to draw water, his jug would be filled with snakes and scorpions that looked like small, red insects, and for some two days we could not draw drinking water from the rivers."

The auguries became reality with the collaboration of several major powers. Pope Innocent XI and Emperor Leopold I organised a Christian army 45 thousand strong, which assembled at Párkány (now Sturovo, Slovakia), about 70 kilometres north-west of Pest, to advance down both banks of the Danube to deliver Buda. Under their protection an indescribable number of boats and galleys, heavy with goods, made their way downstream. The size of their cargo was extraordinary, comprising 186 cannons and mortars, 560 thousand kilograms of gunpowder and 300 thousand kilograms of fuse, 25 thousand kilograms of lead, 112 thousand cannon balls, 54 thousand grenades, 20 thousand bombs, food and supplies, hospital equipment and more. The commander of this force was Duke Charles of Lorraine, who had won every single battle he had fought against the Turks. He led the armies of the Holy Roman Emperor, Bavaria and Saxony; under Buda he was joined by considerable Prussian, Franconian and Swabian forces, in addition to 15 thousand Hungarian soldiers, hussar cavalry, and Haiduks. Italian, English, French and Spanish mercenaries were also present. All in all there were 75 thousand men, each battalion led by an accomplished commander. Observers from various European states accompanied the forces. The recapture of Buda truly became a common Christian and European undertaking.

The Turkish defenders amounted to only some 10 thousand men, but they had the protection of a massive system of fortifications, and were led by an excellent pasha with considerable experience in battle. Abdurrahman, of Albanian descent, was the 99th pasha of Buda, and also its last. Although the Turks could not expect an army to come to their relief, their considerable food provisions and military equipment, and the backing of much of Buda's population – southern Slav Turks and Jews – made their prospects not at all hopeless.

On the Christian side the siege, begun that summer, initially proceeded commodiously with the closing of roads, battery installations, and the repulsion of lesser Turkish forays. The first attacks and small raids took place toward the end of July. Already, the number of casualties proved considerable. Fighting was conducted in any shape or form, and incited savagery on both sides of the wall. Badly placed mines on the allied side exploded to bury masses of their own soldiers, while fire was rained down on the men, and flares that could not be extinguished, scorching their clothes and bodies. On storming the castle walls the troops were met by hails of bullets, stones, arrows, and burning tar bags. The Turks cut off the head of any enemy they could lay their hands on, to be displayed on a pole on the wall as a means of psychological warfare.

On July 22nd a mortar fired a bomb into what was once Friss Palace, which touched off 800 thousand kilos of gunpowder. An eye-witness described the event. "For a full hour the earth around Buda shook. [...] From the weight falling on it the water of the Danube rose over its banks, putting the garrison on the shore to flight, the surging waves in their pursuit. The air was brimming with large stones, and over the opposite shore, too, a hail of rocks scattered." The enormous detonation blew much of the Danube jetty into the air, along with some 1500 Turkish soldiers. Trying to take advantage of the situation Charles of Lorraine called on Abdurrahman Pasha to surrender, but he refused, knowing that he had two untouched powder stores still at his disposal, and that for the time being the breached wall could not be approached by the enemy. There was also the knowledge that the Grand Vizier was advancing toward Buda from the south with a 40 thousand-strong army. The allied force surrounded Buda first with a smaller and subsequently a broader second line of trenches running through the Buda hills. This the Grand Vizier's men were unable to cross, while the allies, following several weeks of canon fire, were able to break through the north-western town wall. On August 29th a reinforcement of over ten thousand men arrived from Transylvania, affording the opportunity to launch the final offensive.

At 3 o'clock in the afternoon of September 2nd the attack began. "Both sides hastened to storm the ruins, displaying an almost unimaginable disdain for the ever-present threat of death," recalled Franz Wagner, the German biographer of Emperor Leopold. "The castle commander himself, with the best of the remaining garrison, defends the breached, dilapidated walls, shouting in the usual manner to heaven to entreat Mohammed for assistance, stirring the enthusiasm of his men, and felling the attackers with well-aimed shots. Among the first to die is Baron d'Asti and the best of the mercenaries, but that does not foil the Germans as they continue their attack over the bodies of their companions, keeping closed ranks amidst a shower of bullets. The losses only increase their ardour. The Turks grimly resist and it seems as if owing to their stalwartness the opposing forces' military fortunes are to remain undecided for some time. [...] The Turks are unable to withstand the pressure, and just as they presage the imminent destruction they become confused and tumble on open ground. [...] Too late do the Turks raise the white banners – some take refuge in the houses opposite, in the Lower Town, while most escape into the Castle area. Few escape their doom. Armed and unarmed men alike fall as the soldiers give free rein to their furore. The streets are swamped with barbarian blood, and the once thriving town is tarnished by the grisly slaughter.

"Lorraine observes all this from the corner tower and [...] orders the soldiers to refrain from killing and pillaging, and to take up battle order in the town. [...] And the fighting ceased only when all the Turks assembled in the square surrounded by the double wall, and casting away their weapons appealed for mercy. [One of the commanders] achieved the acceptance of their surrender, saying that it would be dishonourable for Christians to refuse mercy for those who had proved good soldiers, exhibiting courage to the last. [...] After it was thus decided, both commanders, soiled with the dust of glory, returned to their camp. The

32. *Abdurrahman (c.a. 1615-1686), the last Pasha of Buda, in an etching from the end of the 17th century*

killing and pillaging continued through the night, although fires ravaged in many places, preventing much of the booty from falling prey to the soldiers' greed."

The "breached, dilapidated walls" were to the north-west, next to the Esztergom. This is where the attackers first entered, led by János Fiath, a Haiduk major, who also hoisted the Hungarian colours on the bastion. On the south side a Bavarian lieutenant-colonel named Martin Günther Pechmann is believed to have been the first to enter.

The final offensive and the victory of the allied army took hardly more than two hours. Though the conquest was a masterful feat in several respects, the losses were considerable. Many colonels and commanders fell. Over three thousand men of the allied forces were killed, over three and a half thousand were wounded, and more than a thousand succumbed to disease. The Turks lost around three thousand men in the final assault alone. A plaque commemorating the Italian lieutenant-colonel Michele d'Asti is set in the wall of Matthias Church, and on the Bastion Promenade stands a monument to Abdurrahman Pasha, the fallen defending commander.

There was more to the 77-day siege and recapture of Buda, however, than the losses of soldiers. While the sparse Christian population of the town seems to have informed the allies of their existence in time, the Jews were not pro-

33. *The explosion of the powder store in Buda Castle on July 22, 1686, in a contemporary "picture report"*

tected from danger. Their chronicler Izsák Schulhof described how the inhabitants of the Jewish quarter sought refuge in the synagogue. "Everyone wailed and wept woefully, crying for help, and the lamenting reached the skies – no ears have perceived ever so much pain as that our souls suffered. And in my great torment I stood up hastily, took my phylactery and prayer book, the Sion Kapuit, and weeping loud I cried to my wife and my only son, Simson – praised be his memory. [...] While in the midst of the commotion I gathered them, a great many soldiers stormed in, footsoldiers with their destructive weapons in their hands, firearms and bare swords, Hungarian Hussars, too, they with their crooked swords in hand. And in the house of God they brought sacrifice: spilling the innocent blood of the sons of Israel. As they say: Where there is vice woe will follow. Killing, and pillaging, robbing and slaying, all befell us."

When the fury ended came the taking of prisoners, and then their sale. The surviving four hundred Jews were looked upon as prisoners by the victors. They were redeemed by several West-European congregations, and a

34. *The triumphal procession of Duke Charles of Lorraine on the western slope of Buda Castle, by Heinrich Faust, 1694*

Viennese banker named Samuel Oppenheimer. There must have been a considerable number of Turkish prisoners, since even at the end of the year there were over two thousand held in Buda alone.

After the ancient custom, three days of pillaging were permitted following victory. The fires that broke out in its wake once again devastated Buda. By a stroke of luck the young Count Luigi Ferdinando Marsigli, cartographer, botanist and art collector (and founder of the Academy of Bologna) was a colonel assigned to do battle in Buda. While his fellows pillaged, he gathered codices and documents, rescuing them for posterity. He subsequently prepared numerous drawings and maps of the fortress of Buda, later surveyed a stretch of the Danube and produced a botanical catalogue of the area.

Christianity and Europe celebrated. Messengers conveyed the intelligence, news dispatches and papers spread the tidings, cannon shots fired from Hungarian castles conveyed the triumph. In the towns there were festival illumination and revelry, in the larger towns fireworks; churches celebrated thanksgiving masses, and several dozen commemorative coins were minted. In Valencia, Spain, for example, the academy of literature announced a poetry competition on the occasion.

Inevitably, the Ottoman Empire was being driven out of Europe – but Buda could not regain its previous importance. As the Turkish yoke was being shook off, Hungary was being engorged by the Habsburg Empire, and Pozsony

(Bratislava), with its proximity to Vienna, was retained as the Hungarian capital. Just as four hundred years before, when the Mongolians had devastated Buda and Pest, the chances for a new life were very uncertain. Festivities were held in far-away places, the liberation of Buda was a feat for the west of Europe, just as the object of the feat remained devastated and barren, forsaken rubble in a forsaken place. The festivities ended, and newer triumphs supplanted that in Buda, while the middle Danube was left to decay into a dull provinciality. Yet the dream of regaining its former glory and erstwhile privileges lived on.

In Buda, of course, it became a tradition to celebrate the anniversaries of the victory. That was the town's holiday. Each September 2nd the burghers, with their aldermen at the front bearing the town standard, others with church and guild banners in pursuit, marched over to the long maintained breach in Esztergom Bastion where the Christians first entered. Here the town parson celebrated mass and, in the words of a Vienna paper, "[...] as in every year, an eagle could be seen to soar into the sky."

New Life Emerges from the Ruins

It followed from the circumstances of the siege that Buda came under the authority of the imperial Habsburg army. Reconstruction was overseen by the commander of the castle. Yet the Treasury, the empire's supreme economic authority, was eager to check the increased power of the military. Within a month after victory a Treasury directorate was set up in Buda, headed by Stephan Johann Werlein, an able bureaucrat. Werlein lost no time organising the public administration of Buda and Pest; twelve months later he had compiled a roster of burghers who were compelled to swear an oath of citizenship. Concurrently he named the town leaders, aldermen and senators to oversee the public administration and judiciary, and a mayor for Buda and a chief magistrate for Pest. For close to a century they were of equal rank until, in 1773, the mayor was placed above the Pest chief magistrate.

A military officer became the mayor of Buda, while a Treasury officer was named as the chief magistrate of Pest. Just a few months after taking office and becoming familiar with their towns' past they applied in a memorandum for the re-awarding of the former privileges of freedom from taxation and the right to collect levies. It took a decade and a half for this to happen. In 1703 both towns, each with its own, though similar, charter, after a two-year transition period regained their privileges as free royal towns. Like the letters patent of the nobility they were bestowed their own coats-of-arms, these being their former medieval insignia.

As a first step in the reconstruction the Imperial War Council had its German, Italian and French engineers survey the area and prepare maps. (Consequently more is known about Buda in ruin than about Buda in its former glory as a royal seat.) The survey extended to the plots and to the outskirts beyond the town walls. Buda proper consisted of the Castle and Water Town, the latter having suffered less devastation than the former. Tabán stood as the southern outskirts of Buda, and to the north the settlements extending toward Óbuda were being rebuilt under new names, Országút, and Újlak. The boundary between Buda and Óbuda was along today's Nagyszombat Street.

For some two decades after liberation from Ottoman rule Pest, surrounded by the marshy Rákos-dike and compressed between its town walls, was also considered an annexe of Buda. When it was awarded its charter as a free royal town, it appealed to the Treasury for permission to expand by way of establishing its own suburbs. The first

such outlying area was Pacsirtamező, also known by the German name of Lerchenfeld (both mean Nightingale Field), to the north-east, created around 1730. It was modelled after suburbs of Vienna, as were the subsequently built-in areas, also with German names. As the population grew, so the suburbs increased – but with their village character and agricultural orientation they were quite unlike the town proper. Following half a century of boundary disputes, in 1747 the towns' administrative boundaries were demarcated. Another enduring installation, which was to operate for a hundred years, was built in 1771. This was the "Liniengraben", a link of trenches around the Pest suburbs, where the gardens and farms met the sandy pastures of the plain. The trenches served a number of functions, the first of which was to isolate the population from the frequent epidemics, particularly the plague. The course of these trenches can still be traced; beginning at Ferdinand railway bridge and along Szív and Rottenbiller streets, it ran along Fiume and Orczy roads, and reached the Danube south of the city at Haller Street. Only four highways crossed the trenches into the town, and they were closed at night by barriers. These marked the town's customs frontiers, though duties continued to be collected also at the traditional locations, at one of the town gates. Here the customs officials controlled traffic in so-called "pass-houses", issuing passes to merchants for goods that were subject to duty, to be paid in the customs house near Váci Gate.

In those years when the boundaries of Pest were demarcated, the War Council ordered a new line of defences in

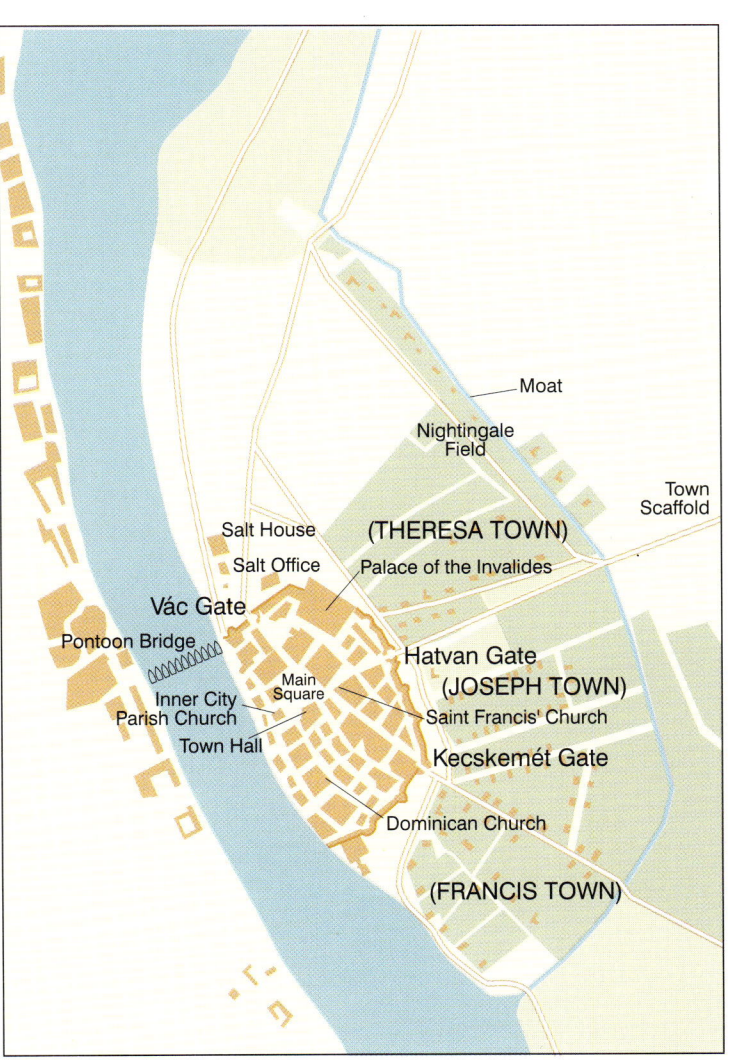

35. A map of Pest from 1764

Buda to be established around the Castle. No construction was allowed within shooting distance of the castle walls. The slopes of Castle Hill remained vacant, while the once open vineyards were divided into plots. By 1772 cadasters were introduced, and there was a new suburb. It was named Krisztinaváros after Queen (of Hungary, and Austrian Empress) Maria Theresa's daughter, the Grand Duchess Christina (1740-1780), who was married to the Governor-General of Hungary.

The reconstruction changed the towns significantly. In Buda houses and a few mansions were raised, and the Church and freshly introduced monastic orders set up attractive ecclesiastic structures that displayed the pomp of the Counter-Reformation in the grandly elaborate baroque style. These included not only churches and monasteries, but various educational institutions and hospices. It was also imperative for the defence of the country to erect fortresses, town walls and gates, the military arsenal (*Zeughaus*) in the Castle, and the Palace of the Invalids, or veterans hospital (built from 1716 to 1741) in Pest. Parts of the Royal Palace had to be built anew, an undertaking that spanned three quarters of the eighteenth century.

The most important administrative and financial structures, such as the town hall, storages, and customs houses, needed to be in place as quickly as possible. The town cores were the first to be completed. On Castle Hill, the Jesuits restored and decorated the Matthias Church, flanked on both sides by their house and school. After the liberation from Ottoman rule, the king granted the Jesuits the exclusive right to run parishes not just in Buda but also in Pest and Óbuda. They contributed to establishing the towns as centres of the arts and intellect in a short time. In the square in front of the Matthias Church the Trinity Statue, as it is called, was erected in gratitude by survivors of the plague. Nearby stood the town well, its fifteenth-century pipes, coming down Svábhegy from the *Városkút* (Town Well), were restored by a Jesuit priest. On the far side of the square the Town Hall was built; with several additions: it functioned as such until the unification of Buda and Pest in the late nineteenth century.

National fairs were held in Buda, in present-day Batthyány Square. The baroque parish church of Water Town, Saint Anne's, was erected on this square. Across from it was the church and monastery of the Franciscans, while on the third side, facing the Danube, was the terminal for long-distance stage-coaches, the Post House, and numerous inns. The most charming of these, with a rococo façade, was the White Cross, a two-story structure still standing today, which is said to have hosted not just the emperor but the Venetian diplomat and womaniser, Casanova. The latter's success – so legend goes – was no less visible in Buda than elsewhere in Europe. Another account has him staying in Tabán, where he became enamoured of the innkeeper's beautiful daughter – and was rebuffed!

The turreted Town Hall of Pest was begun in 1702, and continued to be expanded, decorated and remodelled up to the time, when with the

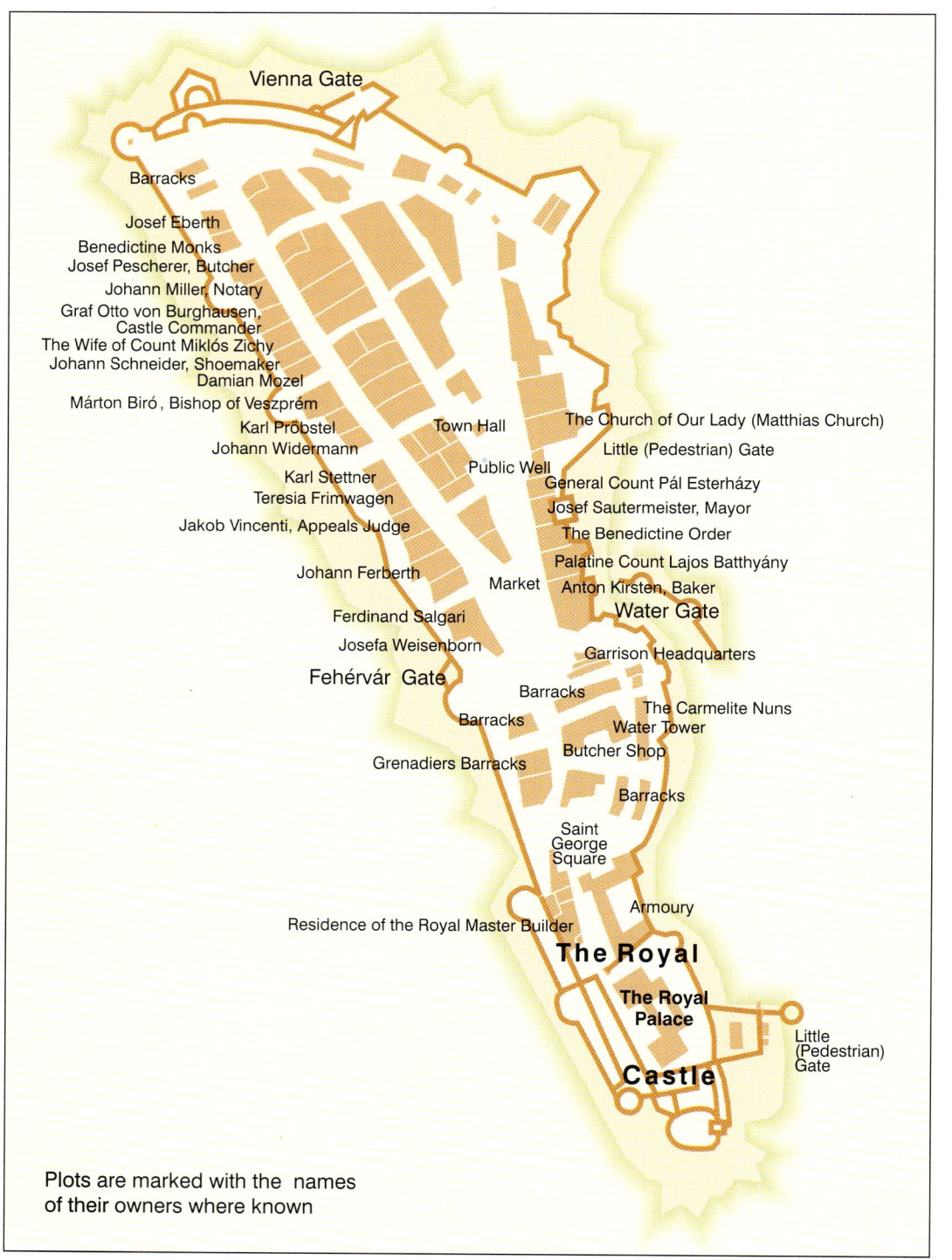

Plots are marked with the names of their owners where known

36. Buda in the 1750s

37. *A photograph from around 1900 of the Town Hall of Buda*

construction of Elizabeth Bridge and the reconstruction of the area at the end of the nineteenth century, it had to be torn down. The tower housed the guards who were assigned to keep continuous watch over the town, and to signal the residents in case of fire. Purportedly their other duty was to cry out on the hour and half hour, "Gelobet sey Jesus Christus!", or "Praised be Jesus Christ."

The building looked down on Pest's main square, which was the central market. The chancel of the town parish church was on one side. The school established by the town, with the instruction entrusted to the Piarists, was adjacent, as was the Piarist monastery. Both stood in their original form until the building of Elizabeth Bridge.

Soon after the Turks were driven out, Greek-Orthodox Serbians were given separate permission by the king to raise their own churches. These were the still functioning Serbian church on Váci Street, and another in Tabán, and during the eighteenth century the Greek-Orthodox patriarch even had his seat in Buda.

Óbuda, since 1659 an estate of the Counts Zichy, resembled more of a market town than an urban centre. It wasn't until the mid eighteenth century that more distinguished buildings were raised here; these include the baroque parish church, the church and monastery of the Trinitarians on the Kiscell Hill, and the Zichy Castle on the Main Square, splendid enough to host the monarch himself.

With Buda and Pest restored to town rank in 1703, the two were finally considered equal to those that had not suffered Turkish occupation and were unhindered in their development. Yet no patent could undo a hundred and fifty years of history. While the new population and the vast ruins waiting to be built upon favoured modern construction and a fresh beginning, commerce and wealth, cultural institutions, civic consciousness and self-regulation remained unstable for lack of tradition and experience. As these towns exemplify, opportunity itself does not make a good self-government. After they were restored their ranks as towns, their aldermen were no longer named but elected. Their twelve-member magistracies had to be augmented by larger "external councils" so that the burghers could exert more direct control over public and financial administration. At the head of the external councils was the *Vormund*, or spokesman, whose duties were much like those of a modern-day ombudsman.

In the end, however, these governments were not granted the influence previously conceived. The appointed counsellors of Buda and Pest, which provided also the mayor and chief magistrate, used their influence to retain their positions once the bodies were elected; they simply appointed spokesmen, while barely a quarter of the votership participated in the elections. In less than two decades, tensions between the cliques and the tyranny of the magistrates became so great and the accrued debt, especially in Buda, was so large that the burghers could bear it no longer. They appealed to the royal chamber for an investigation. With that began a series of reforms of the towns' organisation and spheres of influence. The outcome was that the form of municipal government increasingly lost any resemblance to those in the western parts of the Habsburg Empire. Conditions that characterized the Balkans, such as legal insecurity, corruption, and the exertion of temporary power, became rampant. In Pest, for

example, it happened that men without citizenship who had never taken the civic oath were able to attain high offices. The investigation determined the fraudulent misuse of funds and demanded a considerable sum as retribution – which the delinquents refused to pay. It took a second investigation a decade later to divest the corrupt council of office.

This investigation resulted also in another reform. A 1727 royal decree reinstituted some of the administrative procedures that were in effect prior to the investigation; what had been the "Hundred", a body familiar all over Europe by the Latin designation of *centumvir*, was superseded by a complex external council, and a *Bürgershaft*, or "citizen body". The patricians in the twenty-four-member external council were primarily merchants and wealthy property owners, though the artisans always outnumbered them. The citizen body consisted of suburban chief magistrates, two jurors from each suburb, and the guild master and two senior masters of each guild.

The same ordinance opened the way, however, for Hungarians and Serbians to be elected onto what had been an exclusively German body. With the increase in the Hungarian citizenry, the Treasury at the middle of the eighteenth century would occasionally demand the election of officials speaking the Hungarian language, and after 1763 a Hungarian spokesman had to be elected along with the German one. While in Pest this had been the practice since 1691, it was a novelty in Buda when the master bootmaker József Tóth became the first Hungarian spokesman.

Finally, in 1781, the external council and citizen body merged, under the designation of the latter, with a total of

38. Holy Trinity Square in the Castle District, when it served as a market place, and before Matthias Church was restored. On the right side of the picture stands the Town Hall of Buda. Oil painting by Albert Schickedanz, 1903

39. *The weekly market on Pest's Town Hall Square. Colour lithograph by Rudolf Alt and Franz Xaver Sandmann, 1845*

84 members. New elections were held biennially, always on Saint George's Day on April 24, as had been the custom since medieval times. The magistracy would summon the citizen body to join them in marching to the parish church, and after their return the town clerk would make known the royal mandate. Now the spokesman was elected. Originally, the external council, later the citizen body, nominated three men to the office from among its membership. As there was no limitation to the number of terms of office, it happened that, for instance, a Buda master butcher named Christoph Weiner held the office of spokesman for twenty-five years.

Once the spokesman was decided, the two top officials, the mayor and the chief magistrate, were elected. The mayor oversaw the municipal administration and presided over the council meetings. In Buda he and the chief magistrate could be elected only from the members of the magistracy. Before 1781 the Pest chief magistrate was chosen from three nominees of the external council. The chief magistrate served as deputy to the mayor in addition to presiding over the town court. The court was a tribunal of members from the external council. With the separation of the municipal administration and judiciary Buda's – with Pest conforming in 1773 – was an exceptionally modern administrative system among the towns of Hungary, where the chief magistrate embodied both functions. The magistrates, the officers in the external councils, and members of the citizen bodies were elected for life.

Although both Buda and Pest had identical charters the former required government action against the misuse of power on the part of its leaders, while in Pest it was the arrogance of its burghers that gave rise to crises. The difference had its roots in the way the towns were rebuilt after Turkish rule.

At that time neither Buda nor Pest had any surviving populace; and it was only soldiers and prisoners of war who occupied the two towns' habitable houses. So many Croatian soldiers had established themselves in the northern section of Water Town that it soon became referred to as Croatian Town.

The population grew. While around 1700 both towns together counted fewer than two thousand souls – compared to over a hundred thousand in Vienna – a mere eighty odd years later the number had tripled. Of Buda, Pest and Óbuda the first had by far the greatest population, attracting the well-to-do as the centre of financial administration for the three towns, with opportunities in government administration, and a promising livelihood from the Buda vineyards the Turks had also been fond of. The less affluent went to Pest, itself a poor town without arable land and its once thriving commerce having declined in the centuries of war. As soon as its economy was reviving, the two adversary parties in the early eighteenth-century anti-Habsburg revolts, known as the Rákóczi Wars of Independence, ravaged the town for over six years, exacting ransoms and occasionally massacring the inhabitants. Those who could escaped and took residence elsewhere. Buda remained untouched by these events; its fortifications were sufficiently restored and its garrison strong enough to deter any attempts at assault.

The population of the three towns developed in different directions. Settlement proceeded according to plan, with the Imperial Treasury determining where specific groups were to establish themselves. Buda Castle was to become the home of Germans and Catholics, Water Town – like Pest – was to house Hungarians and South Slavs, mostly Serbs. Protestants or Jews were refused citizenship in Buda Castle – a factor that contributed to the success of the Jesuits in converting many Protestants, Greek Orthodox and Muslims to the Catholic faith.

Arseniye Črnoyević, Patriarch of Ipek and the head of the Orthodox Church and also of the Serbian feudal state of the Ottoman Empire, arrived in Hungary in 1690 with several thousand Serbian families, altogether some forty thousand people. Emperor Leopold I settled them in the devastated parts of the country and granted them privileges. Thus Greek Orthodox and, to a lesser degree, Catholic Serbs came to populate much of Tabán. They surrounded their area, which also included the present-day Naphegy and the northern slope of Gellért Hill, with ram-

parts. On travelling through, Lady Mary Wortley Montague, the wife of the English ambassador to Istanbul, made special note of the unusual atmosphere of this part of town. "Without the walls lie a vast number of little houses or rather huts. [...] These towns look very odd; their houses stand in rows, many thousand of them so close together, that they appear, at a little distance, like old-fashioned thatched tents. They consist, every one of them, of one hovel above, and another under ground; these are their summer and winter apartments." From the diffuse jumble of tent-like huts only a handful of larger buildings stood out: two Turkish baths (Rudas and Rác), adjacent to the former the imperial brewery *(Preuhaus)*, a few watchmen's houses, the Catholic church encircled by a cemetery, and the Greek Orthodox church that the patriarch had consecrated and which was later expanded, still in this form until after the Second World War. The baths drew a multitude of visitors, both the local residents and travellers. They functioned as public baths, visited jointly by men and women – much to the surprise of visitors from western Europe, especially since the dress code prescribing aprons for men and shirts for women was not entirely observed.

Serbs for the most part were involved in trade and crafts, setting up shops in Buda, and also in the military supplies trade. After restrictions were put in place against additional Serbian families settling in Buda, they moved on to Pest in considerable numbers, making up a quarter of that town's inhabitants – comparable to the Hungarian population.

The Hungarian burghers arrived from the west and north-west of the country, mostly from towns, that is from the most advanced areas of Hungary. They brought with them a civic consciousness, a spirit of self-determination,

40. *Houses on the Danube shore in Tabán in the early 19th century*

41. *Indian-ink illustration of Óbuda from 1912*

and skilled craftsmanship. The Germans, who outnumbered the other nationalities in Buda even more than in Pest, came mostly from Vienna, some from Bavaria, and a few from other German regions. Spanish soldiers and officials constituted a significant, though transitory colony.

The once flourishing Jewish population occupied entirely new areas. None of the inhabitants of Buda and Pest from Turkish times remained. Since only Catholics could attain citizenship, an ordinance the towns enforced by every conceivable means, Jews were able to establish themselves only in Óbuda, a market town and aristocratic estate, and in Water Town, where Jewish families enjoyed the protection of the Treasury, which the town council was powerless against. They lived and worshipped in rented houses, since without citizenship they had not the right to own real estate. In 1746 a royal ordinance drove them out of Buda permanently, at which time they moved to Óbuda *en masse*. The Zichy family, as the owners of Óbuda, accepted them and secured them a living, allowed them to prosper and buy real estate. In 1766, when the town passed into the ownership of the Treasury, conditions for the Jewish population improved further. They were granted a new patent, allowing them to trade freely not only on Treasury property but also in the free royal towns. Now it was only a matter of time before they could participate in the economic life of Buda and Pest. In 1781, when Joseph II decreed that Jews must be secured a place in the towns, many moved from Óbuda back to Buda and to Pest. The towns, nonetheless, seized every opportunity to check the influx of "tolerated Jews".

A considerable proportion of the town population were the craftsmen, masters, journeymen, and apprentices. Although in eighteenth-century Buda their number was greater than in Pest, at ten per cent their proportion to the population at large was lower than in less-populated Pest, where at times they reached twenty per cent. The two towns developed into thriving artisans' centres in the heart of the country, thanks to the privileges they were granted. Conversely, the town administration came to serve the interests foremost of the master craftsmen. With Buda and Pest increasingly obstructing the development of industry in the near-by market towns, only Óbuda, as a market town under protection of its overlord, developed the more modern crafts, such as turnery, button-making, locksmithery, or braziery, apart from the traditionally advanced trades, such as milling, butchery, tailoring, and carpentry.

As in the late Middle Ages, the guilds continued to stand as the paramount arrangement for the craft trades. In the western parts of Europe the guilds, impediments to advancement, were already on the decline; the fact that they flourished in this region was actually an anachronism. Immediately following the liberation from Ottoman rule, the towns launched into vigorous campaigns to organise guilds. Initially the joiners, glaziers, stone-masons, bakers and other masters of the two towns established their craft guilds; soon, however, they gathered themselves into nationality groups, setting up German, Hungarian and Serbian guilds. Both towns had well over a hundred guilds. Some trades remained independent, either because they did not meet the minimum of forty masters, or they did not have the financial means to cover the expenses entailed in founding a guild, applying for a patent, later to produce master works, arrange master banquets and a host of other obligations. The guild structure was extremely rigid. Just as the main guilds of Buda and Pest attracted masters from the near-by market towns, they were careful to share their privileges with as few others as possible. They could be ruthless in preventing new masters from joining, one method being to use their influence to have unwanted candidates conscripted.

The guilds looked on the merchants as their main adversaries, their goods creating competition for them. Consequently they sought to incorporate sales privileges into their patents. That enabled them to check the influx of not just foreign but also Hungarian merchants. The town councils under the guilds' sway were eager to construe their regulations accordingly. To offset these actions the merchants of the two towns, in turn, in the 1690s procured their own royal patents, securing the right of retail sale in the towns for their own associations. These associations admitted only Catholic men who had five years of appren-

ticeship and three years as journeymen behind them. Exceptionally they admitted Greek- Orthodox Serbian and other Balkan immigrant merchants – by this time referred to collectively as "Greeks". Merchants from abroad were permitted to trade only during the national fairs. From the Balkans they arrived mostly along the Danube and not before long had penetrated the retail business also. They immigrated to Pest in several waves, which the town government was unsuccessful in thwarting. By the 1730s the overwhelming majority of Pest merchants was from the Balkans and, in conformity with the law, settled their entire families here and attained citizenship. The German merchants were far behind them in number, and only a handful of Hungarians remained.

Merchant Jews resided in Óbuda. The fact that several ethnic and religious denominations and cultural traditions mingled in Pest – and in the other towns – did not give rise to nationalistic clashes; on the contrary, this admixture was a decisive factor in making Pest a major trading centre. In the late 1600s Buda was still the main trading town, and consequently collected considerable tariffs. Just a few years later Pest, though with a much more modest population, gained the upper hand. By the 1720s the income of Pest merchants surpassed that of Buda fivefold. As soon as the interior of the country had overcome the threat of war and business proceeded normally, Pest, with its geographically central location, became a centre of trade as a matter of course. Its national fairs soon became much-attended events of significance to the entire Central and South-Eastern European region. The regular fairs were held on feast days, those of St. Joseph's (March 19th), St. Medardus' (June 8th), St. John the Baptist's (August 29th), and St. Leopold's (November 15th). The livestock fairs on both sides of the Kerepesi highway were especially impressive. Of these, the large Cattle Fair was even surpassed by the enormous Horse Fair, held on an area spanning today's Népszinház Street to Fiumei Street. Conversely, the significance of the Buda fairs declined, and by the second half of the eighteenth century there was not much of them left. Buda arranged its fairs on dates near those in Pest to draw their visitors, which the rebuilt bridge linking the two tows may have facilitated. Initially the bridge was a ferry hauled by ropes stretching between the two shores, approximately at the site of today's Elizabeth Bridge. After 1767 a pontoon bridge was established a little further north.

The St. Medardus' Day Fair rose to first rank with its wealth of goods from different countries, and a series of attractions, which included animal contests. The latter were rather bloody shows held mainly at the so-called "Hetz", or "Heckle", Theatres, of which there were several in Pest in the eighteenth century. The most popular stood

42. Stock im Eisen, *or iron log, from the corner of Iskola and Vám Streets in Buda. Guild journeymen arriving here would hammer a nail into the stump, and with time the wood was entirely covered by nail heads*

43. *An early 19th-century ballot box from Buda's Town Hall. Votes were cast for one of three nominees, whereby voting balls were dropped into the funnels and collected in the drawer below, facilitating their removal for counting*

where the Basilica stands today. The fairs played a crucial role in introducing the various cultures, religions and ethnic groups to society at large, and as such can be considered the forerunners of tourism. The Protestant minister Mátyás Bél took note of the circumstance. When he studied in Halle, Germany he had become acquainted with the new, early eighteenth-century encyclopaedic science of "state education", a kind of civics which he continued to practice on his return. In a comprehensive volume he described the geographic, social, cultural and educational body of knowledge on Hungary available in the 1730s. "Hosting guests may reckon among the main sources of income for Pest. There is hardly a – somewhat better equipped – residence without rooms suitable for receiving guests. They may be engaged at a high price, for daily or weekly rent. In addition there are the meals, notably dearer than one should imagine. [...] Under such circumstances the fortunes of the citizens of Pest are growing considerably. The burghers' customs are easily described. The

Hungarians follow their own customs, but adjust to the fastidiousness of the Germans. The Germans, meanwhile, who are in constant contact with persons of our nationality, are themselves adopting much of what they otherwise disdained. The demeanour of the Hungarian nobility is nowhere more refined. As they converge here from all areas of Hungary, each brings with him from his home region all the culture and manner that he speaks most highly of, and consequently all that stands out in Hungarian conversation either in gravity, or the exquisiteness associated with it. This can be seen in Pest alone as in a theatre. Otherwise Pest is not wont of anything that a comfortable living requires."

It was not seldom that the country's administrative core, the Council of the Governor General, had to interfere into guild matters. Although one of its significant tasks was to reform the guilds, it took almost thirty-five years to meet the challenge, due to resistance from these bodies. The fruits of the reform were reaped in the final quarter of the eighteenth century, when after considerable delay the development of industry was able to take off. Initially a few manufactories were set up, the first in Pest in 1776. It was a state-owned broadcloth and blanket shop in the house of disabled veterans, the building which now houses City Hall. That same year the Italian Valero brothers founded their silk factory in Theresa Town, which within a decade produced fine-quality wares and employed nearly 200 workers. A tannery was founded, which used vegetable matter to work cattle hide, as was a distillery and perfume plant. Silk-making became Pest's most important industry, which by the end of the century employed two thirds of the town's workers. The most significant manufactory of Buda was the faïence factory, established by Domokos Kuny in 1785, which produced glazed and painted vessels and sets of dishes for the entire country and for export, even to Poland. Not much later the country's only "carriage factory", really an assembly plant, opened in the Castle. The influence of Óbuda's silk factory was secured with the state silk industry established here, whereas Pest had a privately initiated silk manufactory. The Venetian A. Mazzucato set up a silk-winding plant, and its unusual, oval building still stands on Miklós Square.

44. *Pest's town coffer from the 18th century*

A Regional Centre
on the Danube

In the 1770s a fundamental change took place in the development of Pest and Buda. At a time when towns were changing into cities in many places in Europe, the two municipalities' combined population of 34 thousand was significant even in the Habsburg Empire. Before the French Revolution London, Paris, Istanbul, Madrid and Naples approached, and most surpassed, the level of half a million residents, with London topping the list at 860 thousand. Indeed, cities such as Amsterdam, Rome, Berlin, Munich and Saint Petersburg had over a hundred thousand inhabitants, and the imperial capital of Vienna boasted a civilian population of 175 thousand in its first census in 1754 (to

which the military added a considerable number). Thus the thriving commerce of Pest and bureaucratic weight of Buda were of no more than local consequence. They were provincial, both in the true sense of the term that implies being separated from the core, and by their having something rural and backward about them. It was the Baroque Age, yet there was nothing of a baroque cityscape in either town, only a handful of ostentatious edifices to represent that style. Nor did any major artist who might be travelling through find anything worthy of note, let alone settle here to work. This was the century of the "grand tours," when extensive journeys through Europe were in vogue. Well-to-do aristocrats from the north or west of Europe would make their way to the south to explore the traditions of western civilisation and experience the world. The English, especially, were fond of travelling, and did so in droves, taking along their sketchbooks to capture in watercolour the atmosphere and particular beauty of some favourite spot. They were interested in southern Europe, with Italy and its classical legacy at the top of their itinerary; and the East, where the exotic world of the Ottoman Empire, and the vestiges of Greek antiquity, lured them. In the course of all these journeys, Europe was described in picture and writing – but Pest and Buda, and much of Hungary, remained a blank spot. This in spite of the fact that though the roads were poor, travel was relatively safe here and there were few tolls to be paid, making a journey in this part of the world quite affordable and expeditious. Hungary had lost its attraction as a place of curiosity that it had held in Turkish times, nor did it have extraordinary wealth, a unique or thriving culture, or anything else to indulge in. In short, Hungary had nothing special to offer.

The seeds of change – and a dramatic one at that – were already sown, nonetheless. What was needed for a city to rise from the average was to become a royal seat, the capital of a realm of whatever size. The administration of matters of state, the building spree extending to public and residential structures, the bustle of people going about official affairs, were the stuff that made a city. If a city's bureaucratic significance was joined by all that a royal court entailed, the recipe was certain to succeed. The military was a major consumer, but even more important was ostentation, which attracted artists and artisans, such as tailors, leather workers, goldsmiths and jewellers; along with their suppliers and trading network, and called for the means of transport, such as carriages and horses. The administration of a larger territory, and the pomp involved by acting as a residence for the monarch and his court, created a need and nurtured the process which, through the diligence and inventiveness of its citizens, could give rise to a city of consequence.

A new set of laws introduced in 1723, called the Pragmatic Sanction, signalled a new era for the Empire and for Hungary, and involved a comprehensive revamping of

45. *Klara Anger, Mother Superior of the convent of Saint Elisabeth in Buda, receives the convent's charter bestowed by Joseph II. The Emperor drove the Franciscan monks out of their monastery in Water Town and gave the building to this nursing order. Painting from around 1785*

a relationship that was so far-reaching that even a hundred and fifty years later Ferenc Deák was able to invoke them in forging what became the Austro-Hungarian Compromise. The law transformed the highest level of the judicial system under which, from 1723 on, the High Court operated. As the monarch's proxy it was the sole tribunal with the power to adjudicate the nobility, in addition to acting as the court of appeal. The institution was of such significance, and handled such a large number of cases, that through its wealthy and more or less sophisticated noble clientele it soon spawned a number of municipal establishments. Along with the ready selection of inns and cafés, the High Court also contributed to stimulating business at the fairs. The city only became aware of the High Court's role in promoting commerce and trade in the course of its operation. Immediately after the law was passed the Pest town council sought out its highest connections to prevent the sovereign from locating the High Court in the city, weary of being forced to provide the facilities gratis, and a set of residences to go with it. Then, since the High Court was already functioning in a rented building, the city entered into litigation to obtain title to set rental and merchandise prices, and withdrew only when it turned out that the Council of the Governor General had secured the claim. Gradually, though, the town council came to the recognition that the High Court in fact increased business and income for the city.

In Buda the royal palace was under reconstruction, though slowly, by fits and starts, but with such exacting care as if the ruler actually wished to live here – wishful thinking on the part of Hungary, for which the Habsburg court gave no cause. Once, when Maria Theresa visited the Buda reconstruction, she is said to have made disparaging remarks about the improvidence involved. Then in 1777, following comprehensive laws on education reform, she ordered the university in Nagyszombat (now Trnava, Slovakia) to relocate to the Royal Castle in Buda. The Cupola Hall was made into an observatory. The ostentatious rooms must have been the world's most impressive educational facility during those six years that it functioned there. After locating the High Court in Pest, moving the university, with its thirty-two full professors and 423 students, along with the university press and library, was again a step in the direction of establishing Buda as the nucleus of the country.

For the time being, however, Pozsony was still the capital. It housed the Council of the Governor General and the town houses of the aristocrats, with splendid new houses continuing to be raised near-by. Not far off, in Nagy-szombat, moreover, was the seat of the archbishop. But once it became inevitable, change progressed quickly. Following the relocation of the university Maria Theresa's son and successor, Joseph II, an indefatigable and reform-minded emperor and King of Hungary (1780-1790) – immortalised in legends in the Austrian lands just as he excited fears and misgivings among the Hungarian nobility – in 1784 ordered the Council of the Governor General to be removed to Buda. The Royal Palace was established as the residence of the Habsburg Palatine of Hungary. At the same time the university was obliged to move again, this time to Pest. The two cities were now linked by a pontoon bridge, made up of 64 boats. With his reforms Joseph wished to establish a centre from which to make the Empire's administration as transparent and effective as possible. Far in excess of his own designs was the return from Vienna of the Holy Crown of Hungary, amidst pomp and ceremony, on February 21, 1790 – just one day after Joseph's death. It was a sure sign that Buda was indeed becoming a capital and royal seat. The new monarch, Leopold II (1790-1792), soon convened the Diet here – though the coronation still took place in Pozsony.

Pest-Buda's attraction as an administrative, judicial, and university centre was mutually gainful, and imparted the handful of aristocrats, who had had the foresight to raise their town houses here, with the pleasant sensation that their influence and wealth were on the rise. A few major houses were built in Buda Castle from the 1740s onward, including that of count Lajos Batthyány, Chancellor and Palatine, on Dísz Square; the Zichy house on 48-50 Úri Street; and the Erdődi family's house on Táncsics Mihály Street. Among the sea of houses on the flatlands of Pest a few splendid mansions stood out, such as the Károlyi House near today's University (then the Order of Saint Paul's) Church, set in its own park; or the since demolished Grassalkovich House at the corner of Kossuth Lajos and Városház Streets. In the vicinity of the two towns (today in metropolitan Budapest) a few truly splendid castles were raised, including the one in Promontor (now the district of Budafok) of Prince Eugene of Savoy, the renowned commander-in-chief in the Turkish campaigns, which later burned to the ground; the Rudnyánszky Castle in Nagy-

47. *The Orczy House, seen from Károly Ring, around 1900*

tétény; and Zichy Castle in Óbuda; on the Pest side in Rákoskeresztúr there was the more modest Bujanovszky-Podmaniczky family castle.

All this caused, and partly resulted from, Pest-Buda being an anomaly among Hungarian towns, which were then at a standstill in their development. Just as the growth in the population of Pest and Buda was taking off in the 1770s, the other towns failed to attract any new residents. In a mere decade and a half Pest-Buda's populace grew by over a third – that of Pest by 55 per cent. The 1784 census (taken on the orders of Joseph II) showed that Buda, Pest, and Óbuda had a combined population of 50 thousand. This growth left its mark on the cities.

It was the first time travellers took notice of a new cluster of towns taking shape. The naturalist Count Joachim C. von Hoffmannsegg in 1793/94 compared Pest-Buda with the capital of Saxony, his home town, clearly favouring the Hungarian capital. Granted, he may have been influenced by the fact that he never experienced such beautiful weather as here. "The two towns together are much larger than Dresden and Neustadt united. Pest is much pleasanter, too. Many new houses are being built here, and in a quite stately form, so that in time it may grow to be a whole little Berlin, its streets and squares being so broad and spacious. With a fair in progress in Pest, the bustle is very much increased; the noise and clamber is as great as at the Leipzig fair, only the market place is much more pleasant here. Pest has ample pretty shops, although they have no

fine merchandise from abroad." Within two decades that last cavil would no longer hold true.

Among all the ordinances that sprang from the spirit of the Enlightenment and from the notion of the sovereign state, the most important for the development of the two cities was Joseph II's set of decrees of 1781. They granted Jews the right to settle there, to worship freely, establish schools, and to practice their trade; these were followed by laws allowing the Protestant and Greek Orthodox communities the right of free worship, the building of their own churches, and the right to take to take office. Just a year after the passing of these laws, Joseph II had most of the Catholic religious orders dissolved, excepting only the teaching and nursing orders.

This soon affected the townscapes. Many Catholic churches and monasteries were immediately converted to secular use. The Carmelite nunnery and church was made into the Castle Theatre – the reconstruction headed by Farkas Kempelen (who was to achieve fame with his chess "automaton") while the complex of the Order of the Clares on Úri Street became the High Court and subsequently housed the Council of the Governor General; the Trinitarian Monastery at Kiscell was transformed into a military depot. Of the Protestant faiths the Lutherans, whose congregations were mainly Germans and Slovaks with a handful of Hungarian aristocratic families and university professors, in 1793 built a chapel on whose site, in 1811, the Deák Square Church was raised. The Calvinist Church had a moderate following among Pest Hungarians and for some time operated under the auspices of Óbuda Church, holding their services in a rented chapel. They began building their church on Calvin Square in 1813. In

once a detached building, owned by the popular and prolific Pest architect Andreas Mayerhoffer. It housed an inn named "The English King", which gave the street its name. When the two buildings were joined, Baron József Orczy – who made his way into history books by establishing Pest's first public park, Orczy Gardens – erected a three-story edifice with several courtyards. In it were apartments, countless storage depots, inns, cafés, different shops, baths, and after 1796 a synagogue, which later became the centre for the Pest congregation. Beginning in the 1780s this became a hospice for Jews coming to Pest, and a storage place for the goods to be sold at the neighbouring Jewish market. The building was alternately referred to as *Judenhof* (German for Jewish Court) and, for its bazaar atmosphere, the Jewish caravansary. "Orczy House offers everything an orthodox Israelite may need all his life and under all circumstances, be that the Pascal flour or a savings bank, a pocket watch cooked according to Jewish law, a Jewish book shop, or a Kosher butcher," wrote Lajos Hevesi, the witty author and newspaper columnist of this time, who bore the name Lőwy at birth but became known in the second half of his life as Ludwig Hevesi, an excellent publicist and art critic for the Viennese press. "[Orcy House] is home to many people, and it is rare to see someone moving out. The entire habitancy of this house has something patriarchal about them, and I dare say one must give not half a year's notice but a quarter of a century's – grandfather gives notice when his grandson is to move out. Thus this peculiar house confers its residents a certain pride, all but a community within a community."

It was only a few years earlier, in 1777, that names had begun to be given to the various quarters of town. Theresa Town was named after the Queen, the second quarter to be given a name received that of her coregent and son Joseph. Within a few years Leopold and Francis Towns had their names, named for two Habsburg monarchs who came to the throne in quick succession a good decade later. (Elizabeth Town was created over a century afterwards, when in 1882 the district seceded from Theresa Town; Elisabeth was Joseph's much-loved queen, popularly called Sissy.) In the 1780s the suburbs saw considerable change as a result of the town wall being torn down, which allowed the city to spread unimpedely, soon to link itself with the outskirts. Váci Gate was the first to be razed in 1780, then the sandy, muddy open land outside was divided into plots, and an enormous building erected on orders of Joseph II. It became known as the *Neugebäude,* or New Building, the function of which neither contemporaries or posterity was able to determine with certainty. What is known is that it was to serve military purposes – several of them – and the district, designed and built to a coherent plan, was named for the new ruler Leopold II, who had recently been crowned.

In the decade of Joseph II's reign, between 1780 and 1790, countless innovations were instituted or begun that were well in advance of their time. This modernising emperor, impatient, and perhaps sensing that he had little time left, was not adverse to displaying truculence if he believed it necessary for quickly and effectively achieving his means. To successfully accomplish his plans for Pest hinged upon his ability to replace the old guard, snug in

addition to Serbians, the Orthodox church in Pest was attended by four other nationalities, Illyrians, Greeks, Romanians, and Bulgarians. The most affluent were the Greeks, who in 1789 built their own church on the Danube bank in the core of the town, and finally left the Serbian church together with the Macedonian-Romanians. The Greek Orthodox church in Buda, with a mostly Serbian congregation, functioned after 1809 as their diocesan church, serving a large territory.

Both town councils were for a long time eager to keep the Jews at bay. The Jews, in turn, sought redress with the Council of the Governor General – not a positive move in the eyes of Hungarians. Their residence continued to be confined to Óbuda, however, until Joseph II opened the way for social equality. The thriving Pest fairs attracted not just Óbuda Jews but many from other parts of the Empire. A rapidly increasing Jewish population settled outside the Pest gates, around the Palace of the Invalids and today's Deák Square, east of the town walls. Within a few years the community had multiplied to the degree that they established the seat of the national convocation of the Hungarian Jewry here. Alongside the open market set up in Újvásártér (New Market – the present Erzsébet – Square) a separate Jewish market was established, and a few inns soon opened around Király Street. Initially the Pest council would have liked to grant Jews the license to settle in a form of ghetto, but a medieval approach of this sort was not supported by any of the other authorities. Still, their settlement in Pest soon took the shape of a Jewish quarter in Theresa Town. On the corner of Király (King) Street, diagonally across from the Lutheran church, stood a huge block referred to as the Orczy House. On its street side was

their positions and opposed to any innovation that might threaten them, with enlightened reformers who shared his ideas and were willing to obey him unswervingly. He already knew Major Moritz Valentine Hülff, a Pest citizen who had attained fortune and influence in the manner not uncommon in the world of guilds, by marrying the widow of a master. He thus seemed an ideal choice for the posit of mayor. The emperor personally urged Hülff to apply for office in the town council – which the town, and even the Chancellery, repeatedly rejected. When charges were brought against the town magistracy – not at all unheard of, to be sure – Joseph II saw his opportunity to open an investigation, which resulted in the mayor and a magistrate being divested of office. Immediately Joseph proclaimed elections, with Hülff to become magistrate and subsequently mayor. The town council and senate objected – but complied. An ensuing investigation brought down the entire council, opening the way in 1785 for the citizens to elect Hülff as their mayor. Buda was spared the same fate only because its council was so interrelated that it was able to elude the divestiture of its members.

Hülff had a few years at his disposal to do what was necessary; in this time he exhibited the authority that bore out Joseph II's expectations of his abilities as the town leader, and also as president of the Building Commission established in 1787. The emperor looked on Hülff as his confidant, even visiting him in his own home to discuss the latter's plans for developing the city. The plans, as far as Joseph was concerned, were overly ambiguous, however. In no way did he wish Pest to gain either in size or influence until its government and urban fabric were modernised. He even looked into such details as house numbering, introduced in 1787. Prior to that time only churches, larger buildings, stores, taverns, or other buildings displaying trade signs, could be depended on for finding one's way around. The talented and original associates Joseph II selected to carry out his reforms would frequently transcend the emperor's own ideas. In Pest Johann von Schilson, for example, who was the director of the District Chamber of Pest, did not shy away from seeking the emperor's approval for his own ideas on urban planning, even if they were to pave the way for the city's expansion. The plan for renewing Pest and building a new suburb – which was to become Leopold Town – grew out of the necessity to establish the market square. The city of Pest, the core of the town within the walls, did not have an adequate market square, as a result of which during national fairs the tents of merchants and artisans crowded the busiest streets. The Council of the Governor General in the summer of 1785 called on the city of Pest to put an end to this unsavoury arrangement by establishing a new market place. As a consequence the area in front of Váci Gate was divided into plots, and the town was then able to cover its share of the cost of the building and improvements from the money received from the sale of these plots.

St. Medardus' Day, on June 8, 1789 was the last time the tents were allowed to obstruct the streets of Pest, two months after this national fair the sites were allocated. The "peasant market" of employment seekers along with their wagons, and the live-stock market were removed to the outer section of the highway toward Hatvan, while the merchants and artisans set up their tents in the New Market Square, where Elizabeth Square stands today.

That same year, when the town garrison marched off to war against the Turks, a citizens militia (*Bürger Miliz*) was organised. This was almost two decades before the Diet calling for a civilian guard to be established in all free royal cities in times of war. Though Pest and Buda retained their garrisons in peacetime, their activities were confined to watch-keeping in the tower of the town council, to conducting exercises, to running the rifle association, and to march in parades during city celebrations. To become a citizen in Pest one had to first serve in the citizens militia, and one had to be in uniform to take the oath of citizenship.

No sooner had the emperor died in 1790, the citizens of Pest called for an investigation against Hülff. The council, hoping to pacify the national desire for vengeance against the king now converging on Pest, and to deflect action against themselves, quickly recalled Hülff. They chose as his successor a wealthy Greek merchant by the name of János Boráros. (A busy Budapest square bears his name today.) Though Hülff was nominated later, he could not hope to be elected. The Building Commission petered out, and the council rejected his plans one by one. It rejected also a proposal by János Hild, who had achieved fame in the Josephine years as the architect of the New Building, that would have drawn up urban planning for Pest as early as the end of the 1790s.

48. Pest tailor Károly Liedke in militia uniform. Oil painting

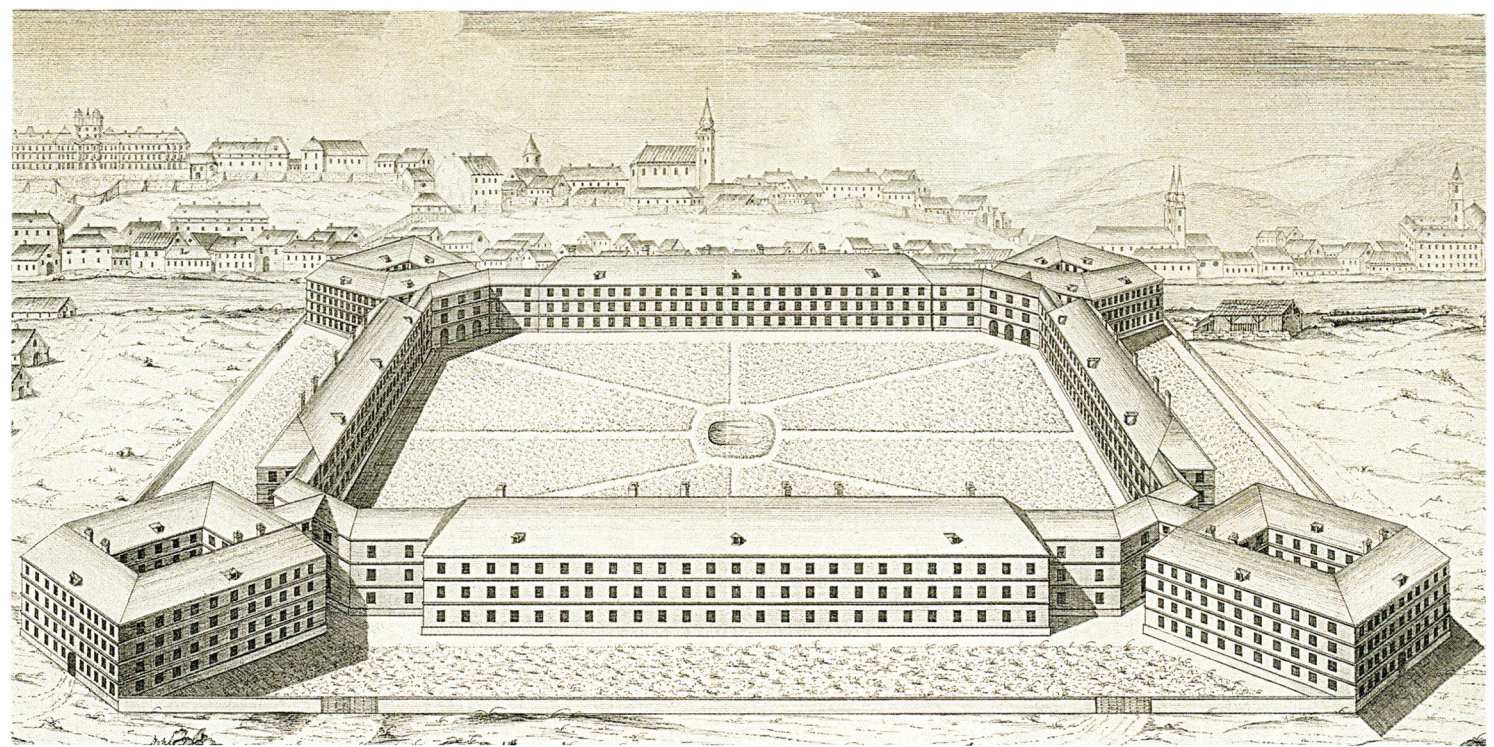

49. *The monumental "New Building" in the late 18th century, still outside the town at this time*

The setbacks not withstanding, however, Pest was definitely beginning to thrive as a city. A clear sign of its growing national significance, and the fact that it was taking on the role of a capital, was that it became the centre of newspaper publication, at this time of course in German. Though short-lived, a Hungarian-language paper, the *Magyar Merkur*, also came out, while publishers of periodicals naturally established themselves in the vicinity of the university.

In 1790, Johann Kemnitzer, a Pest master tanner who had grown rich in his trade, built a spacious, three-story house at the Pest head of the pontoon bridge, where Vigadó Square and Ferenc Deák Street meet today. Its attraction was a grand café, that no visitor, Hungarian or foreign, would wish to miss. It was referred to with civic pride as the equal of the most exquisite of Viennese Cafés, something that Robert Townson, the English naturalist, on his visit to Pest confirmed. "This town has several good ones [i.e. cafés]; but that facing the bridge is, I think, not to be equalled in Europe." Its spacious rooms, marble and imitation marble-covered columns and walls, the stuccoes on the arched ceilings boasting four crystal chandeliers; the ornately decorated fireplace with a clock above it to match; its two billiard rooms, the larger one for smokers, the smaller for non-smokers; and two or three separate sitting rooms, did indeed make the establishment one of the finest of its kind. One side of the large billiard room was opened to offer a view of the bustling activities going on in the kitchen. As Townson noted, "... and very comfortable dinners may be had." He also noticed something else, "And here, according to continental custom, all ranks and both sexes may come; and hair-dressers in their powdered coats, and old market-women, come here and take their coffee or drink their *rosolio* as well as Counts and Barons."

The café played a significant role in being in fact a democratic venue, where people of all social ranks, occupations and sexes could meet as equals. In addition, it had another important function, as a place for the exchange of information and ideas. The Kemnitzer was the birthplace of the

Pest literary café, whose progenitor was the famous writer of early Romanticism and Sentimentalism, József Kármán; he had the contributors to his *Uránia* gather around a table here to discuss the editing of the magazine. The Kemnitzer Café was truly an attraction. A Pest geography professor, András Vályi, described it thus, "Before it stretches the summer promenade where each evening all the genteel men and women from Pest and many from Buda converge, and in the summer fine music is played for the entertainment of the Guests. Those persons, moreover, who, wearied by work, seek refreshment and to find repose for their fancy in the array of objects to be seen, assemble here before this Café, and in its immediate vicinity at the end of the bridge. Likewise meet those who, lacking anything to do at all, pass the time in conversation and indolence." Vályi's is an account of a bustling esplanade in the 1790s.

At this time Pest already had the facilities for the holding of truly grand balls with the restaurant *Sieben Churfürsten* (Seven Electors), in the magnificent mansion belonging to the chief magistrate of Pest, Johann Lenner, on 9 Váci Street. In 1777 the building was procured by a man of affairs, who was known as "the giver of balls and lodging". On the second floor of this not especially striking building were spacious guest rooms; these lodged princely guests, hosted the unveiling of Farkas Kempelen's chess automaton and, a half century later, the first public piano performance by the prodigy Ferenc (or Franz) Liszt. The most prominent section of the building was its ballroom, with a gallery framing the *étage*, which was capable of holding 400. Cushioned settees were placed along the walls, and the ceiling was decorated with frescoes; these were somewhat in contrast to the establishment's name, as they depicted scenes from the abduction of Helen of Troy and the destruction of that city. The room hosted the city's carnival

50. *The small auditorium of the Redoute in the 1830s. Colour etching by Domokos Perlaszka, after a drawing by Carl Schwindt*

balls, attended by the wealthy burghers and aristocracy and, frequently, visitors from other countries. The merriment at times gave rise to diplomatic *faux pas*, as when the Turkish ambassador, in the company of the Palatine, expressed his displeasure at a lady guest having dressed as a sultan. At this time, in 1790, the Sieben Churfürsten became a literary topic, when József Gvadányi produced his satirical poem on the immediately famous "Notary of Peleske" and his travels in Buda.

By the late 1780s Pest-Buda had three theatres. The Jesuit school plays, later the performances that were the climax of large and spectacular popular festivals, and finally, between 1719 and 1745, the dramas on the stage of the Piarist monastery in Pest, were the precursors of theatre in Pest. The first proper stage was established in 1774 in what had been a bastion of the Danube fortification, where a German company was permitted to work. For almost half a century the German theatre performed here, and meanwhile another company began performances nearby. In Buda, Joseph II founded a permanent theatre, the Castle Theatre, in the former Carmelite monastery. The same companies performed in both Pest and Buda – ranking among the better ones in the medium category – and took care to perform comedies or musical plays in Buda whenever they played operas or tragedies in Pest.

Social life flourished to a degree never before seen. For instance, the Pest house of Ferenc Abaffy, a nobleman with vast estates, a parliamentary delegate and Lord-Lieutenant, almost every day hosted a social gathering, on which converged intellectuals and revolutionary-minded young men, who cheered each French victory – and Habsburg defeat – and read the works of the French thinkers who had paved the way to the Revolution, and who had a penchant for the singing of French revolutionary anthems. Buda also had its political *salon*, the *Lesekabinet*, or readers' circle, set up in the rooms of the Fortuna Inn in the Castle District.

In Pest, József Kármán raised the idea of a true, and specifically, Hungarian-language literary *salon*. The idea was enthusiastically embraced by the wealthy widow of General Beleznay, née Baroness Anna Podmaniczky, who opened her house for the purpose. Her rooms resounded with music, literature, and debates and were visited by every learned citizen of Pest, from university professors to (especially Protestant) aristocrats and noteworthy foreign guests. Even decades later, in considerably changed times, these former visitors fondly recalled the *salon* and its significance. A handful of other literary circles organised at this time, with the aim of using the Hungarian language exclusively.

Buda was the royal seat where government offices were located and most of the civil servants resided. The town was virtually a provider of services for the bureaucratic centre. Nevertheless Buda, for centuries the more important town, was beginning to fall behind the lively, business-minded, increasingly affluent and expanding Pest. Buda's attitude and thinking concerning economic matters was different. Its business activities were on a more modest and solid scale, yet until 1800 it drew considerably more income and disbursed a greater expenditure than Pest; after that, however, it began to fall behind. Buda's fiscal balance was generally positive and did not require any special financial transactions in order to sustain its economic equilibrium. In Pest, in contrast, the city had to apply a great deal of financial finesse to keep its fiscal management in balance.

Buda represented the feudal past, with all its positive and negative features, while Pest exemplified everything that was new, a future built on entrepreneurship and capital, banking and commerce. The difference was immediately apparent to any stranger visiting the sister cities. A Russian navy officer passing through at the time of the Napoleonic wars was pleasantly surprised to find that "a considerable part of the population of Pest are merchants, while Buda [...] is the residence of the nobility. The industriousness of the former and the indolence of the latter is not acknowledged equally by the government : therefore the inhabitants of the two towns live in disharmony with each other, and represent two utterly different societies, ways and philosophies of life."

Part of the lag, of course, was the result of a reclusive and exclusive attitude that the aristocracy adhered to. In terms of cultural events Buda often surpassed Pest, but while these were comparable to contemporary high culture and art in Europe, they were confined to the royal castle or to an aristocrat's palace, aloof to the town's inhabitants and the outside world. The palaces of the aristocrats bustled with social life, to the accompaniment of music. The guest in their *salons* were mostly always the same; they shared a love for the arts and their cultivation rather than for literature or politics such as the Pest *salon* visitors had proximity to and an affinity for. A German guest on Tuesdays and Saturdays at Zichy House Palace on Úri Street described such evenings minutely. "We arrive around seven o'clock, around eight o'clock almost every-

one is assembled, most sit down to games, some of the ladies do needlework, while others sit down to the pianoforte and perform music as suits their ability. There is a young man who plays exceptionally well, his talent may be considered truly a heavenly gift, he plays the piano quite excellently, has a very good knowledge of music, memorises entire operas, knows the Magic Flute by heart, and accompanies us from the score. As long as the music lasts it is usually I who sing, at times a few ladies too. Around ten o'clock the games are finished, and many come to sing, even the Lord Chief Justice, but now we perform the operas in parts. Afterwards comes supper, and at midnight it all comes to an end." In many houses the purpose of the regular get-togethers was to make music, but there were some where the lady of the house would also draw or paint. The Buda balls were held in the grand hall of the old house of Parliament, where once the Diet had sat.

In 1790, when the Crown was brought to Buda, Parliament was opened to a busy crowd, and the festivities proceeded under a forest of banners, it was evident that the country had heaved a sigh of relief. There was a sense of victory, that was stoked by a newly awakening national consciousness. In the final years of his reign even those had once supported him turned against Joseph II. The handful of disciples of the Enlightenment and of the idea of bourgeois development – the scant bourgeoisie itself was concerned only with protecting their privileges – joined a clandestine organisation that looked to victorious revolutionary France for guidance. This society was made

51. Parlour in a Buda palace. Watercolour by Countess Erzsébet Festetich, 1847

52. *The execution of Ignác Martinovics in Buda's Vérmező in 1795*

up of people from all walks of life, with the purpose of putting into action a programme that embraced some irreconcilable ideas, and led by Ignác Martinovics, a monk, teacher, later secret agent, from a Pest merchant family. There were followers all over the country. They met in Buda under the auspices of the newly founded readers' circle, the Learned Society, and in Pest at the house of Ferenc Abaffy. The sitting of Parliament was an excellent opportunity for launching the organisation, and within a matter of a few weeks some fifty members had joined from the two cities alone. They were radical intellectuals, civil servants, teachers, attorneys, doctors, university students – many also freemasons, or at least in sympathy with that movement. From the 1770s on, both towns had their Masonic lodges, and with the patronage of Joseph II the freemasons gained significant influence and a broad followership.

The government and the king had no more than a premonition about a growing tension, and a sense that revolution was in the air. They decided on certain security measures, such as mustering troops in the vicinity of Pest-Buda. They had no knowledge about the movement itself and its nature. Later, in July 1794, when the Viennese leaders of the democratic movement, along with Martinovics, were apprehended and the latter soon divulged its Hungarian instigators. A string of arrests thus began in a matter of days in Buda and Pest too. Within a short time, 53 persons

were held in detention in the former Franciscan monastery in Buda, now the headquarters of the Council of the Governor General. Less than a year later, on May 20, 1795, Ignác Martinovics and four fellow insurrectionists were beheaded on the meadow below Buda Castle. Two others followed a few days later. These executions, intended as a deterrent, gave the meadow the name it still has, the Vérmező, or the Field of Blood.

With this Jacobin movement put down, Pest-Buda for several decades once again lost its national significance and its role as a capital. In the almost forty years of Francis I's reign (1792-1835), the twin cities had to endure the king's responses to the changes brought about by the French Revolution and the reign of Napoleon. Although despised throughout the Empire, the conservative Chancellor of this reactionary regime, Prince Klemens von Metternich, was a statesman of genius. Absolutism at this time marched under the banner of the Empire's traditional ideals. This produced no more advantage for Hungary than the absolutism of enforced modernisation that Joseph II had imposed. There was a period of thirteen years when the Diet was simply not convened. When it finally was, it was once again convened at Pozsony.

Neither political repression nor the loss of national importance halted the modernisation of the two cities, with Pest by now clearly heading the way. Pest's own commercial strength, happily matched by the plans, ambitions, and support of the Palatine, Archduke Joseph of Habsburg, were able to surmount the general stagnation that marked these decades.

The Architects of Pest's Future: Palatine Joseph and István Széchenyi

In July 1795, Francis I appointed his brother, Archduke Joseph, as Governor General of Hungary, and subsequently the Diet elected him Palatine. Joseph took up residence in the Royal Palace in Buda. His primary mission was to enhance the beauty, modernity, and cultural refinement of the twin towns – and especially Pest, which he referred to as the capital of Hungary. His aim, in short, was to style them into a genuine metropolis. In celebration of his first marriage to the daughter of Paul I, the Russian Czar, Joseph Haydn, and soon after, Ludwig van Beethoven, gave concerts in Buda. Vienna, as the musical capital of Europe, yielded the limelight to Buda for a brief period. All the while, though, the Palatine envisioned much more than the occasional cultural or artistic affair. He submitted a plan to the monarch for developing Pest into the country's largest city, advancing its favourable location and rapidly growing wealth. It was a matter of years before an answer was given; which, however, was positive. The same cannot be said of the reaction of the town council; after repeated urging, it finally came up with a set of criteria for city-planning but failed to produce a landscaping plan. At that point Palatine Joseph commissioned the architect János Hild, whose work in Pest he was well familiar with and which he esteemed, to prepare a comprehensive plan for the city. This Hild did, and the resulting documents the Palatine submitted to the king. The monarch accepted them on July 29, 1808, and Joseph proceeded to establish an Embellishment Commission (*Szépítő Bizottmány*) to carry them out. This committee was to remain in being for almost half a century, and the result of its labours, the neo-classic Inner City of Pest, for the most part is still standing today.

At this point one may wonder why there was confidence in the success of such a grand plan and why it was hoped that sufficient money would be made available, when countless plans for Hungary had failed for lack of capital and credit.

In 1806 Napoleon imposed a ban on trade with England in Continental Europe, a ban which Austria, defeated and reduced in size, could not ignore. The ban remained in effect until Napoleon's defeat in 1814, and for over a decade the role of the Danube as a trading route for goods from the colonies was advanced, and of Pest as a large Danube port and fair centre. What had once been objects for trade supplied by the British, such as cotton, coffee, tea, scented oils, spices, paints, and a store of other popular commodities, now raised the profits of the Pest merchants. Contemporaries took note of the Napoleonic ban as the source of Pest's wealth. Foreign merchants, too, like Greeks from the Balkans, or major Viennese and German entrepreneurs, were eager to profit from the boom. While the economic strength of the latter two far surpassed that of the Pest tradesmen, the city's commerce also grew substantially in this period. By the

53. *Statue of Palatine Joseph in the square (József Nádor tér) named after him, by Johann Halbig, 1869*

early 1810s, the number of entrepreneurs already topped a thousand, and at least fifty of them had a combined wealth of one seventh to one eighth of the fortunes all the Viennese merchants and bankers together. A considerable difference, to be sure, but not one that could preclude a comparison between Pest and the capital of the Habsburg Empire. Crucial for the development of the city was that the economic boom was accompanied by inflation, and that in turn stimulated real estate investment.

There was another motive, equally as powerful as the economic reasons behind the construction scheme. This was the prevailing desire for advancement, for the country to establish itself as a national entity; an appropriate capital was a precondition for that. At this time, the emergence and the intensity of the national idea was still directed at establishing a culture and a country, at boosting the collective creative drive and the people's willingness to make sacrifices for this end. Rather than segregate various ethnic groups or nationalities, instigating rivalry and viewing the other community as competition – which was what came to the fore in the subsequent decades – the nation as a whole was to exert its creative efforts and achieve success. For the national awakening, Pest was the appropriate city for the capital, not Buda with its ties to the Habsburg court and the imperial state. Buda was increasingly looked upon with mistrust, as representing foreign interests, as opposed to the national idea. Yet,

it was neither the middle class nor the town council that first hit on the national role of Pest, but the reform-minded among the country's nobility.

One of the country's largest landowners, Count Ferenc Széchényi, had been a supporter of Joseph II, and held high government positions. In 1802 he bequeathed his impressive library and other collections to the country to establish a national museum. Palatine Joseph latched on to the idea of a museum. For the time being the collections were housed in the former Pauline monastery – then the seminary in inner Pest – but the same year the Palatine established the Embellishment Commission, the Diet ratified the founding of the Hungarian National Museum. Legislation previously passed by the same Diet decreed the establishment of a Hungarian military academy, the Ludovika. The home of the two new institutions was to be Pest.

The Embellishment Plan for the city involved the area embraced by the present-day Large Ring (comprising Szent István, Teréz, Ferenc and József Körút, or in English, Saint Stephen, Theresa, Francis and Joseph Avenues). A few paved roads already existed in Pest, and three years after Buda, in 1780, a statute was passed requiring street lighting. In a span of ten years the streets were equipped with 375 oil lamps (though with the high cost of oil not all were lit at all times). Since Pest's Inner City was already totally built up, and any restructuring there would have demanded unavailable sums of money. Consequently the Embellishment Plan focused mainly on Leopold Town, at the northern end of the Inner City. Here the land was divided into plots, apartment houses and commercial buildings were permitted only in designated areas, and threshold and building heights were laid down, dams were constructed and the Danube bank adjusted. Proposals were made to stabilise the sand drifts at the outskirts, to regulate the market squares, erect storehouses, raze the still standing town walls and Hatvan Gate, build avenues within the city to connect to the incoming highways, and to plant trees along Üllői Street.

Setting up the Embellishment Commission for the execution of the plan was a politically astute move on the part of Palatine Joseph; in so doing, he was able to take the matter out of the hands of the reluctant town council without inciting their animosity. To preside over the commission he named a member of the Treasury, and the membership was made up of three representatives each from the town council and the citizen body, in addition to an architect, the city engineer, a mason, and a carpenter. In the year after the commission's inception, Joseph also set up a board for the ongoing supervision of the construction work.

To finance the projects (with the exception of the large public buildings) Palatine Joseph set up an Embellishment Fund, whose capital was derived from the sale of plots and a contribution from the city treasury. In addition, he allocated the income from city customs to develop the infrastructure, to fill in roads, pave streets, to build and upkeep wharves,

the promenade, market squares, and sewers. With its annual contribution of five thousand forints, the city of Pest did not exhaust its coffers, and in fact took on a banker's role by channelling its profits from loans into the Fund. This financial scheme, in the first half of the nineteenth century, made it possible for the city to regularly disburse around 30 to 40

per cent of its expenses for its own beautification and communal purposes; indeed in one particular year this figure even reached 65 per cent.

The arrangement, well conceived though it was, was successfully operated only to a limited extent. The abilities of the members of the Embellishment Commission were not up to the scope of the task, and they were negligent and profligate in managing their money, and this was aggravated by the economic crisis that followed the end of the Napoleonic wars. Nevertheless, many of the projects were completed; while others were only initiated, the Commission endured.

By 1814 Pest-Buda was so well developed that by late

October, when the monarchs of the allied powers that had defeated Napoleon gathered for the Congress of Vienna, they visited the twin cities as well. From Buda Castle King and Emperor Francis I, Czar Alexander I of Russia, and King Frederick William of Prussia crossed over into Pest. For the occasion, the pontoon bridge was equipped with nearly a thousand lamps – thick candles fastened on long poles – and the German theatre on the Pest side was decorated with banners, flowers, and allegoric ornaments with slogans like "Hail to Europe's Saviours!", and "Long Live the Indissoluble Holy Alliance!". Palatine Joseph and several aristocrats welcomed the monarchs, but amid the intense cheering the Palatine was prevented from delivering his speech. King Francis gave his guests a tour of the city, visited the Palace of the Invalids (by now known as the "Grenadier" Palace), the museum and the university botanical gardens. The party spent considerable time at the National Museum, which they found so exemplary that subsequently the emperor bestowed praise upon the museum director, Ferdinand Miller.

In the first half of the nineteenth century, the population of Pest, Buda and Óbuda grew enormously. By the 1810s, it had reached 88 thousand people, an increase of 72 per cent over a quarter century earlier. Another decade later it had increased by 25 per cent to 110 thousand, and by the mid 1830s it was approaching 130 thousand. Pest grew more intensely than Buda, by 65 per cent in each of the first two decades of the nineteenth century. By 1830 its population topped 75 thousand. At the same time the number of houses in Pest had increased from 2850 to only 4517, about half the rate of the population growth, and the vast majority of them (more than one third even in the Inner City) were single-story dwellings. The figures indicate that the number of per-

55. *The main street of Inner Pest, Váci Street, in the 1840s, showing the "Great Christopher" statue that gave the adjacent Kristóf Square its name. Lithograph by Rudolf Alt and Franz Xaver Sandmann*

56. *The Wharf Market, today's Roosevelt Square, as the face of Leopold Town. Lithograph by Max Felix Paur and Johann Bergmann, 1837*

sons per house grew considerably, with an increasingly dense population in the suburbs and poverty on the rise; the Inner City had become downright overcrowded. City government, and most of the ecclesiastic and educational institutions remained in the core of the town, while the economic centre shifted to Leopold Town. This part of the city became more and more linked with the Inner City, and soon evolved into a modern town core that existed alongside the old city centre. Office buildings and banks were erected here, as were hotels and fine mansions. The aristocrats, including Count István Széchenyi, built their town houses in this new part of town, mainly on Szél (now Nádor) and Szarka (Zrinyi) Streets. The mansions of the bankers and important entrepreneurs were especially concentrated on Bálvány (Október 6) and Sas Streets. In between apartment houses of greater elegance sprung up. These were three or four-story edifices with wide gates, and entrances arched to accommodate a carriage-and-four. The courts were spacious enough to allow the carriages to turn, with stables for several horses set up at the far ends. The houses had broad, red-marble stairways and galleries with more or less ornate iron railings running along the sides of the courts.

The rest of the suburbs developed differently, however. The atmosphere in the outer part of Joseph Town, between today's Large Ring and Blaha Lujza Square, for example, becomes palpable from the memoirs of Baron Frigyes Podmaniczky, who would become a leading figure in city development. In place of the present-day Ring ran Rákos Creek, spanned by simple footbridges. "Beyond the moat stood, one by one, the outlying taverns where the carters, arriving or departing with their wares, were lodging. [...] These taverns bore all sorts of names or designations, and inside they presented a gleeful picture of various nationalities and costumes, but often also of lasciviousness and sin. They resembled somewhat the sea-town pubs that carousing sailors like to frequent, where savings amassed in months on the ocean are squandered in a matter of hours."

Just as in Joseph Town, the Inner City impressed a foreigner to remark that there, "in the dim of night, artful sirens cast their dangerous nets." Prostitution was spreading, though regulation followed only after it had become pervasive. The first "sufferance permits" for prostitutes were issued by Pest's chief magistrate in 1867, and another thirty years passed before the authorities were to prescribe the medical supervision of these "ladies of pleasure".

Just like the Habsburg Empire and Hungary itself, Pest-Buda embraced many nationalities and ethnic groups, and for some of these for different periods of time Pest-Buda was even a centre of their culture. Traditionally German towns in character and language, Buda and Pest were now becoming the targets of the mounting struggle toward Magyarization. The large Jewish population had various cultural and religious affiliations. By this time there was also a substantial Slovak community that first caught up with, and later surpassed, the Serbs in size. The Habsburg Empire's eastern peoples were all represented to various degrees, some of their leaders awakening to their national identity here in this locus of converging languages and cultures. Jan Kollar, a Lutheran pastor in Pest, became a principal figure in the Slovak national movement and had extensive influence also as a linguist and poet. Ljudevit Gaj, the Croatian politician and publicist, was a member of Kollar's circle when he published his first modern Croatian grammar here, and launched the so-called "Illyrian" movement for Southern Slav unification. The foremost nineteenth-century writer of Serbian prose, Yakov Ignatovich, recalled his student years in Pest in the 1830s when he wrote, "Pest was the centre of the Serbian intelligentsia and literature. The Matica Srbska was already functioning, as was the Tökölyanum. There were attorneys, students of law, and doctors of medicine." A fund

57. *Lunch stand in Pest's Széna (Hay) Market, today's Kálvin Square, in the 1840s. In the background the National Museum. Colour lithograph after a drawing by Henrik Weber*

58. *Greek-Orthodox procession along the Danube shore in Pest. Colour steel engraving by William Henry Bartlett, 1843*

set up by Száva Tököly-Popovics provided a sort of college, giving room and board to Serbian boys studying at Pest university, in addition to an education that forwarded a Serbian consciousness. The intellectual leaders of less sizeable nationalities awakened to their historic calling here in Pest. There were three Greek Orthodox priests, Gheorghe Şincai, Samuil Micu-Klein, and Petru Maior – employed at the Censor's Office of the Council of the Governor General – who advanced the theories on the Latin origin of the Romanian language and on the Daco-Roman continuity; they were to become known as Romanian scholars of the "Transylvanian School". These first writings of theirs, that laid the foundations for Romanian national consciousness, were published by the University Press in Buda, and early nineteenth-century Hungarian scholarly opinion took pride in having the descendants of Rome in their midst. (Conversely, there was at this time a Hungarian university professor in Pest who presented a diatribe on the "fact" that Adam and Eve had

been Magyars, along with the rest of those figuring in the Bible !)

Of the many nationalities then thriving in Pest, it was the city's Hungarian character that showed the greatest growth. The size of the Hungarian population was approaching the Germans', still at over 40 per cent prior to 1830. Pest was beginning to be acknowledged as the Hungarian intellectual and literary centre. At the turn of the century that had not been evident, in spite of the fact that Ferenc Kazinczy was already a leading figure in Hungarian literary circles. Kazinczy lived quite some distance from Pest-Buda, just when his scholarly and literary followers were organising a society in Pest. This group met each day to discuss questions about Hungarian literature and language. István Kultsár opened his house in Pest to an intelligentsia that continued to grow and diversify; he also provided financial support for a variety of cultural undertakings, from the Hungarian theatre to book publishing. It was he who launched and edited the first Hungarian journal, *Hazai és Külföldi Tudósítások* (Reports from Home and Abroad) that ran to a significant number of issues. The crowning point of all this came through Károly Kisfaludy. A man of many interests, he was the first to portray Pest in a piece of fiction an enormously successful satirical novel, which continued to have an effect on successive generations. The eponymous protagonist, Jónás Tollagi, was a young provincial nobleman whose coming to Pest forced him to face up to his backwardness in education and philosophy of life. A playwright, poet and painter, Kisfaludy in 1822 began publication of the literary yearbook *Auróra*, and the circle of writers connected to it laid the foundations for Pest's permanent literary life. István Széchenyi recruited Kisfaludy as editor for his political journal *Jelenkor* (The Present), an editorship which the latter's death sadly prevented. From this point on, nationally circulated journals were published in Pest, and a growing number of magazines, weeklies and periodicals were issued in this city. In the Castle Theatre in Buda, plays in the Hungarian-language were now in the repertoire; in 1837 the National Theatre opened in Pest, in accordance with Széchenyi's concept,

59. *The first Races in Pest in 1827. Colour lithograph after a drawing by Johann Prestel and Alexander Clarot*

adopting the mission to forge a nation. Not much later, the recently completed great classic of the national drama, *Bánk Bán* (Ban Bánk) by József Katona, was premiered.

Around 1830 it was evident that Pest was inexorably, as if by a law of nature, developing into the capital of a modern state. It was also becoming clear that this home to a multitude of nationalities and religious denominations would develop into a centre for all these in the eastern part of Central Europe. This idea was gaining ground, and was greatly advanced by the appearance of a programme that embraced all spheres of modernisation. It was a programme, moreover, that was able to mobilise society, middle class and nobility alike. It was formulated by István Széchenyi; the man who, with unswerving energy and perseverance, gave modern Hungary and its capital so many of its indispensable institutions. An aristocrat, and one of the richest and most influential at that, Széchenyi sought to be a citizen of a country and a capital reborn. In 1829 he took the oath of citizenship for Pest, and two years later was elected into its citizen body. For him a capital had to be a centre in the broadest sense of the term, and the programme he conceived saw Buda-Pest as a complex hub for both culture and transportation. The son of the founder of the National Museum, he had early on been exposed to the notion of working for the public good; even so, it is still difficult to comprehend how he managed to exert so much energy to achieve all that he did, in particular because of his profligacies as a young officer of the Hussars – a lifestyle that combined both bouts of depression and an inclination to taking pleasures to extreme. The commemorative print disseminated after his death frames his portrait with the prolific list of his accomplishments. The most numerous of these were the institutions and establishments he contributed to Buda-Pest: the Chain Bridge, the Hungarian Academy of Sciences, the Tunnel cutting through

Castle Hill, the National Theatre, the Casino as a venue for social intercourse, and significant public inititives such as the establishing horse-racing, steamships, river control, railroad and highway improvements, to list just the obvious.

Széchenyi's thinking was novel, given the traditional Hungarian political environment that always approached questions from their constitutional aspects. As a practical thinker, Széchenyi in fact discovered the importance of infrastructure in the process of modernisation. He also knew how to use the appropriate rhetoric to advance his proposals, and did so through catchy slogans. "We cannot overcome time, and must be patient in waiting to see what it may bring," he wrote in his 1831 *Világ* (World), "but it is in our power to stand in the right place. And for Hungarians the right place cannot be but Buda and Pest, which nature has so designated, because this is the heart of the nation – it must be in order and beat with all its vigour, and gush the lifeblood into the nation's arteries." It was he who coined the phrase "heart of the nation" for Budapest, ever since in popular use in writing and speech. This pamphlet also popularised the name Budapest, stemming of course from his scheme for the unification of the two cities.

60. *Equestrian painting of Count István Széchenyi, which aside from showing his excentric English dress also alludes to his works: the Chain Bridge, and his establishing horse breeding and the Races. Watercolour by Károly Sterio, 1857*

Much of his work had to do with city planning and beautification, and he would have liked to become a member of the Embellishment Commission. This wish, however, Palatine Joseph did not grant and he may well have been right, recognising that Széchenyi's programme looked into a too distant future. As an able organiser and practical thinker himself, Joseph may have perceived the threat Széchenyi's programme posed to the unified Habsburg Empire. Then again, he may have wished to give Széchenyi a free hand and keep him out of the town council's sphere, with its officiousness and its squandering of time and money.

Pest in the 1830s, the scene of Széchenyi's activities, was by now the country's capital, economically and culturally. But the country itself had as yet not developed into an independent and modern European state.

The Chain Bridge: Maker of a Metropolis

One cold day in March 1838 Pest-Buda, now a lovely, thriving and bustling city, was overwhelmed by the icy waters of the Danube. It had long been recognised that, in the absence of river control, the Danube would wreak havoc every decade or so. Along the winding shores and tips of islands, and wherever the water level was low, ice had accumulated to obstruct the river's flow, causing it to spill over into low-lying areas on both sides. In 1775 Pest-Buda had been witness to a devastation caused by the icy river; subsequently a dike was raised above flood level, and both the Pest arm of the Danube and the twin inlet of the Rákos Creek were closed off. With this the authorities assumed the city to be safe. A sewage system only covered the Inner City, and the rapidly expanding Pest suburbs spilled their drainage into their drinking water, with the added effect that the loose, gritty and sandy soil was increasingly weakened.

The winter of 1837/38 brought extremely cold weather and above average precipitation. Already in December the Danube had frozen over at Pest, something the residents was not unaccustomed to, and even welcomed, as it facilitated transit between the two towns. It also provided recreation and entertainment, with the iced over river frequented by skaters and showmen. During the winter, the thick ice at the tip of Csepel Island formed an almost unbreachable dike. Consequently in early March the low-lying parts of Buda flooded and buildings were washed away. In Pest, at the same time, only the exits of the conduits were closed off, and people took walks along the bank to marvel at the high

water. Life proceeded without interruption to its regular course, with the theatre and preparations for the national fair on Saint Joseph's Day. As the ice thawed in the balmy weather, however, the rising water began making its way downstream. Even though the Danube Bend further upstream had already been inundated, the Pest authorities and population still refused to acknowledge the danger. On the evening of March 13, as theatres were filled to the usual capacity, the news broke that the Danube had spilled over the dike protecting the Inner City. The German Theatre interrupted its performance, the National Theatre went on. The water rose so quickly that the audience in the upper balconies were not able to leave their places, and had to spend the night in their seats. During that night, all the dams burst. The Danube broke its banks into the city, and through the pipelines and wells. Irresponsible the town council had been earlier, now it would be rash. Palatine Joseph appointed a royal commissioner to direct the rescue work, to place the populace into shelters, and to organise the distribution of food. Many of the nobles in Pest took a personal part in the rescue operation, offering their palaces as shelters for the homeless. Most heroic of all was Baron Miklós Wesselényi – a leading opposition figure – whose feats are remembered in several works of fiction. Palatine Joseph himself set up a shelter in the royal palace. By the evening of March 15 the water beyond the ice built up at the tip of Csepel Island had risen to three metres above its level downstream. The ice barrier finally gave way, and Pest was inundated for three days. The water went on to flood the settlements to the south. Devastation was enormous; in Albertfalva, for example, not a single house remained intact.

The flood of 1838 was the greatest natural disaster in the history of Pest-Buda. In the suburbs of Buda 204, in Óbuda

61. A scene from the Great Pest Flood "The Town Hall Market on the Dreadful Day of March 15, 1838 in Pest". Colour aquatint by Domokos Perlaszka after a drawing by Carl Schwindt

62. Tea time in a salon *in Pest:* Herbaté *[Herb Tea],*
an illustration to Magyar titkok (Hungarian Secrets), *a once*
famous novel by Ignác Nagy, published in 1845

397, and in Pest 228 buildings were demolished. The water had carried away badly-built adobe houses, and even a new large building on the corner of the New Market Square, which had been spared by the flood, collapsed after the water that had broken into the cellar undermined the foundation. Pest suffered most severely, accounting for most of the flood's 153 casualties, and with over half of its suburbs destroyed. In Francis Town 83 per cent of the buildings lay in ruins; barely a quarter of Pest's 4254 houses remained undamaged. Buda sustained not a single casualty, not so much because of the severity of the flood but because of its more disciplined and organised rescue operations.

As soon as the flood had passed, the cleaning up and damage assessment began. With the help of international relief and donations the towns could hope to recuperate. The king himself was the first to extend substantial financial assistance, and within half a year a board set up for the purpose was able to distribute considerable sums for rebuilding. Regulating construction became imperative, though this was postponed until the true causes behind the damage were assessed. As a result the assumptions that inferior building materials had been used for the suburban houses, that foundations were not set deep enough, and other technical deficiencies, were confirmed. New building regulations were precise and strict, controlling everything from foundations and cellars, to ceilings and firewalls, from measurements to materials. Buildings were permitted to rise to four stories,

63. *A room in the István Főherceg (Archduke Stephen) Hotel. Watercolour by Iván Forray from around 1840*

height was maximised, and ceiling heights were determined at 3.4 metres. Permits were required before commencing construction, and architectural plans had to be submitted. However, in view of the feverish building going on all over town, the regulations could not be imposed entirely. Within two years 859 residential buildings alone had been raised – almost double the annual rate of all construction during the four years prior to the flood.

The deluge left a deep impression on the population and the authorities alike. On the walls of buildings they attached plaques, still extant in many places, with a pointed finger indicating the water level. The Diet of 1839/40 set into law the need to regulate the rivers in the country, though it failed to pass the budget necessary for this, in spite of the fact that the 1838 flood damages amounted to three and a half times the sum needed for river control. Of course Pest was not alone in procrastinating over such action; Vienna similarly postponed the regulation of its own banks. It took another thirty years before the project was finally launched.

After 1838 Pest was rebuilt, and acquired the neo-classical appearance the Inner City exhibits to this day. The achievement, nevertheless, did not take advantage of all the opportunities the devastation and the rearrangement of the city structure. Széchenyi was able to present potent arguments opposing the motion of the city council to fill in the streets of the Inner City with refuse and rubble to protect against a flood. The notion may seem preposterous in the late twentieth century, but was ordinary under contemporary conditions. The Danube bank, for example, was traditionally a place for refuse disposal, and as such one of the city's dirtiest and most odoriferous spots. While this idea was eventually discarded, even Széchenyi could not wrest from the council the acknowledgement that a only stone embankment could provide security.

That Pest presented a harmonious cityscape was only in part due to fixed building regulations: two fine architects largely determined the city's appearance. As a permanent advisor to the Embellishment Commission, Mihály Pollák designed several landmark buildings, including the Lutheran Church on Deák Square; the Sándor Palace in the Castle District (which served as the prime minister's residence until it was burned out during the Second World War); the German Theatre on Vörösmarty Square; behind it the Redoute, a concert and ball room facing the Danube; the mammoth structure of the Ludovika Military Academy on Üllői Street and, most prominently, the National Museum. His apartment buildings and mansions were no less significant, of which about a dozen still stand in various spots in the 5th District. In addition he designed several villas in the Buda hills.

The second notable architect was József Hild, the son of János. His grand, massive constructions left their mark on the city. He was especially known for two, no longer

64. *Hotel Angol királynő (The English Queen). Watercolour by Rudolf Alt, around 1848*

standing, palaces next to the Danube, the Lloyd Palace and the Ullmann House (the latter subsequently becoming into the Europa Hotel); and the inn "The English Queen", the old Kemnitzer House, which he reconstructed and partly redesigned. In addition, the Cziráky Palace (later the National Casino); the Basilica in Leopold Town; and in the same area the Valero Silk Factory; countless residential buildings and, in Buda, the neo-classic building of Császár Baths are all his work.

József Hild also designed what came to be known as the Old Town Hall of Pest, torn down at the turn of the nineteenth to the twentieth centuries. In 1840, the city began searching for a location for a new municipal building. Leopold Town seemed most suitable; the site on Vörösmarty Square (now with the Gerbeaud Café), or the site overlooking the Danube at the Chain Bridge (where subsequently the Gresham Insurance Company built its Hungarian headquarters) were deemed suitable for a building of such stature, but the Town Council rejected these on the grounds of price. In the end, in the 1870s, they built a Town Hall at a somewhat higher cost in crowded Váci Street, a decidedly unpretentious spot that had once held the town brewery. The new building. designed by architect Imre Steindl, who would also build Hungary's imposing Parliament building on the Danube, was referred to as the New Town Hall.

In Buda construction went on at a considerably slower pace, even though its Building Commission, the *Baucomission*, had worked out a set of regulations similar to those of Pest. Densely built-up with many low houses and of a decid-

edly baroque character, the neo-classic that defined its twin city would not do.

The fast increasing density of buildings in low-lying Pest could not, however, shield the city from the sandstorms that sporadically came in from the east. Széchenyi pointedly remarked that the amount of sand a Pester swallowed in a lifetime was enough to make several millstones. Széchenyi devoted a separate work to the subject, *The Dust and Mud of Pest (Pesti por és sár)*. An English gentleman visiting the city, whose beauty and bustling life he otherwise was enthralled by, had this to say: "This sand is one of the miseries of Pest; it is so fine that it enters into everything, destroys furniture, and blinds and chokes the inhabitants worse than the London fog. A sandstorm is something dreadful here."

Palatine Joseph did his best to ameliorate the problem. As a devoted gardener, a man who tended his favourite plants, gardens and parks with his very own hands, he had trees

65. Wind storm in Váci Street. Engraving by Domokos Perlaszka that appeared as a journal illustration in 1844

66. *The foundation stone of the Chain Bridge was laid in a ceremony at 6 p. m., August 24, 1842. Miklós Barabás sketched a watercolour at the scene, but only in the late 1850s was the large oil painting made. Here each public figure of that time is ascertainable, with Count István Széchenyi at the head of the podium stairs*

planted on the slope below Buda Castle, transformed the wilderness on Margaret Island into a well-kempt park, and established what later became the City Park behind Heroes' Square, by planting the area with young trees, as well as a line of trees extending beyond Király Street.

There was one feature, however, that marked the face of Buda and Pest and defined the life of cities' residents more than anything else and this was the Chain Bridge. For a decade Széchenyi had mulled over the idea of building a permanent bridge to link the twin cities. In 1832 he founded the Budapest Bridge Association, and was able to win Palatine Joseph over to the plan. Not long after, he travelled to England to study the construction of bridges and made the acquaintance of a renowned engineer and bridge builder named Tierney William Clark. In 1835 he invited Clark to Pest to put forward his ideas about a bridge, and then commissioned him to make the plans. He already had chosen a constructor to execute the work, also an Englishman and also a Clark – by the first name of Adam and no relation to Tierney William. Széchenyi decided that the construction should be effectuated through a holding company and won over the Viennese banker Georg Sina for the cause. The Diet, meanwhile, had not yet come to a decision on the conditions involved. Indeed, the debates were growing more fervid, since it proved to be a major, and far-reaching, concern whether the nobility, historically exempt from paying taxes, should be required to pay the toll. In addition, the two towns could not agree on the ownership of the future bridge, nor on the joint raising of a further fifty per cent of the building cost to be spent on river control. The voters of Pest were especially opposed to the plan, as they intended to build the bridge on their own. Finally in March 1836 both houses of parliament gave their approval to the plan, and established a national committee to launch and oversee the bridge's construction. Now energies were free to concentrate on debating who should be given the commission to raise the investment money, since a majority stake in the holding company was now also being sought by Salomon Rotschild and another major Viennese banking consortium, the Wodianer-Ullmann Group. Széchenyi continued to support Sina, but was able to convince him to agree to a form a consortium with the other two parties. At this point the bridge-construction bill was presented to the king, and on May 16, 1839 he gave the royal assent. Within a matter of months construction began. The ceremonious laying of the foundation stone took place on August 24, 1842. Adam Clark had agreed to complete construction within five years. Széchenyi closely observed the work, and whenever complications arose – as with the transport of the bridge chains – he would urge the builders on. The initial two-year delay postponed the inauguration ceremony, which finally took place on November 21, 1849. By that time, the cities had lived through the euphoria of revolution and the dismay over the defeat in the country's War of Liberation against Habsburg rule. Széchenyi, the man who had made it happen, was prevented from attending; he was, and would continue to be for the rest of his life, confined to the psychiatric institution in Döblin, near Vienna.

The Chain Bridge embodied much more than the considerable technical deed it was, and more than a pretty addition to the riverscape. As a permanent link between Buda and Pest, it manifested the actual unification of the towns; the administrative merger could be but a matter of time. The Chain Bridge opened the way for Budapest to become a metropolis on a European scale. The bridge signified the point in the country's history when a modern Hungary was born: everyone, regardless of birth or rank, was obliged to pay the toll. It meant a first, and decisive, step toward abolishing birthrights and providing equality before the law. Gyula Krúdy, the great writer of the first third of our own century, expressed the meaning of the bridge: "Beneath the lofty arches of the Chain Bridge old Hungary passed over into new Hungary. The bridge had a hole, and through it our grandfathers cast outmoded catchwords and ideals from their memories into the Danube. On the bridge the wind was strongest, disseminating the seeds of liberty and renewal along the shores, in the hearts and minds of the people."

Yet it seemed as if all the forces that delayed the completion of the bridge had conspired to prevent this symbolic future from coming into being. Construction itself was delayed, then came the War of Liberation, when the Austrian commander defending Buda Castle planned to use demolition charges on it, which retreating Hungarian troops subsequently also attempted. Both these attempts the Chain Bridge withstood with only minor damage. It was inaugurated shortly after the war.

Entrepreneurs, Founders of the National Culture

From the late 1810s on, the number of in trade and commerce in Pest grew considerably; with their amassed wealth, they came to be a decisive factor in the economy of Pest and of the entire nation. Most of them were only able to establish short-lived businesses, but a handful of them achieved a power that extended beyond the boundaries of the Habsburg Empire. Pest evolved into the Empire's wool trading centre, largely due to Sámuel Wodianer's firm which he had relocated from the southern town of Szeged in order to expand it into an Austro-Hungarian enterprise, whose goods reached markets as far north as the Netherlands and England. In the tobacco trade, the firm of Móric Ullmann ruled the market for some time, his vast tobacco storehouses employing 200 to 300 workers. In the wine trade, Frigyes Kappel reached not just Western Europe but established fine Hungarian wines in the United States of America too. In textiles, József Boscovitz Löbl became the most recognised and affluent name. Entrepreneurs established their own banks, and in a manner that was characteristic of the Empire at this time, by dividing their business and banking activities between the two centres of Vienna and Pest.

Most of the important figures in trade, manufacturing and banking of course played leading roles in public life too, founding numerous associations and societies. One of the most venerable, the Civil Commercial Association of Pest (*Pesti Polgári Kereskedelmi Testület*), went back as far as 1699, when it was granted its royal patent. Initially membership was limited to Catholic merchants, who were later joined by Protestants and Greek- Orthodox businessmen. They built a Commercial Hall, designed by József Hild and subsequently known as the Lloyd Palace, which served as the first brokerage house and the National Casino, the latter soon giving way to the headquarters of the majority Liberal Party.

The growth in the number of Jewish merchants at the beginning of the nineteenth century, and in particular because of their exclusion from membership of the Civil Commercial Association, called for a society of their own. In 1815 they established the Israelite Commercial Association of Pest (*Pesti Izraelita Kereskedelmi Testület*).

In the 1840s a number of new societies sprung up. Some avowed economic collaboration, though their actual intention was to provide a forum for political organisation. The Society for Protection (*Védegylet*), the Hungarian Commercial Society (*Magyar Kereskedelmi Társaság*), and the Society of Factory Founders (*Gyáralapító Társaság*) were of this kind, although in the end they did not succeed in their function. Concurrently, several truly economic organisations were

67. A Danube merchant, shown on an iron table ornament made in the Ganz Foundry. 1860s

68. *The Pest railway station painted on a target, 1854*

established, and these did. These included the Industrial Society *(Iparegylet)*, which set up trade schools and was a pioneer in organising three industrial exhibitions prior to the 1848 Revolution. Another was the Wholesale Association of Pest *(Pesti Nagykereskedelmi Testület)*, its establishment sanctioned by the king; this was open to merchants, and bankers of Pest, regardless of religion or creed.

These years also witnessed the birth of the first financial institutions. András Fáy, known as "factotum of the fatherland", a versatile author, theatre patron, politician and active public figure, in 1839 established the First National Savings Bank of Pest *(Pesti Hazai Első Takarékpénztár)*, which in keep-

69. *With life and trade thriving in the capital Pest and Buda were frequently pictured on souvenirs. The glass box, drinking glass and cup and saucer show cityscapes of Pest, while the tarot cards from the 1830s, which are hand-painted woodcuts showing the twin capital, provide insight into Reform-Age thinking: the text below the eagle on the 13th card reads "Industrie und Glück", i.e. "Industry and Luck"*

ing with its name really was the country's first national institution of this kind. Three years later the Hungarian Commercial Bank of Pest (Pesti Magyar Kereskedelmi Bank) began operations as well.

The growth and development of commercial life was accompanied by developments in transportation, made possible by scores of technological innovations. Steam boats plowed the waves of the Danube as early as 1817, and in 1830 the Danube Steam Shipping Society (Donau Dampfschiffahrt Gesellschaft) was formed, setting up regular sailings between Vienna and Pest. This represented a considerable move forward, since goods transported by drawn boats had taken twenty-five days to reach their destination; now they took only three days. This also invigorated trade with territories downstream. Railroads were also being built, with the Pest – Vác line opened in 1846, and the following year the Pest – Cegléd line, initiating a major transport route to the Great Plain in the east.

Pest was growing very much like Vienna, and not just in the eyes of enthusiastic national visionaries, but in those of visiting world-travellers. The Danish writer Hans Christian Andersen noted that "We roam about Pest and have the impression that we are seeing Vienna, or at least a portion of Vienna."

The urge to establish new institutions affected not just economic, commercial, financial and transport. Leading public figures were eager to bring to life national institutions that would benefit the day-to-day affairs of various trades and the arts. The plans originated in Pest, and the societies and associations that were formed all had their centres here.

70. A Pest burgher family in 1848, a painting by Henrik Weber of his own relatives, who can be identified by name. The eldest, reading a newspaper, is Mihály Weber, a respected broadcloth merchant, while behind him to the left is his son-in-law, composer Mihály Mosonyi

Founded by István Széchenyi, the Academy, by the name of Hungarian Learned Society *(Magyar Tudós Társaság)*, was functioning from 1830. The Art Society of Pest *(Pesti Műegylet)* staged annual exhibitions from 1839 on; its arrival meant that artistic activity, once regarded as a private affair of concern only to artists and their patrons, became a public matter. In 1841 the first of the Itinerary Congresses of Hungarian Physicians and Naturalists *(Magyar Orvosok és Természetvizsgálók Vándorgyűlése)* was organised; it dealt with more than just matters of natural science; it embraced the country's geography, history, archaeology, ethnography, and many other areas of science; as such it was the first forum in the country for professionals in these fields to maintain contact between themselves.

From 1836, the Musicians Association of Pest-Buda *(Pest-Budai Hangászegyesület)* was concerned with all areas of music, from staging concerts to music instruction and the patronage of musicians. Their excellent music school later took the name of the National School of Music *(Nemzeti Zenede)*, and continues to this day to operate as a conservatory. The concerts the Association regularly held were mostly in the National Casino, but theatres, and the Redoute were also used as venues. This was when the musical life of Pest became international. The most influential composers and performers were Ferenc Erkel, Márk Rózsavölgyi, and of course Ferenc (Franz) Liszt. Very often Johann Strauss and Josef Lanner came across from Vienna; in the early 1840s Hector Berlioz gave a concert here, as did the Russian child prodigy Anton Rubinstein, the popular French violinist and composer Henri Vieuxtemps, and many other artists from various countries, including England and Norway.

Painters and sculptors, in contrast, did not receive many commissions in early nineteenth-century Pest. The first major sculptor to make his residence here was Lőrinc

Dunaiszky. The Embellishment Commission ordered numerous works from him, resulting in a variety of sculptures, from tombs to public, and from building decorations and church ornamentation to portrait sculptures. István Ferenczy returned from Italy in 1824, where he had been in the workshop of the outstanding sculptor of the period, Bertel Thorvaldsen. Ferenczy established residence in Buda, and exhibited a true artistic esprit in trying to have sculpture treated as an art in Hungary. In consequence he mocked architects, refusing to perform decorating work, and kept aloof from other sculptors working in Buda-Pest whom he considered inferior to him. He received commissions from aristocrats and the Catholic Church, and increasingly sought assignments to create large monuments. Several ideas were put forward, but all were aborted for lack of money, and ultimately Ferenczy was left without any commissions. A society of friends was established, which in 1839 launched an extensive campaign for the raising of a monument to King Matthias I in Pest, to be created by Ferenczy. The debate went on for years in the press about every aspect of the monument, from its location to its material – marble or bronze; finally it was questioned whether assistance for Ferenczy warranted a plan of this financial scope at all, rather than announcing an international competition for it. Another dispute arose as to whether strengthening the national consciousness necessarily involved a monument of this sort; the counter-argument to this was the hope of establishing a national shrine. Every major public figure voiced an opinion, and for once Széchenyi and Lajos Kossuth, the nation's populist icon, were in agreement in expressing their opposition to the illusionistic scheme. The money could not be raised, and neither parliament nor the king was willing to extend financial support. Ferenczy left the completed reliefs and details to the National Museum, destroyed his plaster moulds, and in disappointment went back to his home town in the provinces, forever to relinquish the art of sculpture. The national burden that had been placed on his shoulders, and which his own self-esteem as an artist demanded, exceeded his strength.

Another artist lived and worked in Pest during these years, however, whose skills and talent allowed him to meet the tasks at hand. Miklós Barabás became a painter who was both popular and in great demand, and financially successful. He was a portrait painter whose skills were the equal of any of his Viennese counterparts. His success was something new and unfamiliar for Pest. All his pictures and drawings were executed on commission, including those "national fashion pictures" that made the Hungarian gala-dress popular. Once or twice a year, however, he would paint scenes of Pest for his own pleasure. These watercolours faithfully reflect a thriving city and its mood in the Age of Reform, in the first half of the nineteenth century.

A fine silversmith named József Szentpéteri also made his home in Pest. His silver objects – bowls, pitchers, goblets, plaques for horse races, and devotional objects – are among the most exquisite of the period.

Revolution and Reprisal

With Pest as its centre, information was being made available at a rate that grew intensely. This was largely due to a flourishing press, which now also included illustrated papers. The *Pesti Divatlap* (Pest Fashion Magazine), *Életképek* (Genre Pictures), and *Honderű* (Homeland's Shine) carried supplements on fashion, along with drawings and colour lithographs to illustrate their articles; their coverage of topics concerning daily life constantly grew. The great Hungarian poet Sándor Petőfi was an assistant editor at *Életképek* for some nine months, a position that presented him with an opportunity to publish his own poetry. (His duties obliged him to cross over regularly from the offices in Pest to Buda, where the paper was printed, to read the proofs.) While these journals shaped and synthesised public taste, the political newspapers that carried the new national and reform ideas were of enormously greater portent. From 1841 Lajos Kossuth was the editor of *Pesti Hírlap* (Pest News). His editorials provoked public reflection and debate among his readership, which was something entirely new and the outcome was the formation of the opposition. Concurrently, various political quasi-parties launched their own papers.

These newspapers had their offices in the Inner City of Pest, and employed the local writers; the growing number of printing presses operated mainly in Leopold Town and Theresa Town. Journalists were now becoming prominent figures in the public life of Pest, well-informed young men with an insider's air who knew what mattered to people. Very often their writings carried considerable weight.

The young journalists were a leading voice in society, especially among the politically aware intellectuals and artists. The beacon that attracted them was Mihály Vörösmarty, poet, playwright, literary translator, and newspaper editor in his own right, who supported and united them. His favourite haunt was the Csiga (Snail) Restaurant at the corner of Sebestyén Square in Pest. (It, too, was another victim of the construction of Elizabeth Bridge.) From 1838 his "Circle" of writers, scientists and scholars, actors and artisans gathered regularly in the Csiga, which evolved into a hub of politics. As the group grew larger it changed its name to the "National Circle", and soon outgrew the Csiga, moving into a mansion on Országút (today's Múzeum Ring). Everyone who counted in any area of public life, from young writers to a handful of aristocrats and influential civic figures, frequented the National Circle. They included Lipót Rottenbiller (later to be mayor), the printer Lajos Landerer and the bookseller Gusztáv Heckenast. They organised *soirées* that included concerts, published musical scores and even a volume of Petőfi's poetry. In 1846 they became the "Opposition Circle", with a membership that had swelled to around six hundred. They published works the censorship had prohibited, sometimes printed in Leipzig and smuggled back into Hungary.

In effect they had become a political party, and both Kossuth and Petőfi were members.

An awareness that had been growing for some fifteen years, that Hungary was ripe to become an independent national state with its unique culture and a fast growing, powerful city that was Pest, now had a firm footing. The Viennese court and Metternich with their policy of centralisation, and the relentless repression of any attempt to establish a national identity, only whetted the desire for independence. In the Spring of 1848, a wave of revolution hit Paris, various German towns, and Vienna, and converged on Pest. On the morning of Wednesday, March 15th, a fair day when crowds were even more larger than usual, the young men of Pest were preparing for a demonstration which Petőfi was to address from the steps of the National Museum. The weather was not good, the wind was sharp, and even after eight o'clock the crowd that had assembled was meagre. As the great novelist Mór Jókai grumbled, "A Magyar is no rebel early in the morning." Around nine o'clock, there were enough people present for Jókai to be persuaded to climb on the table at Pilvax Café in inner Pest to proclaim the demands of the nation.

The printer Lajos Landerer, a cautious and well-informed man whose premises were two streets away, had received news the night before that something was brewing, and had stocked sufficient paper to await the young rebels. Wisely, he had also declined the protection offered by the chief consta-

ble, saying that it would be unwise to provoke the mob. The more radical of the young, some of whom were his own authors and editors such as Pál Vasvári, János Irinyi, Mór Jókai, Sándor Petőfi and others, entered the printing workshop (Landerer and Heckenast), and demanded that Landerer print their "Twelve Points" as well as Petőfi's National Anthem. The printer objected vociferously, saying that the manuscript had not been passed by the censor, then suggested – in a more subdued voice – that the young radicals confiscate the press. Most probably it was Irinyi who, setting hand on one of the presses, announced: "In the name of the people we herewith appropriate the press and demand the printing of the manuscript!" Landerer acceded to what he termed the threat, and proceeded to order the printing to be done. Through the diligent labour of five typesetters, the leaflets with the Twelve Points in both Hungarian and German, and the National Anthem, were distributed to the crowd by noon.

Joined by the liberal nobility, the people had the Town Council sign the leaflet "As a Petition to Parliament", and sub-

72. Lipót Rottenbiller, Mayor of Pest at the time of the 1848 Revolution. Daguerreotype from around 1850

73. The Pilvax Café in 1848, where the young rebels gathered and effectively launched the Revolution

sequently set up a revolutionary committee. This body marched up to Buda, to the Council of the Governor General. Petőfi described the event thus, "The honourable Council of the Governor General was quite pale and deigned to tremble, and upon holding council for five minutes agreed to everything." In accordance with one of the Twelve Points, the Council of the Governor General abolished censorship. On hearing the news, toward half past six in the evening, the crowd cheered and proceeded several streets further to free the hero of the free press, Mihály Táncsics, from his incarceration in the Castle. The familiar version of the scene has people unhitching the horses from a carriage and themselves drawing Táncsics amidst the light of torches over the bridge into Pest. Petőfi noted that evening in his diary, "Today Hungarian Liberty was born, because today the shackles are fallen from the press."

The councils of Pest and, a day later, Buda accepted the revolutionary manifesto, the Twelve Points, after initially refusing to do so and succumbing only when the young men presented their arguments to the masses. A revolutionary committee took over the city administration in Pest, presided over by the liberal deputy mayor Lipót Rottenbiller. The national guard was being organised from the city's civilian guard. Parliament passed a new law concerning the cities, which extended the suffrage to a larger group of citizens, and a joint assembly took over from what had been a divided legislature of citizen body and the council. In Pest the mayor was Lipót Rottenbiller, while in Buda a liberal former councilman was elected to the post.

With the revolution Pest became the centre of the country, and continued to function as such as far as the circumstances of the war permitted. In April 1848 laws, assented to by the king, proclaimed that parliament must be assembled annually in Pest, and that Buda-Pest would be the seat of the Hungarian government. The popularly elected national assembly sat in the Auditorium of the Redoute, while the Upper House met in the Grand Hall of the National Museum. The independence movement was also centred in Pest, where the National Defence Committee to direct the War of Liberation was formed with Lajos Kossuth as its president. It was from Pest too that Kossuth set out to recruit soldiers for the army.

The majority of citizens shared the national ideals of the revolutionaries. They did not, however, approve of the young people who had changed their name from the Opposition Circle to the Radical Circle, headed by Petőfi and a teacher named Pál Vasvári, and the ongoing boisterous demonstrations they organised. There were occasions when the young revolutionaries were actually assaulted by disapproving citizens. The guild apprentices launched a strike, calling for the abolition of the guilds. Some of the burghers turned against the Jews who had settled in the city in recent years, and especially against Jewish artisans who were seen as competition, demanding that they be expelled. The

Serbian citizens of Buda and Pest held a joint meeting where they formulated their own demands for national rights and independence. In response young Hungarian writers – who had voiced their faithfulness to the Hungarian revolution – immediately went on the attack in the press. It was the opening to what was to become a bloody confrontation between Hungarians and the national minorities.

In the autumn of 1848 irregular troops were beginning to gather in Pest and Buda. On September 28 a mob murdered the commander-in-chief of the imperial troops in Hungary on the pontoon bridge. In response to this action Count Lajos Batthyány resigned from the prime ministership. The

74. A Pest trade sign showing Alexander Ypsilantis, hero of the Greek War of Independence. The painting from around 1840 made József Kollarits's linen shop on 26 Váci Street famous, and became a symbol in its own right following the Habsburg suppression of the Hungarian War of Independence

75. *The capture of Buda Castle by Hungarian troops on May 21, 1849. Colour lithograph by Károly Klette*

confrontation between the Habsburg Empire and Hungary had developed into full-fledged war. When, following Kossuth's ordinance, the weapons in the city were being collected, and it became known that several members of government had left the country, the people decided to leave too. On news that the imperial army was approaching from the south-west, a regular evacuation of the citizenry began. The National Defence Committee ordered the arsenal and mint, which was printing separate Hungarian bills (referred to as "Kossuth Banknotes"), dismantled in Pest and removed to Debrecen in the east of Hungary. Of the city government leaders, however, there was only a handful of magistrates who abandoned ship, all the rest remained in place. On January 5, 1849 the army of the Habsburg commander-in-chief, Duke Alfred Windischgrätz, entered the abandoned city of Pest, led by the Croatian Ban, Baron Josip Jellačić. The troops remained stationed there until the end of April, when they were ordered to the aid of imperial units fighting in other parts of the country, leaving behind only a four thousand-strong garrison under General Heinrich Hentzi. Although the still incomplete Chain Bridge remained intact, the departing troops set fire to the pontoon bridge. Immediately after the Habsburgs had occupied Buda and Pest they set up military commands. Some of the magistrates came to their assistance in removing those of their colleagues who would not comply, and in rounding up soldiers in hiding.

A hundred and sixty years had passed since the castle of Buda had served as a fortification, since it had last been laid siege to and defended; by the mid nineteenth century it was no longer really capable of acting as a fortress proper, even its gates could barely be lowered. Nevertheless Hentzi had to ready the complex for defence. He closed off part of Water Town with a barrier, evacuated inhabitants from some of the streets, set up a military hospital in the Castle school, and had the planks removed from the Chain Bridge to prevent passage. For added security he had mines placed under the Buda bridgehead. The inhabitants of the closed sections of the Castle and Water Town were called on to store a two month supply of food. Hentzi's arrangements were justified when, on April 24, Hungarian troops under the command of General Lajos Aulich entered Pest.

The main body of the Hungarian army, commanded by General Artúr Görgey soon followed. Although on May 5th an army 30 thousand strong was positioned under Buda, a lack of artillery meant that, in spite of their vastly superior numbers, they were unable to succeed in laying siege to the Castle. Meanwhile Hentzi was bombarding Water Town and Pest, a bombardment that destroyed the magnificent Redoute. At 3 o'clock in the morning of May 21st a flare went up from Görgey's headquarters in Laszlovszky Manor in Buda's Zugliget district as a signal to begin the final, all-round attack. Four hours later Buda Castle was again in Hungarian hands, and Hentzi had succumbed to his wounds before the day was over. The Buda bridgehead of the Chain bridge remained unscathed, even though Lieutenant Colonel Alois Allnoch, on realising the hopelessness of the situation, had thrown a burning cigar into the gunpowder barrel there. The barrel exploded, killing the lieutenant colonel.

Pest and Buda remained under the control of the Hungarian leaders for two months. The government com-

gardens of the National Museum; those condemned were small-time "spies", simple army deserters. The Hungarian military leaders were incarcerated in Arad, while the main political prisoners were held in the New Building in Pest, where the summary court also operated. In its courtyard, Hungary's first prime minister, Count Lajos Batthyány was executed. On thirty-six gallows the names of thirty-six men sentenced to death in absentia were posted on white plaques. The very first was Lajos Kossuth who had gone into exile. Altogether 218 death sentences were proclaimed; although substantially fewer were actually carried out. Later, when the retaliations were beginning to have a negative effect on Austria's foreign relations, the Emperor quickly had Haynau recalled, claiming that in carrying out the executions of civilians he had been acting on his own.

As soon as the fighting ended the military command began fortifying Pest-Buda. On Gellért Hill, construction of the Citadel was begun, on Castle Hill they started to repair

missioner during this time was Dániel Irinyi, a Pest attorney and political writer and one of the young radicals. He set up a summary court to try all those who had collaborated with the Austrians, launched a series of reprisals, and began to draft fresh soldiers for the army. For a few weeks the Hungarian government returned, headed by Lajos Kossuth, who after the Habsburgs had been deposed had become the governor-president of Hungary. The prime minister was Bertalan Szemere. He reassured the population of the two cities that in the new free Hungary a period of peaceful development could be expected; token of this, he launched work on plans for the cities' beautification. On June 24 Szemere passed an ordinance to unify Pest, Buda and Óbuda in a matter of twelve days, which he announced to the governing bodies of the cities in a memorandum. He believed that this would solve the cities' problems once and for all. By now, however, the imperial army under commander-in-chief Baron Julius Haynau was advancing. Over thirty thousand of the citizens of Pest took flight; on July 8th Kossuth and the Hungarian government left Pest as well.

With the assistance of Russia, Austria, far outnumbering the Hungarians, quickly found itself in a position to call for an armistice. Retribution was harsh, to a degree that no one would have imagined. Protests were voiced in all parts of Europe, but the young emperor, Francis Joseph I, was adamant. On July 19, 1849 the military commander in Hungary, Field Marshall Haynau, announced martial law and summary justice. He intimidated the German citizenry, and exacted retribution from the Jews of Óbuda and Pest, ordering them to pay reparations of over a half a million forints for the support they had given to the Hungarian side in the War of Liberation. Summary executions began in the

the ruined walls. As a form of psychological pressure to break the population's resistance, important Austrian and Russian military officers were elected honorary citizens. A ban on assembly was in effect, and so enforced that the Academy of Sciences was not able meet for several years. Censorship, which the revolution had done away with, was not re-imposed; but was replaced by a regulation whereby texts had to be submitted to the police for review after printing, which effectively curbed the dissemination of books and newspapers. Hungarian coats-of-arms and flags were no longer displayed, the Habsburg Empire's colours of black and yellow with its double-headed eagle were omnipresent. Beards were shaven, or its bearers charged with revolutionary conduct, house were searched wherever questionable writings were suspected, newspapers were closed down for using the word "king" – only "emperor" was permitted. In short, the victors wished to regulate the minutest details of daily life. This worked for a few years, until the regulations became so hackneyed, and supervision became less strict, until the bureaucrats imported from Bohemia and Austria learned enough Hungarian to grow ever more snug in their life in Pest. In 1854 the imperial authorities lifted martial law. Municipal elections were postponed for many years, however, and a succession of appointed mayors and bureaucrats of various ranks and designations attended to matters of local government.

Adversity not withstanding, the development of Pest continued. Many significant buildings that continue to characterise Pest today were raised in this "dark decade". Among these is the huge synagogue on Dohány Street, built by the Viennese architect Ludwig Förster on commission by the congregation, based on the plans he submitted in an open

competition. The monumental building tastefully combines important Jewish religious architectural traditions, and subsequently served as a model for several of the world's great synagogues, such as the Central Synagogue in New York City. Adjacent to it stood, until the end of the nineteenth century, the residential building in which Theodor Herzl, the founder of the state of Israel, was born.

In place of the demolished Redoute the Vigadó was erected in a peculiar Romantic style. It evinces a strong desire to find a style of architecture that is specifically Hungarian, so much so that it was described as "gypsy music carved in stone". The Berlin architect August Stüler designed the neo-renaissance building a little further up on the Danube that houses the Hungarian Academy of Sciences. In Buda the Tunnel, running under Castle Hill as an extension of the Chain Bridge, opened in this period, while in Pest many aristocrats were having their town houses built in the immediate vicinity of the National Museum. A share company set up by aristocrat entrepreneurs erected an indoor riding school, and not far off, in today's Bródy Sándor Street, a temporary House of Representatives was built. A major event in the

77. Young ladies after the ball. Painting by József Borsos from 1850, the year contemporaries termed the "darkest" following the suppression of the War of Independence

mid 1850s was the establishment of swimming pools in the Danube. These were wooden floats with pools in the middle that let the water of the river flow through. More and more sprang up along the Pest shore, and became increasingly popular as people came to realise that rivers could be used not only as trading routes but for sports and recreation, thereby supporting a healthy lifestyle.

Health and healing were just growing into a regular concern of the municipal government, not least owing to the fact that in Pest-Buda the death rate was exceedingly high. Small hospitals operated with few doctors, and only one larger healthcare institution stood in Pest: the public hospital of Saint Roche's. Its obstetric ward was headed by Ignác Semmelweis, who came to be known by the epithet "saviour of mothers" for his discovery of the pathogen that caused post-partum fever resulting in a great number of deaths.

City officials of Pest

*Johann Lenner von Lennersberg,
chief magistrate, 1715-1719*

*János Boráros, chief magistrate,
1790-1807*

*István Szilágyi, button maker,
member of the citizen body, 1826*

*Jakab Pisztory, magistrate,
1834-1843*

*István Staffenberg, spokesman,
1838*

*Mihály Farkas, chief master of the
carpenters' guild, 1851*

City officials of Buda

*Ignác Kramerlauff (Kalmárffy),
chief magistrate, 1790-1792, 1797-1825*

*Ferenc Balássy, chief magistrate, 1795-1797,
mayor 1800-1828*

*Ferenc Házmán, mayor,
1867-1873*

City Leaders of Budapest

Károly Ráth, prefect,
1873-1897

Károly Kamermayer, mayor,
1873-1896

Károly Gerlóczy, deputy mayor,
1873-1897

István Bárczy, mayor, 1906-1918,
Prefect, 1913-1919

Ferenc Heltai, prefect,
1912-1913

Tivadar Bódy, mayor,
1918-1920

János Buzáth, deputy mayor,
1920-1930

Jenő Sipőtz, mayor, 1920-1934,
prefect, 1934-1937

Ferenc Ripka, prefect,
1925-1932

Endre Liber, deputy mayor,
1930-1934

Károly Szendy, deputy mayor, 1934,
mayor, 1934-1944

The Fathers of the Metropolis: Gyula Andrássy and Frigyes Podmaniczky

The Revolution and its aftermath had little impact on the rate of Pest's development, which was not in the least stifled. The city's geographical and economic advantages no political power could resist, at least not for long. Vienna was unsuccessful in its attempts to prevent Pest's influence. The rate by which the population grew actually accelerated. (Between 1830 and 1850 the population of Pest grew by 57 per cent, in the twenty years that followed the growth was 62 per cent. The two cities of Buda and Pest – Óbuda had been incorporated into Buda in December 1849 – in 1851 had a combined population of 178 thousand, swelling to over 270 thousand by 1870.

The pace of growth was enormous, and the increase in numbers substantial. During the same period Vienna, initially two and a half times the size of Budapest, added 180 thousand inhabitants, Berlin almost doubled, and Saint Petersburg – rarely mentioned – increased at an annual rate of 50 thousand people. This, then, was the time when Budapest became that fast developing juvenile city that constantly outgrew its clothes – to use the fitting analogy by the late Hungarian historian Péter Hanák. In contrast to the growth of other large cities, Budapest's was healthy, and was not threatened by the social and functional calamity that for example Saint Petersburg experienced. In 1867 Hungary concluded an agreement with Austria known as the "Compromise". Budapest was made a capital city, and when in 1873 its administrative unification officially went into effect, another spurt of growth followed. By 1890 the number of inhabitants topped 490 thousand which constituted a 76 percent increase over two decades. Most of it, of course, came from immigration, and this endowed the city with a freshness and strength, an entrepreneurial spirit in the true sense of the term.

William H. Seward, President Lincoln's Secretary of State who had acquired Alaska from Russia, went on a journey around the world following his term of office. In the summer of 1869 he arrived in Pest from an unaccustomed direction, coming up the Danube from the Balkans. His comment expresses surprise at what he saw: "How striking is the contrast of European and Asiatic civilization! Though Buda-Pesth is an inland provincial town, with a population of two hundred and fifty thousand, the tonnage in its port, altogether of steam, is greater than that of Cairo, Alexandria, or Constatinople. We were not prepared for a scene of such activity. [...] Here we feel, for the first time, that we have left the East behind, and have only Western civilization around and before us."

The coronation that followed the Compromise, whereby Francis Joseph became King of Hungary, took place on June 8, 1867 and, of course, involved both Buda and Pest. The coronation took place in the Matthias Church; on the Pest side of the Chain Bridge, on the square between the Lloyd Palace and the new Academy of Sciences building, a coronation mount was set up, from which and in keeping with tradition, the newly crowned king had to cut the air with his sword in all four directions of the compass. (The

78. A bird's-eye view of Pest-Buda. Lithograph by Rudolf Alt, 1857

square was named after Francis Joseph at that time, and is now Roosevelt Square.) The king then ceremoniously knighted individuals in the medieval Garrison Church, Mary Magdalene's in the Castle District. With the coronation accomplished, Budapest had to be made fitting as a royal seat, which Francis Joseph would hence have to occupy alternatively with the imperial seat of Vienna. To this end the remodelling of Matthias Church into a Coronation Church, and the expansion of the royal palace at the turn of the century, were among the most conspicuous of the undertakings.

In Pest large projects were launched. The city raised enormous loans to build its waterworks, a slaughter-house and to launch a long-term project for constructing elementary schools. Concurrently parliament was busy forging a whole series of laws to modernise the country under the new circumstances the Compromise produced in its wake. One of them was proposed legislation that would deter-

mine the legal status of the two cities and their administration. This raised suspicion and concern in both Pest and Buda, since the approach adopted in creating a government structure for the metropolis was taken from the perspective of a county administering a small provincial town. During the parliamentary debate on this legislation, two members, one for Pest and one for Buda, submitted a joint motion to unite the two cities. The Pest M. P. was Mór Wahrmann, the first ever Jewish member of the Hungarian Parliament; political equality for Jews was passed into law in 1867, the year of the Compromise. Wahrmann, popularly known for his sense of humour and fondness for telling jokes, was a businessman and banker, a descendent of an old Óbuda family that included several rabbis. Wahrmann was an appropriate symbolic figure in Pest society, of which Jews made up 20 per cent, second only to Catholics. The M. P. from Buda was Ferenc Házmán, a respected politician who for twenty years or so had been a representative of various Buda districts. His own plan for unification had been drawn up as far back as 1848.

Parliament accepted the motion for debate, which ultimately led to the ratification of Act XXXVI/1872 calling for a united Budapest, that went into effect the following year. With the new municipal elections accomplished and the city government in place a ceremonial assembly was held on November 17, 1873. Now the new administration was ready to tackle the government of a metropolis. A year of transition was announced, made necessary by numerous details that needed to be resolved. A committee of thirty-four members worked out

Uj házasság.

Herr von Ofner. Alsdenn Fräul'n, mir sollen uns heirad'n. Mátyar emper hat kurás ! Ich liebe Sie !
Fräulein Pestella. Eh schon wissen, kraupetes Bubi. Jessas, an ungrische Eh'! Und alles wegen die talketen Schnrnalisten.
Herr von Ofner. Píszom, píszom ! Muszájn lenni hószafiság ! Tudja kisaszon mótyarul ?
Fräulein Pestella. Tudom.
Herr von Ofner. Látok.

the division of the city into new districts, accepted a coat-of-arms and flag, the composition and agendas of the municipal government committees, the assembly meeting schedules, and much more. It was as if the administration of a small country was being set up. Meanwhile voices protesting against unification persisted. Headed by the former mayor Mór Szentkirályi, the Pest party insisted that a German Buda, incapable of development, would only impede the modernisation of their city. They had their counterparts on the other side of the Danube.

The law specified the minimum taxes to be paid as a precondition for voting in the municipal elections. The general assembly consisted of 400 members, who elected the Prefect for a six-year term, from three candidates nominated by the king. The Prefect was the representative of the national government within the city body, responsible for ensuring that the interests of the state would be expedited. The mayor, on the other hand, was the head of the municipal government and presided over the city council. He was assisted by two deputy mayors. The council was made up of the leading municipal officials and was responsible for the supervision of the public coffers. The districts were headed by district chairmen and had their separate councils.

Budapest's first Prefect was Károly Ráth, a Pest attorney with business links to the haute bourgeoisie, who had risen to the coveted post within a matter of a few years. Károly

Kamermayer, who had served in civil service positions in both cities, was elected mayor. He was re-elected again and again until his death at the end of the century, and his term as mayor enabled him to restructure the municipal administration of Budapest. The post of deputy mayor went to the former town clerk Károly Gerlóczy. He held that position for a similarly extended period, in which he introduced a health care system of European standard in Budapest, founded cultural and art institutions, organised two large national exhibitions, and acquired the Károly barracks (the former Palace of the Invalids) as a home for the City Hall. The quarter century or so that the three men were in office is referred to by Budapesters as the "era of the three Károlys". The other deputy mayor, Mihály Kada, oversaw the day-to-day affairs of government.

The unification of Buda and Pest was, by this time, a legal and administrative step that concluded a long and inexorable course of development. Although it officially snubbed the idea, Pest took steps to prevent an unfavourable outcome for itself. As a first step, the town planning formulated at the beginning of the century was re-examined. A chief engineer at the building department

81. *The last meeting of the Budapest city council in the Old Town Hall on February 8, 1900*

82. *Ferenc Reitter's plan for a canal in Pest, where instead today's Large Ring runs*

of the Governor General's office, Ferenc Reitter, in the early 1860 had devised a plan to convert the arm of the Danube, which ran along today's Large Ring, into a canal. Modelled after Vienna and Paris, this waterway would have expanded docking facilities, improved the transport of goods, along with other benefits, to which he added plans for a railroad network and bridges. Lajos Kossuth had toyed with a similar idea himself, and Mihály Táncsics devised an even broader proposal concurrently with Reitter.

By the time these plans had advanced from the concept to the design phase, Count Gyula Andrássy, who had been made Prime Minister at the time of the Compromise, took charge of organising town planning. He had conceived a scheme of his own prior to 1848 for the future of Hungary, in which he assigned the capital a key role. With the predictable collapse of the Ottoman Empire and the Turkish withdrawal from the Balkans, Hungary's influence within the Habsburg Monarchy seemed certain to rise. Andrássy believed that the trade routes for the agricultural and industrial products and the merchants of the Balkan countries would converge on Budapest, if only its advantages could be exploited. In a long-term plan such as this the support of the largely traditional middle class, whose immediate interests lay in real estate speculation ultimately leading to increasingly small and crowded parcels of land, did not matter, while the upper middle class was barely visible at this time. In May 1868 Andrássy convened a Pest-

Buda commission to whom he outlined his ideas on dividing the city into zones, including an industrial zone, a boulevard of Parisian elegance that would connect the City Park with the core of the city, and first and foremost the necessity for a law on eminent domain as a precondition for urban design. This was the background to the passing of Act X/1870, after numerous intermediary steps, establishing the Municipal Public Works Council as the central organisation for urban planning.

83. *Count Gyula Andrássy. Oil painting by Gyula Benczúr from the 1880s*

86

84. Baron Frigyes Podmaniczky around 1905

85. Pest in the midst of a fervour of construction, shown in an 1873 cartoon in the satirical journal Borsszem Jankó

Podmaniczky. Szent Rend! jöjjön el a te országod Pesten is.

That was when the de facto unification of Buda and Pest occurred, and everything constructed in the ensuing half century was conceived and staked out at this time. Huge loans subsidised by the state secured the necessary capital. It was a rare moment in Hungarian history when the steps leading to the completion of a plan were predictable, and not contingent on the whims of political and economic groups with their volatility and principal purpose of raising a monument to their own immortal greatness.

The thrust that propelled the undertakings to success came largely from Baron Frigyes Podmaniczky, who for over three decades presided over the Municipal Public Works Council. An aristocrat with a bohemian spirit who delved also into literature, he was one of the well-known figures in Pest's art world, not least for his eccentric dress. But as a public figure, the man in chequered trousers was more than simply conscientious: he had a passion for the city. He was indeed "Budapest's groom", as the writer Gyula Krúdy called him, who with unflagging energy developed the plans for the city, had them passed, and launched their execution.

The projects included the regulation of the Budapest stretch of the Danube, with docks, storage facilities, bridges, and boulevards, a central rail station and a railway overpass, as well as the regulation of main transportation arteries. Ferenc Reitter, who was now working for the ministry on the detailed programme, at this point proposed the building of a Large Ring (thus discarding his proposal for a canal), which was to be concentric to the Small Ring embracing the Inner City. The complex program was, therefore, preceded by comprehensive city planning. In 1870 a public tender was announced for the specific projects, with a map indicating the construction already under way. The tender involved both broad and detailed assign-

ments, and also called for an estimation of the projected growth of the city, with the future integration of outlying towns in mind.

Of the ten tenders submitted nine were written in German – these being the local tenderers, the tender in Hungarian was by a London firm. The commission was awarded to the architect Lajos Lechner, whose family had for several generations been active in building the capital into what it was. Lechner was soon after named the director of city construction, as such he established the principles for city planning and the principal means to carry them through. For the most part they became reality.

The building of the Boulevard, known from 1890 to this day – with minor interruptions – as Andrássy Boulevard, was begun on expropriated land in 1871. That same year legislation to build the Large Ring was passed. Soon after the construction of a second Danube bridge, Margaret Bridge, was begun, and a great many of the Pest streets were broadened, extended and regulated. For many years the Inner City became one large construction site, a spectacle that historian Péter Hanák, in comparing Budapest – the "workshop" – to Vienna – the "garden" – described thus, "Pest was driven by the desire to rise as a capital to European rank. Its sheep pastures were converted not into gardens or parks, but crowded apartment buildings, streets, and factories. It was industrious and became industrialised."

Buildings grew out of the ground like mushrooms: in 1870 there were 9,400 structures, two decades later there were 16,200. Not only did the city expand horizontally, it grew vertically as well. Traditionally there had been single-story houses, within twenty years the majority of buildings had two or more stories, and in the central parts of town houses were at least two, but often three and even four stories high.

Budapest's Calling Card: Andrássy Boulevard

The haute bourgeoisie and the generation of the *Gründerzeit* (the "foundation years" in the 1860s and 1870s when the Monarchy went through a period of industrial and commercial expansion) shaped public taste and the cityscape of Budapest. The monuments to these years are the buildings along Andrássy Boulevard and the Large Ring, and on the Buda side the countless villas and summer homes on the slope of Svábhegy, in Zugliget and Hűvösvölgy. Pest's building boom saw scores of new buildings being raised in Leopold and Theresa Towns.

The Boulevard was developed in an organised manner, and was given a homogenous appearance, the likes of which Pest had not known before. Plots expropriated under right of eminent domain were re-divided, and after 1871 the Municipal Public Works Council sold them under condition that they would be built on within a brief span of time. Most of the Boulevard was completed within fifteen years, in a neo-renaissance style.

The Boulevard's full length of two and a half kilometres has three distinct sections of equal length. The first, between the Small and Large Rings, has two-story apartment buildings with rows of trees on either side. The houses look like mansions, but their owners, bankers and entrepreneurs, had built them as investments rather than for their own use. They themselves continued to live in the Inner City or Leopold Town, and only after the end of the century did some of them move into town houses on the Boulevard's outer, truly elegant section. Thus it was an exception when someone like the former textile magnate András Saxlehner, who had made a substantial fortune from producing "János Hunyadi Bitter", took up residence in his own building at 3 Andrássy Boulevard, in a ten-room apartment on the second floor – with his five-room office adjacent. It now houses the Post Office Museum and visitors to can still appreciate the magnificent entrance and stairway, and the decor of the apartment.

This first stretch of Andrássy Boulevard was initially the most elegant section. Gyula Krúdy captured the street's essence when he wrote, "On its three fathom-deep asphalt every gentlewoman in Pest who could boast an impeccable toilette, had the opportunity to present herself. [...] Every burgher without any hope of entering either the Magyar nobility or a baronage was eager to obtain the rank that can be obtained on one's own strength – a landlordship on Andrássy Boulevard. [...] Real Andrássy Boulevard is where the asphalt is always immaculate, the parquet that is the carriageway is sprinkled with dust-repellent oil, the constable's frock-coat is always pressed and his gloves white, the carriage wheels are red and have noiseless tires, the cafés are bustling with life, in the restaurants they are constantly cooking, eating, the people are forever smiling..."

Between the Oktogon and Körönd Squares, terraced rows of buildings remain extant. They are one level lower than in the first stretch, and include public buildings and art academies, such as the Old Academy of Music established by Ferenc (Franz) Liszt, as well as apartment houses. From this point on a carriageway was built on either side, with a pavement between it and the Boulevard, lined with double rows of trees. The third section extended to the City Park, and its detached town houses are set back in gardens and were originally two stories high.

The Boulevard, with its residential and public buildings, its grand cultural establishments and a modern public utilities system, is the epitome of Budapest's development, and the driving force and sophistication behind it. The vast amounts of money consumed by all this feverish building and expansion had been accumulated in the commerce and banking sectors. The Balkan countries of Bulgaria, Romania

86. Andrássy Boulevard, with the Opera House in the foreground and cafés around it. Photograph from around 1900

and Serbia, having just shed the Ottoman yoke and rich in agriculture and animal husbandry, passed through Budapest to reach the European markets. But with its advanced milling and food industry the Hungarian capital was not just a transit station, but a place where goods could be sold or processed. Conversely, Budapest was the main conveyor of industrial merchandise from Germany and England to the Balkans. The central location that had made Pest a town of consequence for a thousand five hundred years, a liberal economy and the period of peace that extended between the third quarter of the nineteenth and the early twentieth centuries, advanced Budapest into a city of wealth. Now it could produce the enormous capital that was needed to make it into a metropolis fit to be a regional centre. Money invested in construction earned additional income: rents rose even more steeply than the population, encouraging house owners to invest in additional construction.

The town houses of the upper middle class built at this time were just as large and exclusive as those of the old aristocracy. Outwardly similar in grandeur and pomp, the interiors differed only in that the eclectic interiors the aristocrats resided in contained family heirlooms, antiques and paintings, while the items in old styles the haute-bourgeoisie surrounded themselves with were newly manufactured, often commissioned to suit the interior design. At the same time, many of the rich art collections compiled in the final years of the nineteenth century were established in these haute bourgeois residences, and particularly on Andrássy Boulevard.

87. The writer Mór Jókai in his study in Bajza Street. Photograph by Mór Erdélyi, 1892

At the intersection of the Boulevard and the Large Ring is the Oktogon, an eight-angle square, adjacent to which was the town house of an aristocrat modelled on the magnificent renaissance Strozzi Palace in Florence. The neighbouring buildings were nothing of the sort, however. They were, exclusive, middle-class apartment buildings and shops, rather than town houses, but elegant in their own way, nonetheless.

From the 1880s on bathrooms were included not only in the city's more fashionable apartments but also in the common, four- or five-room middle-class ones, at least in the inner districts. The need for a good public utilities system had become pressing. Water pipes and sewage were being built so quickly that while in 1880 only 25 percent of the Budapest houses had running water, a decade later the ratio was 67 percent. The acceleration slowed when the network reached the poor and badly constructed buildings in the outskirts. After the turn of the century rented housing for workers was being built; the apartments consisted of a room and a kitchen, often with one communal toilet.

Street lighting became common at this time. By 1885 there were almost eight thousand gas and oil lamps along the streets, squares and in public buildings. It was the duty of the concierge to place the rubbish bins in front of each house at six in the morning. The collection of these commenced at this time, followed by the sprinkling and sweeping of the streets. Various materials were used to pave the streets and squares: they included wooden blocks, basalt stones, and, even then, asphalt, depending on the expected traffic. Pavements were built from 1868 on, for the purposes of separating pedestrian and wheeled traffic and of safety.

Public transport in the form of horse-drawn omnibuses first appeared back in 1832, between Vörösmarty Square and the City Park, but the creation of a network had to wait until after the 1867 Compromise. Running on tracks, passenger cars shuttled between Calvin Square and Újpest, and on the Buda side between the Chain Bridge and Óbuda, the line branching off to the popular excursion spot in the Buda hills called Zugliget. The Buda and the Pest lines were linked when Margaret Bridge was completed in 1876. In 1887 a new public transport company brought yellow electric trams along the Large Ring. This innovation, whose future was truly long-term, had banished the horse-drawn cars before the century was over. In 1870 a steam-powered funicular railway rising from the side of the Tunnel to the top of Castle Hill was in place, and it was followed four years later by a cogwheel railway up to Svábhegy. Soon city transportation extended beyond the inlying areas to connect several neighbouring settlements,

88. *A drawing-room furnished with valuable art objects in the Erdődy-Hatvany House at 7 Táncics Mihály Street in the Castle District, around 1900*

which would later become part of Budapest. Újpest, established forty years earlier on the flat and barren estate of Count Károlyi, was quickly growing into an industrial and commercial district; it was not long before it had a horse-drawn railway of its own. In the second half of the 1880s a network of local railways connecting the rest of the outlying towns was established. Known by its acronym, the HÉV on the Pest side extended to Soroksár and Cinkota, on the Buda side to Szentendre, thus making Budapest into a metropolitan area.

Rail transport was not the only technological innovation to span distances; there were also the telegraph and the telephone. Several dozen companies were established to set up telegraph networks. In 1874 the Central Telegraphy Company opened in the Lloyd Palace, which is an indication that the system's main clients were merchants and the Stock Exchange. Five years later the telephone network was started, and in 1893, recognising the telephone's potential to disseminate information, the Hungarian engineer Ferenc Puskás launched his "voice news." He acquired a world patent for his innovation, which became available in many large cities. With the invention of the radio not much later, this technically more feasible "wireless" supplanted the telephone as a news medium.

Journalists were quick to recognise the tremendous advantages of both the telephone and telegraph in transmitting fresh information within a matter of minutes. Reporters had their headquarters in the Lloyd Palace, since this where the most recent economic and political information arrived. Daily papers at this time had reached circulations of over ten thousand copies, and these papers competed to increase their readership. The speed with which information was transmitted became crucial. Back in the 1870s, the dissemination of a speech by the prime minister somewhere in the provinces would involve the parliamentary reporter taking it down in situ, and then boarding a train equipped with a special car where he would dictate the text to reporters. For longer speeches dictation would continue at the Lloyd Palace, where it would also be translated for the German papers. Now editorial clerks would shuttle between the Lloyd and their offices, carrying first the manuscripts, then the proofs, and by the following morning the national dailies, published in Pest, would carry the prime minister's speech. With the introduction of the telegraph all this changed. For the more important events occurring in the provinces a separate telegraph office would be set up for the press; a court proceeding in the morning, for instance, would appear in the papers that same afternoon. Circulations soon tripled, *Pesti Hírlap* and *Budapest Hírlap* were becoming businesses and their owners influential public figures and some of the capital's largest tax payers. In a few years the main streets were loud with the voices of newsvendors, dashing through the crowds of pedestrians while shouting out catchy headlines – and selling ever more copies. Before the century was over the tabloid was born. The streets were filled with masses of people, public transport alone carried over 200 thousand passengers a day. What a young emigrant from Leopold Town named Joseph Pulitzer had brought to New York thirty years earlier, sensational journalism (known after 1895 as "yellow journalism"), was now popular also in his home town of Pest.

The newspaper became an established part of middle-class social life, together with the café and the theatre. On the square at the intersection of Kerepesi (now Rákóczi) Street and the Large Ring, was erected the People's Theatre, "Népszínház", which was later to become home to the National Theatre. On the József Avenue corner rose the headquarters of the *Budapest Hírlap*, which housed the printing press, publishers' and editorial offices, and its advertisement bureau. On the facing corner at Teréz Avenue stood the buildings of the Atheneum Publishers and Press. At three o'clock in the afternoon the newsvendors would set out from this square to reach, in one and a half to two hours, as far as Újpest. Further along József Avenue, extending outward from the Ring, was the red-light district, which already had a history of many decades. Several cafés and restaurants were located along this stretch of József Avenue. On Teréz Avenue, on the other side of Atheneum headquarters, an insurance company

000366

Magyar vigszinház-részvénytársaság.

RÉSZVÉNY 400 AZAZ NÉGYSZÁZ KORONÁRÓL

Knoblauch Richard
mint ezen részvény birtokosának vagy jogutódjának mindazok a jogok biztosíttatnak, melyek a társaság alapszabályai szerint minden részvényest megilletnek.
Budapest, 1895. julius 1.
MAGYAR VÍGSZINHÁZ-RÉSZVÉNYTÁRSASÁG

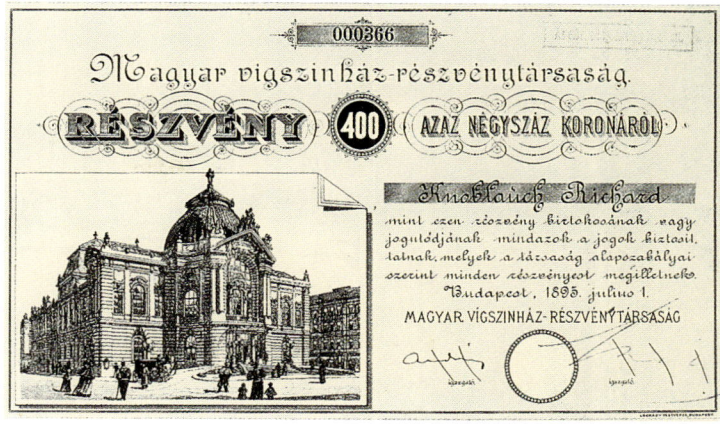

89. *A 400-Korona share certificate issued in 1895 for the construction of the Vígszínház Theatre*

90. *The Large Ring with the New York House. Photograph by Mór Erdélyi, 1896*

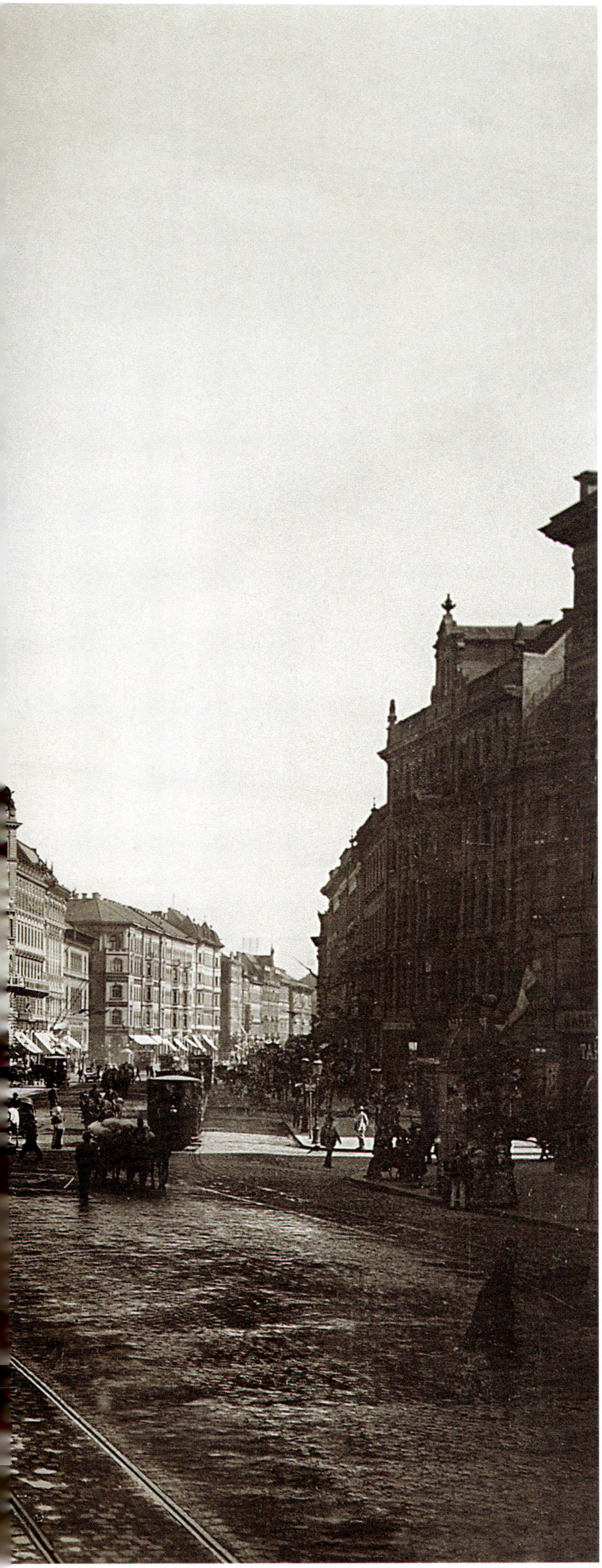

built a block that housed what was to become Pest's most fashionable café, the New York, a home for writers, journalists and actors.

Pest's traditional bohemian district with its restaurants, cafés and night-clubs was on Nagymező Street (intersecting Andrássy Boulevard just west of the Oktogon) and extended into Király Street. Artists, journalists and writers, actors and their patrons frequented this part of town and its establishments. Here the middle class public could mingle with artists and all sorts of questionable elements, including "dancers" otherwise excluded from "society". Pest's best-known place of entertainment, the Somossy Orpheum (which today houses the Operetta), had stood here for many years. Built by the fashionable Viennese theatre construction company Fellner and Helmer, which designed also the Vígszínház (still standing on Szent István Avenue) and several other theatres in Pest, the Orpheum was an enormously successful undertaking.

Along this stretch of Andrássy Boulevard were several cafés, including the Japán on the corner of Liszt Ferenc Square, which after the turn of the century was for many decades a popular meeting place for painters, musicians and writers. Gyula Krúdy described the atmosphere of this

91. *Pest's most famous café, the Gerbeaud*

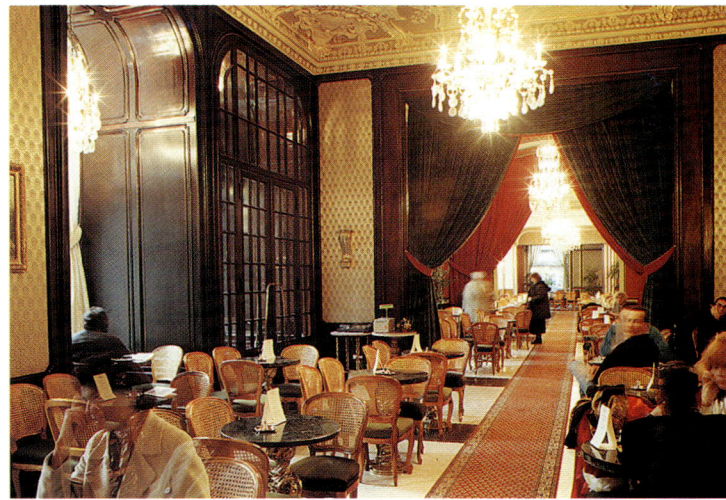

92. *The "Table of Scholars" in the Café Centrál in inner Pest around the turn of the century*

93. *The café as the main setting for social life in Pest: "Scene in a Budapest café". Cartoon by János Jankó in the comic journal* Borsszem Jankó, *1890*

part of the city. "In the cafés on Andrássy Boulevard so-called frivolous women and young men with penetrating eyes converse about literature, music, painting, and the founding of banks and enterprises."

The café was much more, however, than a bohemian hang-out. It served the bourgeoisie as a surrogate for the salon, a place for socialising that the average middle-class apartment lacked the facilities for. The café, in Péter Hanák's words, "served as a place for eating, reading the papers, exchanging information, socialising, playing cards and billiards, conducting business meetings, and enjoying musical entertainment, even for drinking coffee. It was bureau and editorial office, a rendezvous spot, and lavatory. In this part of the world the café became an integral part of daily life, from punch at dawn to café-au-lait before noon, the merriment to the exhausted strains of gypsy music lasting until the wee hours of morning."

The Climax of National Pride: The Millenary Celebrations

In 1884 Budapest's first Opera House opened its doors on Andrássy Boulevard. Designed by Miklós Ybl, the most important architect of the final third of the nineteenth century, this exquisitely ornamented neo-renaissance building displays seated statues of the period's two great Hungarian composers, Ferenc (Franz) Liszt and Ferenc Erkel in niches at its main entrance. For its opening, excerpts from Erkel's two national operas, *Ban Bánk* and *László Hunyadi,* were performed, with the first act of Richard Wagner's *Lohengrin* between them, almost as a rejoinder to the feud that was going on in this decade to attain independence for Hungarian culture and the Magyarization of Budapest by doing away with everything German. At the end of the decade, the musical director, Gustav Mahler, was driven away under the claim that he spread "musical Germanism".

Concurrently with the unification process of Buda and Pest, town names in the country were changed to Hungarian ones. After 1844, when the Diet ratified the country's official name as "Magyar", the suburbs within and around Buda and Pest were gradually given Hungarian names. First the hills, valleys and springs around Buda were reassigned – often just invented – their "old Magyar names". In 1861 the old German names of streets and squares in Pest were changed. Nevertheless German names continued to be in use up until the mid 1870s. The map which accompanied the announcement of the Municipal Public Works Council's city planning competition still contained German names; just two or three years later, when the unification of Budapest was in progress, maps showed the official names to be in Hungarian. Mostly, of course, these were faithful translations of the German names.

While visitors, too, saw Budapest as a Hungarian city now, it still retained its distinct image of embracing a colourful variety of cultures. Extreme nationalists and those who demanded the quick and coerced assimilation of all minorities, alleged with increasing persistence that Budapest was a foreign city, one that had obliterated the Hungarian national spirit. The director of Johann Strauss's *Fledermaus* actually transferred the opera's setting to ancient China so as to avoid its taking place in Vienna with German names. (The latter, by the way, were changed to Italian!) Grotesquely, among those accusing Budapest of foreignness were individuals who had come from German or Jewish families, and had chosen Hungarian names for themselves in place of their original German ones. Their doing so was not by coercion, however. It was an intuitive desire for assimilation, hastened by Hungary's, and especially Budapest's, economic achievements, and the attractiveness of Hungarian culture and arts, coupled with an ambition to rise on the social ladder. It simply was pleasant to belong to the majority in the successful capital of a nation that looked toward a promising future.

In a Budapest which was Hungarian/German/Jewish and, due to nineteenth-century immigration, also Slovak, a citizen could not easily determine who was who, or even who he himself was and where he belonged to. This unique situation gave rise to the wonderful genre of the Budapest Joke, a blend of Hungarian anecdotes and Yiddish jokes, and their medium, the comic journals. In the environment shaped by the Compromise and Jewish emancipation *Borsszem Jankó,* a comic journal that retained its popularity over several decades, came into being. More than anything else it confronted the various members of heterogeneous Budapest society with each other. Week after week caricatures brought to life everyday figures, with their peculiar features and manners of speech that neither outsiders nor they themselves could always decipher. Comic journals presented a complex and faithful portrait of Budapest society, albeit in a twisted form. These figures made their way into belles-lettres and were evoked even in political speeches.

94. *The interior of the Opera, watercolour after a drawing by its architect Miklós Ybl from the 1880s*

95. *Caricatures of some typical Pest figures: Laci Titán, the primordial genius; Iczig Spitzig, the lower-middle-class character from Theresa Town; Absentius Bukovay (Absentius de Fail), student of law; porter Mátyás Lábatlan (Matthew Footless); Vendel Sanyarú (Wendel Wretched), a junior clerk; Zirzabella Kotlik Lengenádfalvay (Zirsabell Brooding-Swayreed) poetress undergoing emancipation; police officer András Mihaszna (Andrew Goodfornaught); Monokles, the aristocrat; and Berci Mokány (Bert Spunky), a gentry figure*

96. Colour postcard on the occasion of the Budapest première of Ferenc Lehár's operetta The Merry Widow in Király Theatre in 1907

The operetta used similar figures chiselled into stage characters, and also the jokes. Imported from Vienna and sustained by the atmosphere of the Monarchy, operetta took on distinctively Pest characteristics.

On June 8, 1892 Francis Joseph observed the quartercentenary of his coronation as King of Hungary. The capital became the site of splendid festivities, and the monarch chose the occasion to bestow on the city the title of a royal seat, thus officially proclaiming that Budapest was in this respect of equal standing with Vienna. Budapest was officially referred to as "royal seat and capital", a designation later fused into "capital seat".

The climax to Budapest's history, however, came in the year 1896. The nation-wide celebrations on the thousandth anniversary of the Hungarian state was centred on the capital, and as a thriving metropolis it was able to benefit equitably from the whole enterprise. The initial idea was to stage a World Fair in Budapest, something that would have soothed the pride of the nation and the city. In addition, the fact that Vienna had hosted a World Fair in 1873 persuaded the people of Budapest that this was worthy of their efforts – but, finally, a national fair was deemed just as acceptable.

The fair buildings went up in the City Park, which itself was developed on a grand scale for the occasion. Running from the very centre of Pest underneath Andrássy Boulevard directly to the site was the Continent's first underground railway, which Francis Joseph, on his arrival for the fair, formerly opened. A number of the buildings erected for the Fair, some memorials to the country's past, others a tribute to the recent achievements in agriculture, industry and commerce, along with cultural, regional and municipal landmarks, have remained to this day; they accommodate a museum, a popular wedding chapel, and a courtyard where summer concerts are held. The 1896 celebrations, where the consumption of wine reached 5600 litres and 32 thousand pairs of sausages on a given day, were staged in the City Park and in Buda's Vérmező park. From Vérmező a 1700-strong mounted escort, representing each town and county in Hungary, proceeded to the Castle to salute the King, then to Matthias Church to pay tribute to the Holy Crown, and crossed the Danube to the House of Parliament, then still under construction; from there they rode along Andrássy Boulevard to reach the Fair grounds proper. They were wearing armour over Magyar gala-dress and carried ornate weaponry, the heralds bearing banners and blowing bugles. Parading after them came the city representatives, dressed as the members of the great historic aristocratic families of Hungary. Thriving capitalists, beer brewers, mill and distillery owners, proprietors of machine factories, and scores of other citizens marched in a medieval pageant.

In preparation for this grand event, Parliament had decreed the raising of a gigantic monument at the far end of Andrássy Boulevard, on what has since become Heroes Square. The design of the Millenary Monument was com-

97. Jacques Offenbach in Hungarian gala dress, on his guest performance in Pest in 1861

97

98. *The historic Millenary procession at Margaret Bridge*

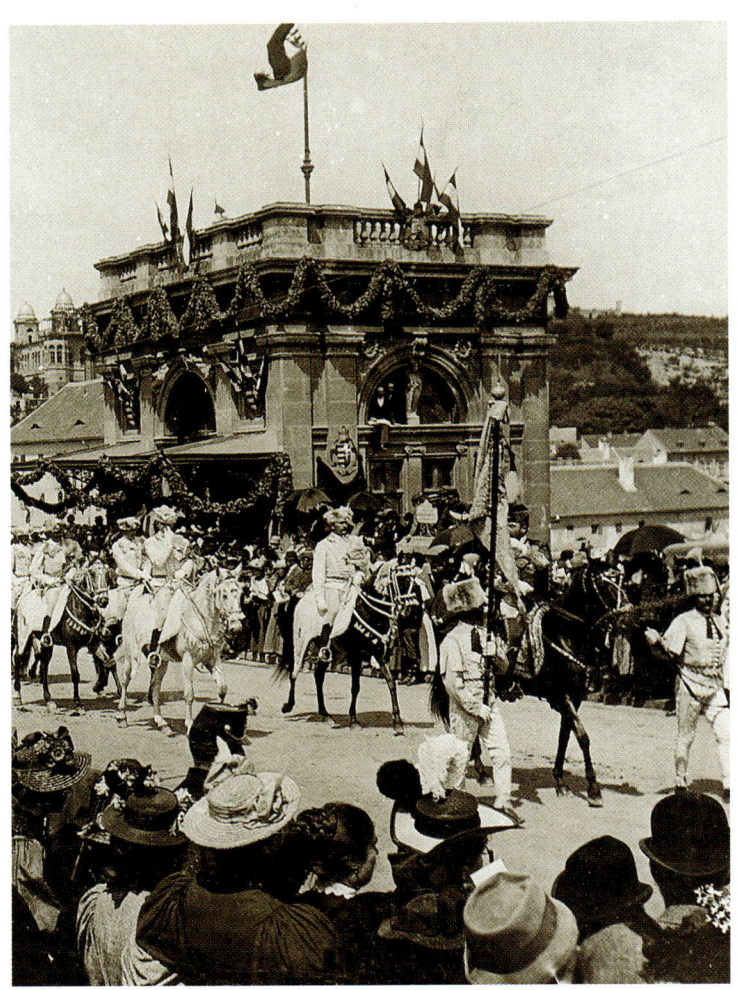

missioned to sculptor György Zala and architect Albert Schickedanz. The complex took 23 years to complete, and includes huge sculptures personifying War, Peace, Work and Welfare, as well as Knowledge and Glory, in addition to the mounted statues of the chieftains of the Magyar tribes, and an arc of statues of the country's most notable rulers. On both sides of the complex are museums, and behind it, on the island in the City Park lake, the popular architect of Pest's eclectic style, Ignác Alpár, created reduced-scale copies of historic structures from various parts of Hungary. That compound was called Vajdahunyad Castle (whose original is the birthplace of the renaissance King Matthias I) after its most prominent structure.

On the Danube bank at Leopold Town the Parliament building was in a sufficient stage of completion (though the inauguration was not until 1902) to permit the ceremonial assembly to sit in the Grand Hall beneath the central cupola. The enormous edifice, reflecting its creators' yearning for the Gothic, was conceived in 1880 to accommodate its anticipated status in a future Danubian Empire. In size it competed with the Parliament of England. If not for its status, as an

99. *The 1896 Millenary Exhibition Complex painted from a bird's-eye perspective*

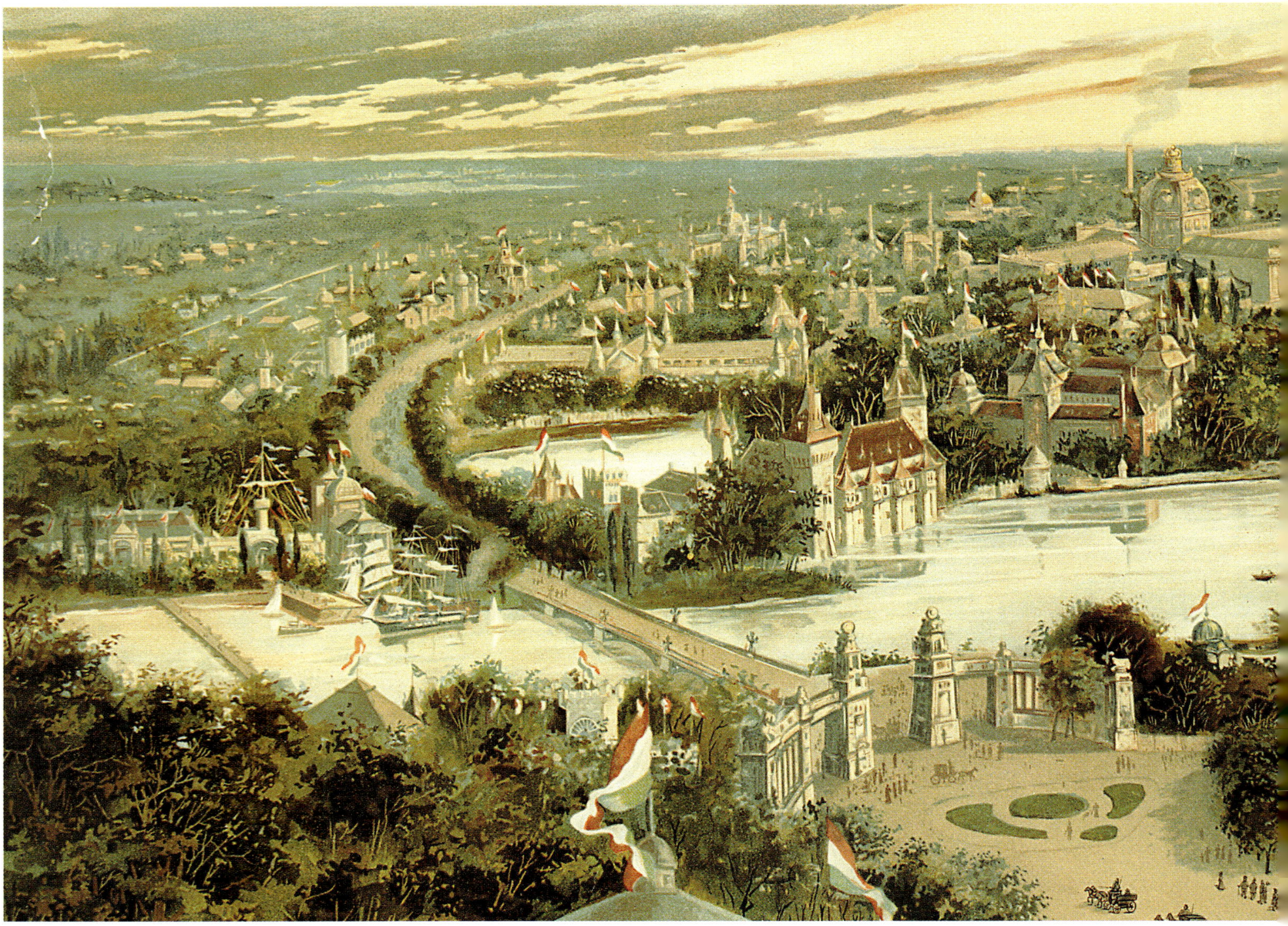

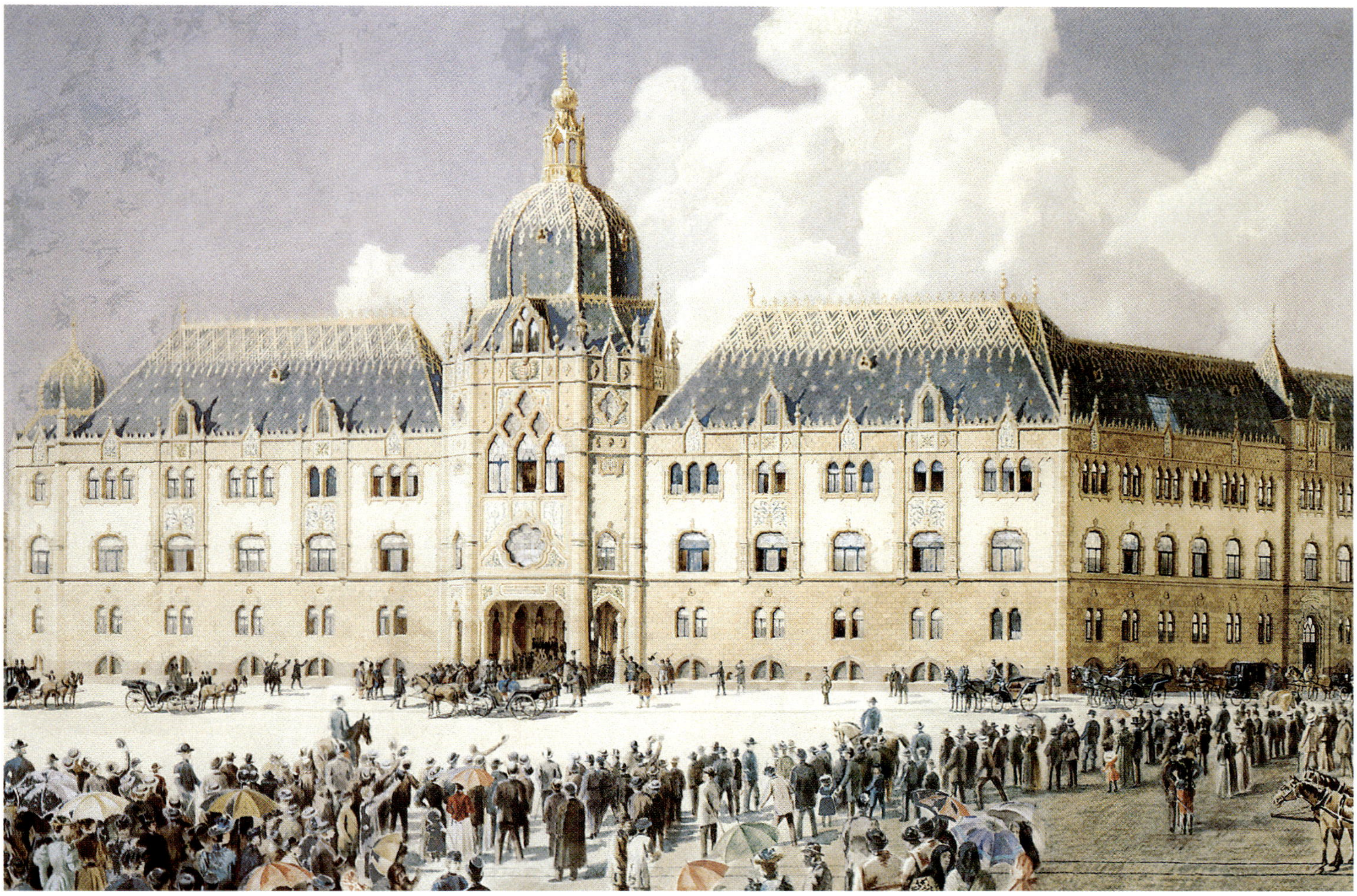

100. *The Museum of Applied Art, an outstanding piece of art-nouveau architecture in Hungary, designed by Ödön Lechner. The watercolour shows the arrival of Francis Joseph I for the building's inauguration in 1896*

101. *The "Millenary" Underground Railway, seen in a cross-section underneath Andrássy Boulevard*

attraction the building certainly remains a photogenic land-mark of Budapest. Designed by architect Imre Steindl, its ornamentation has contributions by all major Hungarian artists of the late nineteenth and early twentieth centuries.

Across the square from the main entrance to Parliament stands another large and ornate edifice which housed the

102. *One of the first mass demonstrations: the procession passing through the Large Ring for the funeral of Lajos Kossuth in 1894. Photograph by György Klösz*

103. *The Austrian-Hungarian Bank on Szabadság Square. Water-colour by the building's architect, Ignác Alpár, from around 1900*

Supreme Court. It was designed by Alajos Hausman, the architect who planned the remodelling and enlargement of the Royal Palace. The Inner City by this time already extended to Saint Stephen Avenue, and here the Pest bourgeoisie had its own theatre, the Vígszínház, erected. Near the other end of the Large Ring stood the Museum of Applied Art, and a new bridge, Francis Joseph (today's Szabadság, or Freedom) Bridge was formally opened.

104. *The National Flag Monument on Szabadság Square, with sculptures as testimonials to the Trianon Peace Treaty in the background. Photograph by Ernő Vadas from the 1930s*

The new Museum of Applied Art brought in a new era in architecture. Designed by Ödön Lechner the unusual building with its oriental ornamentation and coloured ceramic tile roof introduced the *Sezession* style to Budapest. This style, an *art nouveau* specific to the Habsburg Monarchy, was a revolt against the confines of the academic school; as such it was also an expression of bourgeois equality in defiance of the aristocratic models feeding on the past.

Sezession family residences and villas were built in a functional arrangement and size, refusing to mimic the kinds of expansive rooms found in palaces. A distinctly Hungarian *Szecesszió* evolved, where rationality and objectivity fused with the national idea, specifically, to discover in the country's own past the forms and motifs that are its own, and not adaptations of a style that originated in some other part of Europe. Artists, architects, folk-tale collectors, and musicians in search of ancient melodies (most prominently Béla Bartók and Zoltán Kodály) flocked to the Székely region in Transylvania, where folk art and customs were retained in their most archaic forms. There were countless individual structures, including public buildings (the Geology Institute, the Post Savings Bank, now a wing of the National Bank, and some schools), several family homes and villas (most around the City Park and in Buda), and the core of the state-built Wekerle housing project in Kispest, which succeeded in conveying the newly popular Magyar motifs. Even if as a trend it never caught on as an independent style of architecture, it left a great imprint on the furniture, glass, porcelain, jewellry, and other works of applied arts at that time, and is both gaining in popularity and inspiring other styles today.

The City Park with Heroes Square and the Millenary Monument at its heart, is Budapest's display of the country's matured national pride. In another part of the city is a site that projects, in contrast, the consciousness of Budapest's upper middle class. Szabadság Square can serve as a symbol for the city's modern history.

This once waterlogged and sandy part of Leopold Town entered history in 1786, when it was chosen as the site for the New Building (referred to by its German name as Neugebäude), an enormous complex the size of a large city block. Decades later István Széchenyi planted a row of trees along its side with the intention of establishing the town's first promenade here. A few years after that the building saw the reprisals against Hungarians for their War of Liberation, and was the site where the country's first prime minister was executed.

The Millenary generation, with its confidence in a great future, razed the building and placed a memorial with an eternal flame on the execution spot. Where the edifice stood, Szabadság (Freedom) Square was conceived, with the streets converging on it to bear the names of the generals executed after the War. On the square's western end, several apartment buildings of equal height were erected in the early years of the twentieth century, while along the eastern flank the Austrian-Hungarian Bank (subsequently the Hungarian National Bank), and facing it the Stock Exchange were built.

Both public buildings, designed by Ignác Alpár, were very large, that of the Stock Exchange downright monumental. When the old Town Hall was pulled down as part of the reconstruction of the core of the Inner City, the same citizenry of Budapest that saw no need for a new town hall fitting for a municipality of this scale, clearly attributed more importance to having a Stock Exchange at this conspicuous location and in a size that nearly matched that of the parliament building. (The same rivalry was seen in Vienna between their parliament and town hall, and the city government fared not at all worse than the national legislature.)

With the new buildings the portentous history of Szabadság Square was by no means over. Following the First World War, the site became a symbol of the country's fate, when statues representing those parts of historic Hungary lost under the terms of the Trianon Peace Treaty, with the national flag flown in the centre and the soil of each county of historic Hungary encased in the flagpole pedestal, was erected here. At the tip of the national flag a hand, modelled after that of Hungary's regent Miklós Horthy, pointed toward the sky, raised in oath. Events of significance for the country's diplomacy were taking place in Szabadság Square almost all the time now, an expression of Hungary's political efforts to regain her lost territories. With the Soviet occupation after World War II the statues were, of course, removed. What was once the flagpole was remodelled into the new occupiers' heroic monument, which has remained in place. In 1956 the Hungarian Revolution shook the Soviet Union's power in Central Europe, and again Szabadság Square played an important role. After the crushing of the Revolution the Embassy of the United States of America, situated here, offered refuge to one of the staunchest foes of the system, Archbishop József Mindszenty, who remained in the building for two decades as a living symbol of the uprising. Then, to complete the picture, came the transformation of the capitalist symbol of the Stock Exchange into another influential twentieth-century institution: it is now the headquarters of Hungarian Television.

Destitution in the Metropolis and a New Approach in Municipal Government: István Bárczy

One tends to think of Budapest at the turn of the century as a large city with a middle-class way of life. In the words of writer-historian John Lukacs, "The working classes were the largest portion of the people of Budapest; but by 1900 the tone of Budapest was that of a bourgeois city. Perhaps in all of Eastern Europe it was the *only* bourgeois city." Behind the grand construction projects, the large stores, and the thriving intellectual and artistic life there existed, however, a belt of outlying districts.

Both industry and industrial workers converged on the capital, and the consequences were social as well as economic. Industrial areas developed along the transport routes for raw material, these being the main highways leading into the city and along the Danube. By the turn of the century there was an industrial region in the north of Pest along the highway to Vác, with dense rows of factories and plants that employed a total of 12 thousand workers. On the other side of Pest, in Kőbánya, 8 thousand people worked in the large machine factories and the workshops and plants for the State Railway. In the southern industrial area along Soroksári Street, there were large steam mills, food processing and

chemical plants employing 9 thousand. On the other side of the Danube, Óbuda became a main industrial area with its textile and tobacco plants and shipyard, which at the dawn of the twentieth century provided work for some five and a half thousand people. The last area to become an industrial centre was around Kelenföld and Lágymányos in the southern part of Buda; this was partly due to the plants that had been demolished during the expansion of the residential area in Leopold Town being rebuilt here.

Industrial areas extended beyond Budapest's limits, and consequently the towns along the peripheries, especially Újpest, Palota, Erzsébetfalva, Pestszentlőrinc and Kispest, and Csepel to the south, were practically attached to Budapest. As the population became denser and industry expanded, metropolitan Budapest effectively existed even before the First World War, with half the population living in the outskirts of the city or more outlying sections.

Tens of thousands of the proletariat lived in dreadful conditions, packed together in various areas around the peripheries. There were scores of sociological studies and newspaper articles describing the ankle-deep mud along unpaved, unlit streets, barely one or two kilometres from the elegance of Andrássy Boulevard. "Most houses are single-story barracks, and many are wooden shacks that serve as living quarters. Most of them have a single room. The apartments in the barracks are packed in rows, like cells in a prison. The yards are usually filled with dirt and mud," runs the dry account in one sociological study. Destitution, in daily contact with big-city splendour, made its way into Budapest fiction, most notably in work by Sándor Bródy and in the young Ferenc Molnár's novel *Az éhes város* (The Hungry City).

The municipal government took some action to address the hopeless situation and to soothe tensions. In the late 1890s several homeless shelters were set up, and several housing projects for blue-collar workers were started in the

106. *The workshop hall at the Láng Machine Works.*
Photograph by György Klösz from around 1900

outskirts of Budapest. Many of these were two-story houses that offered workers' families substantially better and healthier living conditions than they had left behind, but they fell far short of the numbers the situation demanded. The largest of these housing projects, built with state funds following a parliament decree, was commenced in Kispest in 1908. Named after the prime minister, the Wekerle Colony consisted of over a thousand houses with almost 4800 apartments. By this time, however, the trade unions and the Hungarian Social Democratic Party that had been active since 1890 were increasingly successful in shaping the workers' political awareness, and had organised themselves into effective movements. Throngs of workers marched in demonstrations and made their way into the middle-class parts of town. In September 1905 more than a hundred thousand workers paraded in front of Parliament; two years later they announced a general strike. On May 23, 1912 a wave of work stoppages began that culminated in streetcars being overturned and barricades being erected. Mounted police responded with the flat of their swords, the usual reaction when the goal was not to kill. Still the unrest claimed five casualties, and was later referred to by workers as "blood-red Thursday". A poem of Endre Ady's warned that "We are running into revolution." The birth of the twentieth century, with its advocating of human and political rights for the masses, was directly experienced by the Budapest middle classes also.

Ironically Budapest again had, after a long hiatus, a mayor in the person of István Bárczy, who was a man with a broad vision and determined to pass major reforms. Prior to his 1906 election, the upper middle class had for many years grown accustomed to advance only its own immediate interests. There was, however, also an opposition in municipal party politics that concerned itself with the pressing social questions, rather more than what can be said for the national government, whose sole preoccupation was to define the country's relationship with Austria, and how to shape that relationship to further Hungarian interests.

Municipal government was undergoing a change, signalled in the 1901 parliamentary elections by a sweeping victory by Vilmos Vázsonyi, whose programme was shaped by the interests and demands of the lower middle class in the Pest district of Theresa Town. Vázsonyi had for some years headed the Community Democratic Party of Budapest, which represented city interests and liberalism in opposition

to the growing threat of agrarian conservatism. However in 1905 and 1906, a political crisis unfolded across the country, where the leading figures of the former opposition, now in power, frequently spoke of the need to castigate Budapest, and voiced their ire against the capital. In such a precarious situation various parties in the municipal government agreed to elect István Bárczy, a city alderman in the education department, as mayor. The advancement constituted an unusually large leap up the government hierarchy, and would not have occurred had there not been a crisis.

Before long Bárczy had worked out a programme which shows his acumen for democracy; in this he committed himself to take on social and cultural responsibilities and fused concepts which had hitherto been considered as contradictory. His agenda revealed a wide understanding of the mechanics of city government and a fine sense of strategy; all this was complemented by his administrative abilities, a prerequisite if his goals were to be achieved. He was popular among both the economic and intellectual elite of the city

108. *The Freemasons' Symbolic Grand Lodge "Hungary", a mansion in Podmaniczky Street. Photograph by Mór Erdélyi from around 1900*

and, the subject of many paeans of praise, as an individual he become an important symbol of the time. A team of polished and broad-minded professionals was what was needed to bring the great transformation about. Among the civil servants in city government a new generation was emerging. They were young and skilled, well informed about what went on in the world, and put progressive left-wing intellectuals into top positions. This, however, was by no means considered as an advantage for Budapest. Parliament, with its conservative majority, and the still traditional provinces, became utterly convinced that their animosity against the capital was well-justified. Budapest followed a path foreign to the nation, radically urbanist and cosmopolitan.

By the end of his tenure in 1918, the most far-reaching achievement Bárczy had carried through was the sweeping reorganisation of city administration. City government operated much more efficiently, and what was at least as important, its credit rating had improved. The city's income had grown, while Bárczy's projects consumed additional amounts of money. Both foreign and local banks, which set rather strict conditions, were repeatedly

called on to provide substantial loans. As a result, in the 1910s, one fifth of the city's expenditures went to loan and interest payments – still less than what was expended on school improvements, however.

Without these enormous loans, Budapest would not have developed at the pace it did, and would have fallen behind the modern large cities of Europe. "Budapest a Metropolis" became the municipal government's slogan, and it was in this spirit that the municipal government acted. No one could have known that with Hungary's defeat in the First World War and its tragic consequences, a debt topping a hundred million crowns was going to drag the capital into financial crisis. Bárczy was accused of overspending, and the crisis was directly attributed to this. After the end of the war in 1918 he was deprived of the opportunity to run for re-elec-

109. The Jewish market in Újvásár (New Market, today's Köztársaság) Square. Photograph from around 1900

110. The interior of the Central Market Hall. Photograph from 1897

tion. His detractors would not admit that the city owed much of its modernisation before the war to just this "overspending," without which none of the vast projects would have succeeded.

One of Bárczy's greatest schemes was the creation of metropolitan Budapest. In 1908 he commissioned a study to determine the feasibility of integrating thirty outlying settlements. With time running out it was no longer possible to develop or carry out the plan. Another scheme was completed, however. It involved the establishment of a public school system, and there was one three-year period when 55 schools with almost one thousand school rooms were created, mostly in the underdeveloped outskirts of Budapest.

Although Budapest's educational institutions and teachers had been recognised internationally for many years, their initial influence was mainly on the upper and middle classes. After the 1867 Compromise the reforms and comprehensive modernisation of higher education institutions, including Budapest's University of Arts and Sciences with its faculties of religion, humanities, law and medicine; the József University of Technology, which incorporated the old technical institutions; the Eastern Academy launched in the final decades of the nineteenth century which, following World War I, merged with the economics faculty of the university; and several art academies, were so successful that they could produce scholars and scientists who were acknowledged throughout the world, including several who were to go on to be awarded Nobel Prizes. To commemorate his father (the first Hungarian government's Minister for Religion and Public Education, who after the Compromise had developed

and launched a public education reform that involved a network of secular institutions) the then Minister of Culture Baron Loránd Eötvös in 1895 established the Eötvös College. It offered talented but underprivileged university students, who were democratically chosen, the chance to receive an elite education. Several generations of famous university teachers were to come from this institution. A secondary school system, involving the *gimnázium*, where education in the humanities was stressed, and "real schools", which focused on the sciences, was modelled after the Austrian school system devised in the 1850s. After the 1880s several state gymnasia were opened, and in 1869 the country's first higher women's school, headed by Mrs. Pál Veres, was founded.

The oldest religious gymnasium was the in the hands of the Piarist fathers. Established in Pest in 1717, it also functioned for a time as a college of theology. Several major figures in Hungarian intellectual and political life, in particular, many writers received their education in this progressive-minded gymnasium: István Széchenyi, Mihály Vörösmarty, József Katona, János Vajda, and Baron Loránd Eötvös were among them. Some of the highly capable teachers included countless familiar personalities, from the eighteenth-century author András Dugonics up to the contemporary writer and philosopher István Jelenits. Its provosts included the poet Sándor Sík.

Tolerance and intellectual refinement combined characterized the Lutheran church, and thus produced an especially great number of professionals, scholars, and well-known artists. Their school stood first on Deák Square and later moved into a new building on Városligeti Avenue. Among its students were the poet and revolutionary Sándor Petőfi, who died young in the War of Liberation; the influential political journalist of the second half of the nineteenth century; Miksa Falk, who as the editor-in-chief of *Pester Lloyd* was

111. The Wekerle housing project, built between 1909 and 1912, and designed by the notable architect of the Hungarian art-nouveau style, Károly Kós, and his colleagues

112. *Writer, newspaper editor and dramatist Sándor Bródy*

113. *The Vígszínház Theatre's two permanent authors, Ferenc Molnár and Jenő Heltai, versatile figures in Pest's literary life and journalism, around 1910*

114. *Poet Endre Ady, the leading figure in progressive literature. Photograph by Aladár Székely, 1908*

115. *Dezső Kosztolányi, poet, novelist, essayist, translator of fiction and publicist, the authoritative master of modern Hungarian literature*

awarded a knighthood; there were also the painters Adolf Fényes and Oszkár Glatz; the famed operetta-composer Imre Kálmán, the conductor Antal Doráti; the philosopher György (Georg) Lukács; the mathematician known for his game theory and contribution to computer science János (John von) Neumann; the nuclear physicists Leó Szilárd and Ede (Edward) Teller; and the Nobel laureate in physics Jenő (Eugene) Wigner.

At the end of the nineteenth century a fund was established to set up a Jewish gymnasium, whose construction was begun near the City Park under Bárczy's mayoralty, but which did not open its doors until after World War I.

"A Courtly Mistress Falling To Disrepute"

Launched in 1910, Budapest found itself with a daily paper, *Az Est* (The Evening), of the dynamism and professionalism that only American newspaper publishing had. Established in conjunction with a hitherto unknown advertisement campaign by Andor Miklós, who had been financial editor until his dismissal from *Pesti Napló* for alleged profiteering and bribery, *Az Est* came out in the early afternoon and was distributed almost exclusively by street vendors. Soon it had a circulation of a quarter million copies a day, with its famous and feared reporters uncovering and writing up government corruption and common crime. Its offices had several separate telephone lines, over which reports coming in from abroad would be received and typed. When the government attempted to prevent the paper's distribution, a mass demonstration ensued. Despised by those in power, *Az Est* gained increasing popularity, both for its investigative style and its reliability. During the First World War, its circulation at times approached half a million copies – it took half a century for another Hungarian paper to top that. *Az Est* was even quoted in the press of countries antagonistic to Hungary. Its success was financial as well, making a millionaire mogul out of a man who in his childhood had known only poverty. Andor Miklós acquired the Atheneum Publishers and Printing Press along with two other major dailies, and until his death in 1933 headed the *Az Est* syndicate. He also owned valuable Pest real estate and a prized art collection.

In the evening of July 23, 1914 a group that included all the editorial staff of *Az Est* was seated at a long table in the New York Café. "Never have I heard as few jokes as on Thursday evening. Coming to think of it, I believe I heard not one," recalled Ferenc Molnár, the author and a reporter for *Pesti Napló*. "The time was half past eleven. An automobile stopped in front of the café. At the reporters' table everyone rose. The café was jam-packed. There was a sudden silence, at some tables people jumped to their feet. Tonight remarkably few women are in the café. A gentleman comes running in, the next moment the long table is empty. As the public charges after them it sees only that they are holding on to the automobile, some standing up in it, others gripping the outside. The machine gives out a roar and rushes off with its black cargo. One word lingers among the gathered crowd in the street, the first moment's frightful exaggeration – War! This strange, brief, thunder-like word now rises in the crowd, which rushes back into the café with the news. Everyone is standing at his table. This one word amplifies into a howl until it reaches a terrifying crescendo, joining the thuds of many chairs pushed back at once – a sudden, frantic jumping to the feet, and then one great, prolonged cry: War!"

The First World War, in which Austria-Hungary fought as Germany's ally, terminated an extended period of

116. The Opium Smoker's Dream, *painting by Lajos Gulácsy, 1913-1918*

peace. The country had not been a *place d'armes* for 65 years, Hungarian soldiers had seen action only in the Balkan wars. This may have been a factor in the public counting on a quick and triumphal war. Enthusiastic recruiting parades, with colourful uniforms and banners, were seen daily in the capital. At first it was only posters and newsvendors that signalled the presence of war, but soon the streets themselves advertised it; in 1915 a National Benefaction statue was erected in Deák Square. This was a large wooden equestrian statue into which bronze nails or small bronze plaques were hammered to represent donations to support the war. During the short-lived Communist regime that followed the war, the statue was damaged, and in the mid twenties was removed to the side of a wing of the Ludovika Military Academy.

The prolonged fighting produced a growing number of casualties, while triumph became increasingly elusive. Neither Budapest nor the area around it were threatened by the fighting, but as a centre of the hinterland the war became tangible and made its way into the daily life of the

know that the conventicles of those groups of people who worked at the coming upheaval gathered in dark apartments in dark houses in the dark streets of Pest, in the afternoons and evenings."

Military failure at the end of 1918 was followed by the collapse of the state. The Austro-Hungarian Monarchy had disintegrated, its former peoples and nationalities – at least the larger ones – established their autonomous national states. Hungary had gained its independence from the Habsburgs, but lost two thirds of its territory and now had one third of Hungarians living outside the state borders. In addition Hungary was now surrounded by nation-states that considered it their most adverse enemy. The new state of Hungary, and of course the revolutionary and counter-revolutionary governments that followed in quick succession, retained Budapest as their capital. The metropolis, not so long before a cheerful and thriving city in a bourgeois milieu, was overtaken by a new atmosphere: its streets and squares were filled with ad hoc military units and the mobs converging on the city centre from the outskirts.

118. *Procession on Dísz Square for the coronation of Charles IV, Hungary's last king. Coloured photograph, 1916*

populace. Church bells were taken down and carried off to be cast as canons. A daily transport of wounded soldiers arrived from the frontlines, hospitals were soon filled beyond capacity and school buildings had to be converted into military hospitals. Schools were merged, and children had to attend classes in alternating morning or afternoon shifts (a practice that remained in effect for almost a half century). Food rationing had to be imposed, and soon vouchers were issued not just for food but for household goods too; the lines in front of the stores grew longer and longer. Budapest had not witnessed anything like this before. Then came the refugees from the occupied territories, many of whom sought shelter in Budapest. Their numbers grew by the day, as did those of army deserters who had abandoned their retreating units. When the school gymnasiums no longer sufficed as shelters, classrooms had to be used for this purpose, and even railway carriages. The latter were to serve as temporary housing for years to come for families that had been forced out of Transylvania, Ruthenia and Upper Hungary, when these areas were annexed by Romania, the Soviet Union and Czechoslovakia. In the words of the historian John Lukacs, "One gets the impression that sometime in late 1917 those shafts of sunshine that illuminated, if only temporarily, the streets and the squares and even the spirit of the city during the first years of the war had disappeared. [...] We

On March 21, 1919 the Communist government, or Council of Soviets, which styled itself after the eighteen months old Russian revolutionary regime, came to power and brought with it a 133-day social and administrative experiment along Communist lines. Its leaders were former Russian prisoners of war and radical leftist intellectuals. The Council of Soviets held out the promise for the deprived masses that they were to own everything from that moment on. Parks, including Margaret Island, previously only accessible on payment of a high entrance fee or previously closed to the public at large, along with palaces and the art collections they contained, were nationalised and opened to the masses. Hardly a day went by without rallies, propaganda lectures and meetings to explain the new legislation. One that drew an enormous crowd was the celebration of "The First Free May Day". Long overdue reforms and the individual ideas of newly influential, educated professionals, journalists and university professors were suddenly adopted as official and were shaped into a policy that had been ideologically-deduced. A surge of terror accompanied the process: in the name of the class struggle everyone who owned anything at all could be branded an enemy, and it mattered not whether the motive was individual revenge or if it endangered the very lives of the individual so pilloried. The class struggle was an excuse for free-booting and murder by armed squads; the apartments of those awaiting execution in the cellars of Parliament, or who had fled abroad, were handed over to proletarians or comrades. Finally all journals except the *Vörös Újság* (Red Newspaper) were banned.

With the approach of the army of the newly established state of Romania the paralysed and terrified city underwent a marked transformation. On August 1, the Revolutionary Governing Council, meeting in the auditorium of the New City Hall on Váci Street, resigned and announced the dissolution of the Council of Soviets. Two days later Romanian troops were marching through the streets of Budapest, and the population gaped at the their officers wearing lipstick and face powder and lavishly sprinkled with cologne, as they came to take up quarters in any house they took fancy to. Budapest, with its cultural and technical treasures was in greater danger than ever. The National Museum's art collection was saved only by the resolute action of an American general of the Allied Control Commission, commemorated in a statue that stands on Szabadság Square. Less fortunate were the radio installations maintained by the Hungarian Post Office, or the postal directorate's cash boxes, along with several thousands of telegraph and telephone apparatuses, automobiles and mail coaches, and over 70 thousand telegraph poles. Taking up the tradition of "three days of free pillage", a centuries-old prerogative of victorious armies, the troops extended it to three months.

On November 16, owing to the insistence of the victori-

119. *Festive decoration in front of the Western Railway Station for the Mayday celebration in 1919*

ous powers, the Romanian army withdrew from Budapest. The same day the National Army of the counter-revolutionary government, formed in the southern Hungarian city of Szeged, marched into the city. At their head, riding a white horse, was their commander-in-chief, Miklós Horthy. The months of terror and censorship continued, only the colour had changed from red to white. With the abuses and murders carried out by squads of military officers, traces of anti-Semitism, and revenge inflicted on the "city of sin", Budapest's woes were far from over. Over one eighth of the capital's population was charged with siding with the Communist regime. Many of the young and

120. *The Pest reporter, as the hero of a projected picture show. Poster from 1912*

121. *A poster for a film with the characteristic title* Börzekirály, *or "King of the Stock Exchange", at the Royal Apollo cinema. Imre Földes, 1915*

broad-minded Budapest intellectuals, scholars and artists, who had survived or endorsed the "red terror", fled the military-enforced restoration and left the country. The 1919 wave of emigrants from Budapest made a name for themselves as professors or scientists in European and American universities and research institutes, or artists, some of them in fledgling branches, such as the English and American film industry. Among them was the painter and Bauhaus artist László Moholy-Nagy; the sociologist and philosopher Károly (Karl) Mannheim; the philosopher and art historian Arnold Hauser; and film director and producer Sándor (Alexander) Korda.

Nevertheless, in 1921 life began to seep back into Budapest. Public administration and politics gradually regained its footing. Budapest had entered the new era under extremely difficult conditions. For the first time in two hundred years the population was declining, and markedly at that. In 1917 it had approached 1 million, in 1920 it was below 930 thousand, which included hundreds of thousands of refugees and many of the 100 thousand ex-

122. *Poster promoting the Zoo. Ervin Voit, 1912*

prisoners of war. The face of Budapest had changed. The city, which before the war had been the most bourgeois in the entire region, was now noted for its depression and impoverished districts. "Pest is like a courtly mistress fallen to disrepute, abandoned by her benefactor," was Gyula Krúdy's laconic comment on the Budapest of this time.

In the 1920s Budapest was the only large city in Hungary, the disproportionately large capital of a much reduced country. It was accused of siphoning off the country's economic and cultural strength, and depriving the nation of its oxygen. Figures show that while in 1910 a bare five per cent of the country's population lived in the capital, the proportion had now jumped to twelve per cent. The political and ideological attacks on Budapest were constant, at first coming from the right-wing parties in government, later on from the increasingly stronger extreme right, which organised itself into the Arrow-Cross, the Hungarian fascist party. While one group was concerned about the outlying communities of metropolitan Budapest which were attracting an ever growing number of pro-social democratic, and partly pro-Communist, factory workers and their consequently increasing influence, the other denounced the metropolis and its middle-class traditions as being devoid of the foundations needed to establish any movement based on racial ideals.

In Budapest's administration, which mirrored the national government, right-wing and explicitly Christian parties came into power. After the 1920 elections these parties, merged into a separate Budapest party, under the name of the Christian Community Party, became the city's leading political force. Its leader Károly Wolff worked out its programme and put it forward with highly effective rhetoric. To a degree, however, the political environment of the capital differed from that of the rest of the country in that the liberal opposition in Budapest continued to play a

123. The passion for flying caught on quickly. Poster for an international flying contest in Budapest by Dezső Bér, 1910

124. The start of an automobile long-distance race from the Tattersall riding school. Photograph by Gyula Jelfy, 1909

125. *A 1934 soccer match between Ferencváros (popularly Fradi), the team with the largest number of fans, and MTK Hungária. The teams would be rivals for decades to come*

larger role, and the Hungarian Social Democratic Party was represented in Parliament.

The national assembly repeatedly amended legislation on the capital; a 1930 statute was a significant step toward creating a "national metropolis" by acknowledging greater planning and social tasks, changing district boundaries and creating new ones, and partly reducing the capital's autonomy while strengthening centralisation.

Establishing the right course and opportunities for development was not always easy, and it was not always the lack of financial resources or even political vision that prevented Budapest from finding a way back to the success it had lost with the war. The initial production of aircraft in Hungary occurred in the 1910s. As early as June 1910 an international flying competition took place at the newly built Rákos airport, and two years later aeroplanes were being manufactured here. Following the First World War,. the victorious Allies destroyed all Hungarian planes that had survived the war, and enforced a set of strictures to prevent the operation of an airline in Hungary. Eventually, in late 1922 the Hungarian Air Traffic Company was formed, and though its international flights were limited to Vienna, internal traffic was successfully launched. In 1937 an international airport opened in Budaörs and, two years later, the construction of Budapest's present international airport Ferihegy was begun. Its inauguration, however, had to be postponed until after the end of the Second World War.

Public transport in Budapest knew no such restrictions. The city's size and the large number of vehicles made regulation and its enforcement much more cumbersome than in the country's other cities. Initially mounted police over-

saw traffic, and although in 1926 the first traffic light was set up at the intersection of the Large Ring and Rákóczi Street, police officers using hand signals remained the main traffic regulators. On November 9, 1941, (later than in the rest of the country) Budapest traffic switched over to driving on the right.

In the all too brief period between the two world wars, Budapest's character as an industrial metropolis grew quite distinct, with new industry sectors being formed. The number of those living in the outlying communities was surpassing that of the city proper. At the same time, Budapest's suburbs proper accounted for some 400 thousand people of metropolitan Budapest's total population of one million. There were, however, several additional signs indicating the city's changed role and spirit. In the early thirties, the number of banks and credit institutions in Budapest had fallen by over a third of that in the last year before the outbreak of the First World War some twenty years earlier. The number of visitors to the city was beginning to approach the earlier level, but they spent considerably less time here. Museums recorded less than half the number of visitors, the Zoo only one third. Art patrons spent barely one seventh as much. This was indeed the low point from which Budapest tried to rise to its feet.

Buda, which for over half a century had been overshadowed in significance by Pest, was now coming to the fore in city planning. Ever since 1885, the idea that Pest's Large Ring should be continued on the Buda side had come up again and again. Now this was to become a reality. The Margaret Ring was completed as the continuation of Margaret Bridge, with a series of new buildings erected along it. The plan also called for the restructuring of the two old sections of Buda, Water Town and the Tabán. In Water Town significant construction was launched, in the Tabán most of the buildings were torn down. Only a few detached buildings and a single complex were left standing; succeeding generations retained a tinge of nostalgia for this once Mediterranean-style neighbourhood. In the

Buda hills and valleys, entire communities with new villas were springing up. Some, like those designed by Aladár Árkay, showed the influence of the *Sezession* style, while others were more in line with the German *Bauhaus*. In Pasarét, a model project launched a construction scheme for detached family housing involving several well-known architects, such as Lajos Kozma.

Angyalföld in Pest, which had become an industrial area significant for its mills and factories, was incorporated into Budapest as its 13th District in 1930. To the south, a new section of the city known as Újlipótváros (New Leopold Town) housed white-collar workers, with over six thousand modern apartments built over the course of two decades. The writer Antal Szerb drew a superb portrait of this community: "When I was young, this part of town consisted of fences. Underneath the fences dogs would jump forward extending half their trunks, their barking making you slip on the ice, and feel embarrassed as you stood up. But it was pretty, and you could walk a long distance in the direction of Újpest, which I knew only from stories and anxieties. Today it has the flattest modern mansions. In the mansions young psychoanalysts on couches expose each other's souls, the dashing amazons of bridge parties fantasise in the deep reaches of snow-white bathrooms, the highly intelligent clerks of private firms tune into Moscow on the radio. On winter Sundays the entire community treads toward Svábhegy-Mountain bearing long wooden planks, leaving only the widowed barber behind. Everything here is modern and uncomplicated and detached and uniform. The entire district is two rooms and a hall, its inhabitants concealing doggedly, youthfully and with *élan* the single honest truth of their tedious lives: that they, none of them, have any money."

In the mid 1920s, there was a surge in the construction of apartment buildings, the number of apartments in the capital rising by five thousand every five years. By 1941, on the eve of Hungary's entry into the Second World War, there were over 288 thousand apartments. Though this gradually alleviated the city's long-standing housing shortage, there were still an average of two persons per room. This meant, in effect, that one third of Budapest's population lived in rented quarters. While spacious middle-class apartments continued to be the norm in the inner city, housing in the suburbs was almost as decrepit as before. After the Compromise in 1867, the government began to exploit the city's famous thermal and medicinal springs. Various parliamentary acts pertaining to health and the utilisation of water were passed, and scores of professional organisations and associations were involved. Around the turn of the century several major spas were built, including that on Margaret Island, the Széchenyi Baths in the City Park, the Császár Baths; the Szent Lukács Baths and Sanitarium; and part of the Gellért Baths and Hotel. In 1929 Parliament passed a separate law on medicinal baths, and established the National Commission on Spas, headquartered in Budapest, thus recognising both the health and tourism benefits of the baths. From 1934 on, Budapest was advertised both at home and abroad as a city of spas, three years later it hosted the International Spa Congress. Health tourism at once started to thrive. In this decade the number of visitors arriving for this purpose increased tenfold.

Although the arts and artists had lost some of their former allure, there were events, usually with an organised movement behind them and involving the mainstream of people, such as book fairs and athletic events, that gained in popularity. Libraries, connected to educational institutions and especially those attached to the newly established Budapest library network, drew a vast public. While the total number of theatre seats rose many times, the theatres were generally only able to sell less than a quarter of their seats and only remained in business because of significant municipal budget subsidies. The once enormously successful Király Theatre, located at 71 Király Street, which had established the operetta in Budapest (premiering in Hungary one of the Monarchy's most popular operettas, Imre Kálmán's *Czardas Queen*), lost much of its audiences at this time and was soon forced to close down. Only years later was a new Operetta, which grew out of the Fővárosi Színház (Capital Theatre), able to fill the void.

Even the cinema industry underwent a crisis that lasted for a decade. Films had been Budapest's most popular form of entertainment even before the First World War, when over a hundred cinemas were in operation. Cinemania led to a thriving film industry in Budapest, and even during the war over a dozen silent feature films were produced each year. Budapest had two major film studios, the Star on Pasaréti Street specialising in adaptations of literary works shot by famous directors both Hungarian and foreign; and the Corvin Studios on Gyarmat Street in Pest's Zugló district, which made films of high artistic quality based on Hungarian fiction. Corvin was headed by the director Sándor Korda, who later became a leading film-maker in England, where he was eventually knighted under the name of Sir Alexander Korda. Other internationally known names who worked in Budapest during these years included director Mihály Kertész, who as Michael Curtis made Hollywood's *Robin Hood* and *Casablanca*. The war, the revolutions and ensuing reprisals, dispersed much of the creative talent abroad; because of this and economic difficulties, the industry came to a near standstill. But following the arrival of the talking film in the first half of the 1930s, the industry suddenly experienced a revival. A generation of new stars and talented directors contributed to a boom that was to be tragically short-lived. Before the end of the decade, impending war and the legal restrictions that preceded it brought an end to film-making in Budapest.

As far as the city's musical life was concerned, two contradictory currents ran side by side. While concert halls were always filled, the audience was basically always the same middle-class public with strictly conventional tastes. The compositions of Béla Bartók were premiered in Hungary only after a substantial delay, and music lovers had to travel abroad to hear a new Bartók work well before it was performed in his native country. Bartók, too, left Hungary for New York. Zoltán Kodály's more melodious and, as such, more digestible treatment of folk tunes and those works of his that more recognisably resonated to national themes were more readily accepted. Ernő (later Ernst von) Dohnányi, the composer and conductor who was appointed as music director for the new mass medium, the Hungarian Radio, was extremely influential in introducing contemporary composers and in shaping musical tastes.

City and Citizens Under the Shadow of Doom

In the Inner City, the lustre and tranquillity that had been the trademark of the Budapest of the 1900s seemed to be returning. Everywhere there were cafés filled with artists, journalists and bohemian types. Avant-garde artist groups diverted themselves in deliberately outraging middle-class morals. The writer Miklós Szentkuthy, for example, in the 1930s, after a night of conversation and revelry, donned a cardinal's costume, ordered a carriage, and had himself and a friend taken to the top of Gellért Hill, where he bestowed a blessing on the city as the first rays of the sun appeared.

In 1938 a refound fin-de-siécle Budapest attempted to recapture the splendour of the millenary celebrations. The year was the 900th anniversary of the death of Hungary's first king, Saint Stephen, in whose honour Leopold Town took on the official name of Saint Stephen Town (just Szent István Avenue and the name of a park in the district remains of this). The Catholic Church's Eucharistic Congress was planned to take place concurrently. Heroes' Square was arranged so as to accommodate a crowd of 100 thousand to attend open-air mass, and the entire city was decorated. A system of floodlights to provide festival illumination was completed. Yet there was a sense of foreboding that cast its shadow over all this splendour. On the very day the Eucharistic Congress opened, the Hungarian Parliament passed its first anti-Jewish law, that set a quota for Jews in civil service positions and especially in the press. It was an unambiguous sign of the official endorsement of Nazi ideals.

The war had been in progress for some time and the Budapest Jewry, some 20 per cent of the city's population, was still relatively safe, at least as far as its physical well-being was concerned. On March 19, 1944, however, Hitler's troops occupied Hungary, and shortly afterwards Adolf Eichmann's SS units set about implementing the "final solution". Now Jews in Budapest were obliged to wear the Star of David on their clothing; in the countryside deportations began. Most of those who tried to find safety in the capital were captured by the SS before they were able to reach their destination. On July 7 the Regent, Miklós Horthy, succeeded in halting the deportations from the capital and thus saved the lives of the majority of the Budapest Jewry. Three months later, on October 16, when the Hungarian Nazis, the Arrow Cross Party, came to power and expelled Horthy, the persecution resumed.

In Budapest the Jews set up a Zionist rescue committee which, considering the enormous sums it paid out, was only able to achieve meagre results: the SS allowed one group of 300 Jews to leave for Switzerland. A handful of diplomats and their assistants, including the Swiss consul Carl Lutz, the Spanish chargé d'affaires San Briz, the Vatican nuncio Angelo Rotta, the Swedish and the International Red Cross and especially the latter's Friedrich Born, the Lutheran priest Gábor Sztehlo, and most effectively of all a secretary at the Swedish Embassy, Raoul Wallenberg, proved considerably more successful in offering foreign passports, false identification papers, and setting up children's shelters. In November, however, the Arrow Cross "national leader" Ferenc Szálasi commanded the deportation of everyone of working age, and set up the Budapest ghetto.

In New Leopold Town, between the area of Szent István Park and the Large Ring, certain buildings comprised the so-called "international ghetto" and were deemed to stand under international protection and thus designated as "safe"; those possessing letters of safe-conduct who sought refuge here were allowed to remain. The authorities moved the Jewish population *en masse* into the central ghetto, allowing them to take only as much of their personal belongings as they could carry. This ghetto was located between Dohány and Király streets and Károly Avenue. Arrow-Cross details lingered around the area, and many who ventured out were taken by these details to be shot and thrown into the Danube. There were frequent assaults on the people within the ghetto itself, but it endured until the arrival of the Soviet army. The Budapest ghetto was the only one in Central and Eastern Europe which survived to the end of the war, offering at least a degree of safety for its inhabitants.

The Second World War brought to Budapest a degree of destruction almost as complete as that visited upon Berlin or Warsaw. From November 1944, when the Soviet troops were drawing steadily closer, the German command decided to resist until the end, going so far as to plant mines on all the city's bridges. The Arrow-Cross government captured and executed the leader of the Hungarian resistance movement, Endre Bajcsy-Zsilinszky, and his companions. The government proceeded to dismantle and transport to Germany the assembly lines and fittings of factories, plants and hospitals, as well as raw materials, the country's gold reserves and art treasures. Not long after, elections were held in those areas from which German nationals had been cleared out, and in Debrecen a Temporary National Assembly was convened; on December 16 the Red Army began to invest Budapest. With constant air raids and blanket shelling of industrial and military establishments, the German army's resistance began to be broken and on January 18, 1945 the Soviets occupied Pest. In Buda, they were able to advance only by fighting from street to street.

The population of Budapest survived the siege under destitute conditions in underground shelters. Throughout history, Pest had always suffered more than Buda, but now the Castle District endured the longest and most critical attacks. Residents were forced to take to the cellars and the centuries-old network of caves that run beneath them. The Hungarian authorities had set up a spacious hospital underground, while the German defenders had established a military hospital for themselves. When the supply of medicine was depleted, surgery and amputations were conducted without anaesthetics. On the other side of the walls – a hastily raised single row of bricks – the men, women and children in the shelters were forced to hear the

126. *The main altar set up on Heroes Square for the 18th Eucharistic Congress, designed by Jenő Lechner. Coloured photograph, 1938*

patients' anguished screams. The shelters, that had originally been used as cellars, were built to store firewood and coal, and were not equipped with sewage, running water or electricity. Double the permitted number of people were crowded inside, with a constant stream of new refugees from many parts of town arriving to seek shelter from the bombing and shelling. Fresh air was lacking and temperatures reached 40 °C, leading to unbearable conditions amidst the humidity of the surrounding rock. Initially there were candles to provide some lighting but they soon ran out. Water came from melted snow or wells, brought in by those who put their lives at risk to the bombing and shelling. Tea made from roots, baked potatoes and dry beans were all there was to eat. People's tongues stuck to their gums for lack of drinking water. They could not wash or change clothes, only run to the surface for a few breaths of fresh air whenever the sound of strafing aeroplanes could not be heard. At night, when families huddled together across wooden chests or cables, the water dripping on them from the rock prevented them from sleeping, thus compoiunding their suffering. Finally, on February 13, there was silence. Filthy beyond recognition, pale and exhausted, the cave dwellers stumbled to the surface, to find what had once been their homes in ruins. Even thirty years afterwards, unexploded bombs were still being found.

The extended siege cost the lives of 25 thousand civilians; in the Castle District one in ten had been killed. All the Danube bridges were destroyed. Some 20 thousand Hungarian soldiers had fallen during the siege of Budapest, and in occupying the city Soviet troops took 138 thousand prisoners. Three quarters of all the buildings were damaged or destroyed. The historic Castle area, the seat of government, had suffered by far the greatest destruction; only four apartments in the nearly eight hundred houses remained unscathed. Public utilities were damaged, there was neither gas nor electricity nor running water, and no public transport. The city's roads were for the most part plain rubble. In the Castle a narrow-gauge mining railway would carry away the rubble for years to come. Vérmező below the Castle Hill was filled in with it and eventually made into a park. The Royal Palace was burned out, the National Archives were largely destroyed in the bombing. There was, however, one small consolation amid the destruction: with the plaster coming off and in the course of the reconstruction work. a great many medieval ruins came to light, whose existence had not been suspected. In the ensuing decades a new historic monument complex was reconstituted. Today the Castle District is a tourist attraction and has been declared a World Heritage site.

As fighting still continued in Buda, the People's Tribunal began its mission in newly liberated Pest, with summary proceedings and executions carried out in Oktogon Square. In the name of the new ideology, the masses were driven to fanaticism.

It was at this time that Voroshilov, the Soviet Marshal and chairman of the Allied Control Council, ordered the internationally known sculptor Zsigmond Kisfaludi Strobl

115

127. *Members of the congregation in front of the Catholic church in Theresa Town, wearing the Star of David*

to see him. Kisfaludy Strobl had already created several monuments, alongside portrait sculptures of scores of prominent figures in the arts and politics, including several members of the English royal family. Voroshilov now commissioned him to prepare a monument to the liberation of Hungary. With political acumen Kisfaludi Strobl made a few sketches of Voroshilov as well.

Kisfaludy Strobl's studio was located in what had been Budapest's most elegant section, on the once fashionable sycamore-lined Stephánia carriageway. In a matter of days the damaged studio was restored, and the street was soon renamed Voroshilov Street. Kisfaludi Strobl created his *Genius of Liberty*, and together with a Soviet painter and architect designated as his associate he made it into the *Liberation Monument*. The artist was widely hailed, especially for the speed with which he had accomplished the huge work. In February 1947 it was erected on top of Gellért Hill, where it still stands; the Red Army soldiers on the pediment were removed in 1990.

Hungary came under Soviet occupation. The intruders demanded more than just sympathy from those who saw them as liberators from persecution and the threat to their lives; they wanted to be recognised not merely for their power, but expected expressions of affection from the people they had vanquished, a people who since their defeat in the 1849 War of Liberation had dreaded the Russians. Now the Hungarian public expressed its love with ardent

zeal. A Hungarian writer who came home in a Soviet officer's uniform discovered a Russian hero who was destined to soothe bad memories. A commemorative plaque, commissioned by the Hungarian People's Army and placed on the corner of a street in Leopold Town named after him, declared that it was in honour of "Captain Guszev and his comrades, who fought together with our people in the War of Liberation in 1848/49, who challenged the tyranny of the Czar, and died as martyrs." It was only many years later that the discovery was made that this hero had never had any existence outside the imagination and political acuity of his inventor. Guszev Street retained its name nonetheless, and only after the end of the era in 1989 did it regain its former name of Sas (Eagle) Street.

Directly after the war, the public did not recognise the signs that should have warned them of what was to come. Both the people and the municipal government of the city were eager to clear away the rubble and begin reconstruction. In a brief three years, under the leadership of a civic and workers' party coalition, the people of Budapest revelled in a sense of optimism, the zeal for work together with a willingness to make sacrifices: quickly and perceptibly Budapest was reborn. Temporary bridges were thrown across the river, the first being Kossuth Bridge near the Parliament, designed to be used for ten years. House owners were ordered to repair their roofs, and for larger construction they were offered loans. At this time, large apart-

128. *Úri Street in Buda at the end of World War II*

116

ments were sub-divided on government orders, and in consequence statistics soon showed more apartments than before the war. By the time the house and apartment owners, most of them in debt and their surviving valuables invested into the reconstruction, had more or less repaired the major damage, nationalisation began. Any citizen labelled a "class enemy", mainly aristocrats and high-ranking officials, was deported to the countryside. They included several city officials in the post-war coalition government, among them the first mayor, János Csorba, but also many who had just returned from the death camps. All in all 4136 Budapest families, including the sick, the elderly and children, were taken by the "State Defence Authority", the Secret Police, to far-away villages, where they were quartered in a single room in a better-off peasant house. Frequently someone, a relative of a party functionary perhaps, would express a liking for a fine villa or family home,

and the residents would simply be deported to make room for him. The deported were the lucky ones; others were taken to the secret police headquarters on 60 Andrássy Boulevard.

"I was beginning to sense that what went on around me was not mere organised terror but an enemy more dangerous than anything, against whom there was no defence – stupidity," recalled the writer Sándor Márai, who eventually emigrated. "[...] Everything they plan and execute here is not just avaricious and brutal, but deeply and hopelessly redundant and stupid." Recognition and fear again – for the umpteenth time – forced the cream of the country and its capital to find refuge abroad. The conductor György (George) Solti, the writers Ferenc Molnár and Artúr Köstler (Arthur Koestler), the psychologist Lipót (Leopold) Szondi, the art historian Károly (Charles de) Tolnay, and the philosopher Károly Kerényi, the conductors Ernő (Ernst von) Dohnányi and Ferenc Fricsay, the biologist and Nobel-laureate Albert Szent-Györgyi, the nuclear physicist Zoltán Bay, the archaeologist András Alföldi, the internationally recognised Hungarian economist Lipót Baranyai, and the young György (George) Soros were among the

129. Budapest's city limits before and after the annexation of suburbs on January 1, 1950

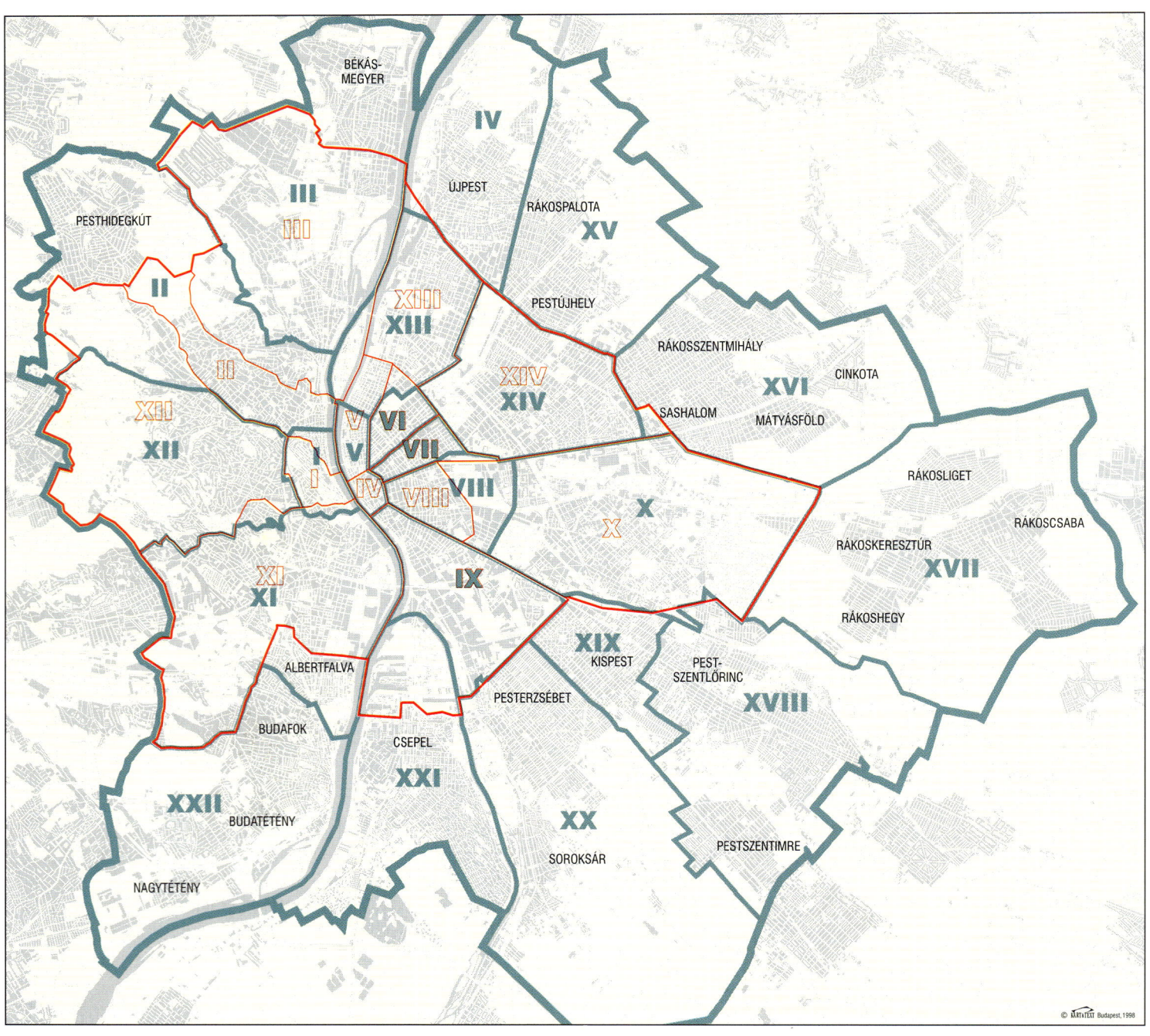

130. *The Freedom Statue on Gellért Hill has become part of Hungary's political symbolism. Poster by Tibor Gönczi (Gebhardt) for the 1950 festivities commemorating the country's liberation by the Soviet army*

131. *Festival stand below the statue of Stalin during the 1953 Mayday procession. The bronze for the monument came from sculptures of historical* personae non grata, *figures become inadmissible in the ideology of "people's democracy". The Stalin statue, in turn, was sawn to pieces by demonstrators during the Revolution in 1956*

many who left at this time. Those who came back, many from Moscow, arrived with the task of restructuring the country along the Soviet model; among them was the philosopher and cultural policy-maker György (Georg) Lukács.

Budapest became the capital of a "popular democratic" Hungary, whose reconstruction and transformation into a centre of heavy industry was to be shouldered by the entire country. That was the prominent goal set in the three-year plan, announced in July 1947.

The social structure of Budapest was also expected to take on the image that the leadership expected. Law XXIX/1949 established metropolitan Budapest with the integration of seven towns and 16 communities, enlarging its area two and a half times and raising the number of its inhabitants to 1.6 million, one and half times the pre-war

figure. Budapest now ranked seventh in population among the cities of Europe, with a social structure in which workers in large factories predominated. For the two decades to come, additional industries would be concentrated in Budapest, resulting in a rapidly increasing population. One fifth of the country's inhabitants were now living in the capital, and this soon led to a distortion between Budapest and the rest of the country that affected every sphere of life.

Finally, in 1950, a true Soviet-style form of municipal government was installed. Budapest was administered by a Municipal Soviet and its Executive Committee. This remained effective until 1990, when the old form, the Popular Assembly, was reinstituted.

The almost unreal tempo of reconstruction, and the state administration created by the Communist Party, a hallucination in which the borderline between desire and reality became blurred, sometimes gave rise to grandiose plans. Hungary has a history of great success in sports, there was talk of the Olympic Games being staged in Budapest. To further this, the enormous People's Stadium was built, and a project to construct a new Metro line was launched; the latter proposal was postponed for many years due to a lack of money and insurmountable technical hurdles. In place of the Olympics and other monumental developments, the socialist-realist style was channelled into lesser projects, such as public sculptures, monuments, trade-union headquarters, and housing projects in an attempt to meet the needs of the incoming population.

To Obliterate the Quelled Revolution

By 1956 the Hungarian people, the workers and peasants claimed as supporters of the Communist system as well as the intellectual and professional classes, had had enough of dictatorship and the Soviet military presence. Of the Central and Eastern European and Balkan countries occupied by the Soviet Union in the wake of the Second World War, Budapest was the first capital to rise in armed revolt. The revolution shook the entire system, and its reverberations instigated its transformation. The Hungarian Revolution began on October 23 with an initially peaceful student demonstration. That same night shooting broke out in front of the building housing Hungarian Radio. Shortly afterwards, the Hungarian military sided with the rebels, and rebellion became an outright war of liberation, which for a few days attempted to forge a "socialism with a human face". The Prime Minister, Imre Nagy, and the short-lived multi-party coalition he led were, however, waging an impossible battle against a world power whose strength was many times that of Hungary. The assault the Soviets launched on November 4 marked the beginning of the second devastation of Budapest by the Red Army, barely ten years after the end of the world war. Fighting was especially savage along Üllői Street, the Large Ring, and around Széna Square in Buda. The armed insurgents, including teenagers with their home-made Molotov-cocktails either succeeded in fleeing abroad or faced life-time prison sentences – or, as did the Prime Minister, execution. The retribution was similar to that in 1849, this time a larger number were executed, and interred in unmarked graves in Lot 301 of Rákoskeresztúr Cemetery. One Hungarian politician showed himself ready and willing to charge himself with the retributions: János Kádár, who as Minister of the Interior had successfully collaborated in the first comprehensive show trial in 1949. The execution of Imre Nagy was an act Kádár found no convincing explanation for, even to himself. Three decades later in his last public appearance, he was to behave as the antagonist in Greek classic drama, his mind confused, his words disconnected, as he struggled with the shadow of his nemesis.

In addition to the blood-letting, the loss in productive minds and talent was enormous: 200 thousand people crossed the border into Austria, to settle in Western Europe, in North America or Australia. The Party, under a new name, continued to hold its grip on power, but it no longer concentrated on the ideological struggle, or on the major – and astutely adjusted – economic indicators and structures. Instead, it was forced to deal with society at large, with people's actual living conditions. To alleviate the acute apartment shortage in the capital, large-scale housing projects were launched. Using a new technology, factories in the mid 1960s began to produce concrete building panels, which allowed apartment blocks to be assembled on site. Within barely a quarter century, these often mammoth-size concrete blocks formed a belt around inner Budapest. What may now look inhumanely colossal to the eye seemed, at the time, not colossal enough. In the documentary *Nehéz emberek* (Heavy People) filmed at this time, a team of architects consider themselves the hard done-by victims of professional intrigue after the rejection of their concept of a building almost twenty-kilometres-in length, that would have covered the distance from Árpád Bridge to the town of Szentendre, to the north of Budapest.

In forty years, 240 thousand apartments in housing projects of this kind were built in Budapest. In the decade after 1970, such complexes came to over 70 per cent of new apartments. Mass-production of apartments became the goal, quality and durability were not of concern. It took years before the building authorities came to recognise the need for common facilities, such as basements for storage or for activities, or landscaping. People were transplanted into a concrete wasteland where neighbours did not know each other – and no provisions were made for them to get acquainted. Monotonous hallways with endless rows of doors, cramped living quarters all to the same design, became the homes and castles of tens of thousands. They had overcome the apartment shortage, their lives were no better for it.

132. *Demonstrators in the Large Ring during the Revolution of 1956. Photograph by Gyula Nagy*

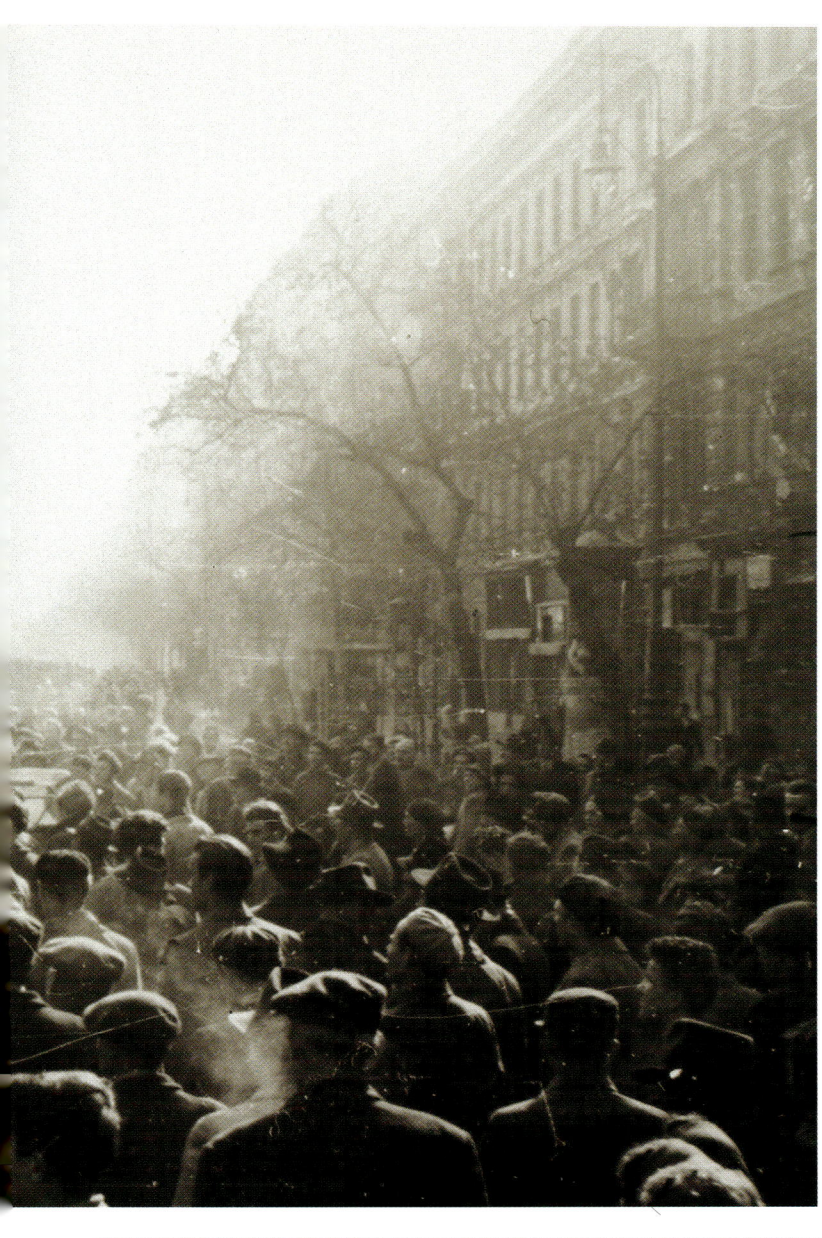

Another consequence of the housing projects was that, with the authorities concentrating their efforts on massive construction, they lost sight of Budapest's inner sections. Here, in these most valuable areas which had suffered the greatest damage during the war and revolution, the houses were deteriorating, with no one responsible for their upkeep. Many of the houses carried the scars of the fighting on their walls, even if restoration was undertaken the materials used were of such poor quality that the destruction of the original architecture was all that remained. The bureau in charge of monument protection vainly attempted to preserve traditional buildings and the architectural heritage. They succeeded splendidly with the Castle District and a handful of buildings in various parts of the city, but monument protection was not a matter of concern for the city. The particular ambience that had marked fin-de-siécle Budapest, the capital at the millenary, the buildings and public places with their fine installations, the street signs, the lamps, the benches, the painted glass windows in the stairwells, the sundials in the courtyards, and so much other trivial details were dismantled and lost. A check was put on this in the 1970s, when Mihály Ráday, an editor for Hungarian Television, launched a series – and coined the expression "city preservation" – in which he drew attention to the treasures embodied in the city's

133. *Demonstration for an environmental cause in April 1989 in Mártirok Street (now Margit Ring)*

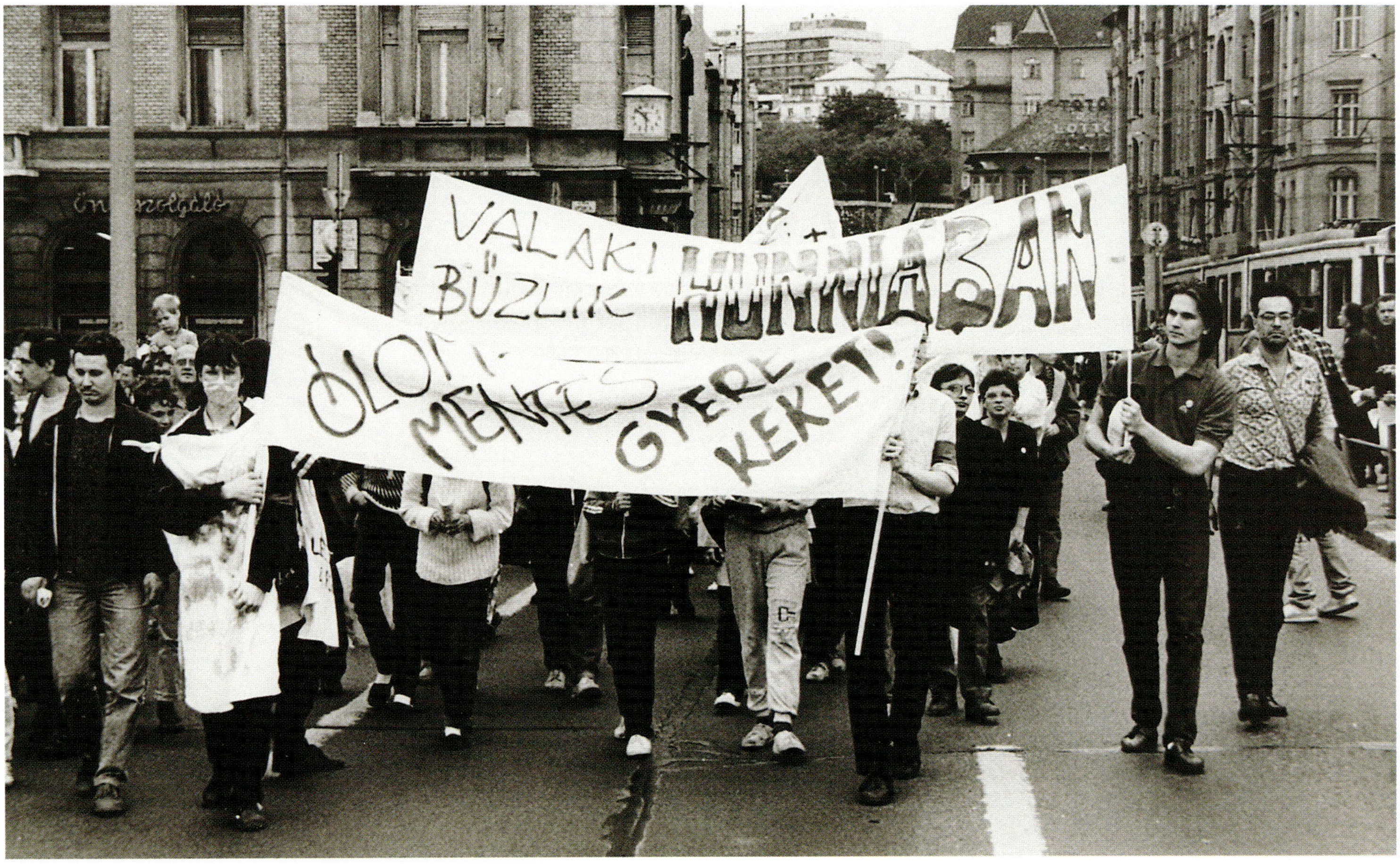

architecture. He gathered supporters for the cause who offered financial and professional backing, companies willing to manufacture items based on old models or photographs. This caught on nationwide.

Gradually the Inner City regained some of its old glory and elegance. A few new buildings sprang up, in the out-going 20th century's modern and post-modern style. Most of these buildings, including the two large hotels on the Danube, the office centre on the corner of Andrássy Boulevard and Bajcsy-Zsilinszky Street, the Hotel Kempinski on Erzsébet Square, and the glass-encased bank on Szabadság Square, were designed by the architect József Finta's company. In contrast to Finta's international style stands Imre Makovecz, who reaches back to old Magyar ornamentation, organic materials, and art-nouveau motifs. His mark is to be found on villas and community buildings in the Buda hills, and elsewhere in Hungary.

János Kádár's long reign, while smothering rights and problems, accorded Hungary the most open system of administration and relative prosperity and security within the socialist bloc. Hungary was called "the happiest barracks in the peace camp" and Budapest was showcased for the West as the success and superior qualities of socialism. Major Western European journals advertised Budapest with the promise that "Communism is less perceptible here than elsewhere". Péter Esterházy, the novelist, remarked about this period that "Budapest was an exception, there was colour, if not taste. The colour of socialism is grey, which can overwhelm even a dazzling city like Prague, golden Prague. Budapest is never grey."

134. Before their departure from Hungary the soldiers of the Soviet army put everything up for sale. Sellers of uniforms and badges turned up sporadically in the most frequented streets of Budapest

In 1973 the Skála chain of department stores and supermarkets, going by the name of ABC, opened their doors, conveying to Hungarians and East-European visitors the illusion that here too was a rich selection of goods known only in the West. Budapest residents were beginning to accumulate relative wealth; in addition to their housing-project apartments they could now save up to buy a weekend house near Lake Balaton or the Danube Bend, to escape the dreariness of the work week. Hungarians, unlike their counterparts in the other countries of the socialist bloc, had the chance to travel to the West once every three years, when they could purchase a limited amount of "hard currency". Conversely, western tourists could enter Hungary without special difficulty, enjoy the excitement of having crossed the Iron Curtain, Germans from both sides of the divide could safely rendezvous here with their compatriots, relatives and friends.

The various bodies of both the state and the Party were all headquartered in Budapest. From his offices in the Party Building on the Danube, known as the "White House", the cultural policy-maker and commissar György Aczél directed the country's intellectual life. Under the – unofficial – motto "prohibit, tolerate, support", he stifled anything that would have constituted innovation or exceptional quality in the fine arts and prevented the public's access to such works. In music or cinema, on the other hand, a large number of internationally acclaimed artists were allowed to flourish.

From the outside it looked as if there basically were no problems and that, even if slowly, everything was progressing in the right direction. But the best writers began to feel a sense of alienation. Budapest had always been a city of writers, and in each generation it had its admirers and at least one author who made Budapest a literary centre. That was no longer true now. The novelist Péter Nádas remarks,

"The city – it is an unmistakable tone, attitude, whereby certain sentences are permitted and others are not. [...] Budapest's tone persisted until the mid sixties. Perhaps Theresa and Christina Towns up to the end of the sixties. Many awful things happened in this city, but the covenant with its citizens held up until then. After that it no longer did. Budapest was depleted, or had lost its sense of balance. At the same rate that its civic spirit was dying out, its level of aggression rose."

Everyone believed that the dictatorship, cheerful and lax and hardly perceptible anymore in daily life, continued to exist simply because Soviet troops, under the terms of the Warsaw Pact that the Central and East European countries had had to adhere to in 1955, were still stationed on Hungarian soil. Yet a cautious underground opposition, while reckoning with periodic reprisals, was already functioning. AB was one of the most influential underground publishers, which from 1981 on was producing its own periodical *Hírmondó* (Courier) – its motto "Read it, copy it, pass it on"; its guiding light was Gábor Demszky, who has been mayor of Budapest since 1990.

By the late 1980s this laid back centralised dictatorship

135. *The new young city leadership became a symbol of the new democracy that replaced the gerontocratic Kádár regime. The Lord Mayor Gábor Demszky stands to the right, seated behind him on the podium are Deputy Mayors Miklós Marschall and Gábor Székely, and City Clerk Zsolt Tiba, at a public session in the New Town Hall in 1992*

had turned lax. Its leading figures had grown snug and were concerned rather with their own material well-being than with promoting the ideology. The Soviet Union was visibly weakening as well. No one believed that the horrors of 1956 would return once Mikhail Gorbachev, who to appeared to have a grasp of the situation and experimented with far-reaching reforms, came into office. Massive demonstrations took place in Budapest in the years 1988 and 1989, mostly centred on Heroes' Square in protest against the building of a dam on the Danube; to celebrate an ecumenical mass; in support of Transylvania; and in a

136. *The democratically elected municipal government passed a decision to dismantle statues and monuments from Communist times from public squares, and to establish a sculpture park in the 22nd district where they would be displayed*

touching commemoration of the heroes of the 1956 Revolution, marked by the re-burial of the executed 1956 Prime Minister Imre Nagy and members of his government. This last drew a crowd of 250 thousand, who listened in silence, passed the symbolic raised biers in orderly rows, and held back their breath when a young speaker named Viktor Orbán, the subsequent president of the Alliance of Young Democrats (FIDESZ), declared that the Soviet troops must go. This time there was no response from Soviet tanks, the last Red Army units left Hungary on June 30, 1991. The day has become Budapest's very own holiday, celebrated in a procession and fair on the last weekend each June.

Following national elections, municipal elections were held in the autumn of 1990. Budapest for the most part voted for the candidates they knew from the underground movement. A young team, mainly under the age of forty, tried its hand at city administration – and to tackle the unprecedented problems inherited from a decayed system. A new economy had to be staked out, there were the abandoned and incredibly derelict Soviet bases, neglected city districts, an infrastructure that was weak and full of gaps. Streets and squares, named after heroes or events commemorated by the workers' movement, had to have their old names restored, the monuments to Communism had to be removed. These last were taken to a sculpture park created for that purpose on the outskirts of Budapest. The city shed the grey decades of socialism in no time. What remained is the lingering question of whether four decades can be erased from the mind. For the moment, the commercials that pound the brain on countless, though indistinguishable, television channels seem to hold out the answers.

The year 1996 marked both the 1100th anniversary of the founding of the Hungarian state and the centenary of the Millenary Celebrations – Budapest's golden age. Vienna and Budapest had agreed to jointly host a World Fair in that year, so considerable plans had been made. As the date drew nearer, however, it turned out that Hungary's dire economic situation and huge national debt precluded the success of an undertaking of this scope. Nevertheless, the "Mille-Centenary" was observed, even if the scale of the celebrations was nowhere near what it had been a hundred years earlier. Nor did the capital expand on the scale it had a hundred years earlier. And yet, not for half a century had a government spent as much on its museums as in 1996. There was also a new bridge, the Lágymányosi, a new university complex on the site of the planned Expo, an expansion of Hungary's international airport, and the start to the construction of a new metro line, all to prove that Budapest has never lost its sense of being a city of the world. Perhaps it is symbolic for Budapest that Hungary's first Internet Café was opened in the Múcsarnok Palace of Exhibitions on Heroes' Square: the café as the traditional venue of public encounter and the transmission of ideas, linked through the technology of the end of the millennium with universal mankind.

137. Budapest by night, seen from Gellért Hill

The Chief Magistrates, Mayors, Prefects, Lord Mayors and City Council Chairmen of Buda, Pest and Budapest

The Chief Magistrates of Buda, 1707–1871

1707–1711 J. Zaunackh, merchant
1711–1719 F. Sautermeister von Sautersheimb, merchant
1719–1722 R. K. Kepeller, town official
1722–1724 F. Ch. K. Vánosy, town syndic and prothonotary
1724–1730 R. K. Kepeller
1730–1737 X. F. Depré, deputy town chamberlain
1737–1738 B. Bobner, deputy town chamberlain
1738–1739 A. Christen, surgeon
1739–1741 (deputy chief magistrate to A. Christen, at this time under house arrest:) A. J. Cetto
1741–1751 A. J. Cetto, merchant
1751–1754 F. T. Neuhauser, town official
1754–1755 J. Perger, deputy chief magistrate
1755–1765 J. Klinglmayer, town official
1765–1769 Á. Balásy, town official
1769–1770 F. Szlatinyi, deputy chief magistrate
1770–1782 F. Szlatinyi, counsellor of the County of Pest
1782–1788 J. Pavianovics, town official
1788–1789 F. Szlatinyi
1789–1790 J. Margalics, chief constable for the County of Pest
1790–1792 I. Kramerlauff (Kalmárffy), town official
1792–1795 F. Laszlovszky, town official
1795–1797 F. Balásy, town official
1797–1825 I. Kalmárffy
1825–1826 I. Perger, deputy chief magistrate
1826–1827 M. Mayer, deputy chief magistrate
1827–1828 F. Gammel, deputy chief magistrate
1828–1837 Ch. Szeth, town official
1837–1848 F. Schreiber, town official
1848–1862 K. Bajcsy
1862–1867 V. Greiffenegg
1867–1871 A. Áldássy

The Mayors of Buda, 1687–1873

1687–1688 W. A. L. Prenner von Ebenhoffen, captain general
1688 N. Küchl and H. Leink, deputy mayor
1688–1692 P. Salgáry von Salgár, postmaster
1692–1695 J. G. Ungar (Unger), merchant
1695–1698 F. I. Bösinger, apothecary
1698–1701 F. Sautermeister von Sautersheimb, merchant
1701–1702 F. I. Bösinger
1702 F. Sautermeister
1703–1705 F. I. Bösinger
1705–1710 F. Sautermeister
1710–1712 J. Ch. Baitz

1712–1723 J. Zaunack, merchant
1723–1727 F. Sautermeister
1727–1730 F. Ch. K. Vánosy, town syndic
1730–1737 J. S. Dillmann
1737–1739 J. B. Perger
1739–1741 L. Schultz, deputy mayor
1741–1751 J. E. Sautermeister von Sautersheimb, merchant
1751–1754 A. J. Cetto, merchant
1755–1768 J. E. Sautermeister
1768–1786 J. Klinglmayer, town official
1786–1787 J. Pavianovics, deputy mayor
1787–1789 F. Szlatinyi
1789–1795 J. Margalics
1795–1800 J. Laszlovszky
1800–1828 F. Balásy
1828–1848 F. Oeffner
1848–1849 J. Walheim
1849 E. Feley
1849–1854 J. Walheim
1854–1856 L. Pletka
1856–1859 F. Kalina
1859–1861 L. Paulovics
1861 E. Feley
1861–1867 L. Paulovics
1867–1873 F. Házmán

The Chief Magistrates of Pest, 1687–1871

1687 J. J. Watula, customs office superintendent
1688 1. Petschmann, deputy chief magistrate, captain
2. J. V. Knipper, lieutenant
3. J. Ch. Karpfenstein, military officer
1689–1692 J. H. S. Herold von Blumenfels, apothecary
1692 Ph. Eschenbrucker, inn-keeper
1693 J. Proberger, beer-brewer
1694 S. Herold
1695–1697 J. Proberger
1697 1. Ph. Eschenbrucker
2. S. Herold
1698–1701 J. Proberger
1701 S. Herold
1702–1709 J. Proberger
1709–1715 S. Eyserich von Eisenthal, iron merchant
1715–1719 J. Lenner von Lennersberg, carpenter
1719–1723 F. J. Sautermeister, merchant
1723–1725 B. J. Neander, director of war provisions
1725–1727 S. Eyserich
1727–1731 F. J. Sautermeister
1731–1741 K. A. Partl
1741–1749 T. Kerschbaumer
1749–1751 K. A. Partl
1751–1759 J. Mosel
1759–1762 T. Kerschbaumer
1762–1769 J. Mosel
1769–1771 G. Josephy
1771–1773 J. Mosel
1773–1777 G. Josephy
1777–1783 J. Papich
1783–1785 T. Lehner

1785–1787 (M. Kregár, de facto:) M.V. Hülff, deputy chief
magistrate
1787–1790 M. V. Hülff, major
1790–1807 J. Boráros, barrister
1807–1819 F. Szlatinyi
1819–1825 F. Steinbach
1825–1826 (folowing the resignation of F. Steinbach:)
J. Veidinger, formerly deputy chief magistrate
1826–1836 A. Makk
1836–1838 J. Eichholcz (changed to Tölgyessy in 1839)
1838–1843 J. Havas
1843–1845 Gy. Tretter (changed to Járy in 1843)
1845–1848 (following the resignation of Gy. Járy, formerly
Tretter, in 1845:) M. Szász, until the elections
deputy chief magistrate
1848   F. Gräffl
1849–1861 E. Szekrényessy
1861   1. F. Gräffl
           2. F. Horváth
           3. E. Makovecz
1862–1865 K. Tölgyessy
1865–1867 P. Thanhoffer
1867–1871 M. Agorasztó

The Mayors of Pest, 1773–1873

1773–1783 J. Mosel
1783–1785 J. Papich
1785–1787 M.V. Hülff, major
1787–1803 M. Kregár
1803–1807 (following the death of M. Kregár:) J. Boráros,
formerly deputy mayor
1807–1813 J. J. Kögl, military judge
1813–1819 J. Veidinger
1819–1827 B. Fellner
1827–1829 (following the death of B. Fellner:) J. Boráros,
formerly deputy mayor
1829–1838 K. Seeber (Széber)
1838–1843 J. Eichholcz (Tölgyessy)
1843–1848 F. Szepessy
1848   L. Rottenbiller
1849   1. K. Lechner
           2. L. Rottenbiller
           3. F. Koller
1850   1. S. Ságody, deputy mayor
           2. Sz. Terczy
1851   Gy. Friedrich
1852   J. Appiano, deputy mayor
1852–1856 J. Krászonyi, deputy mayor
1856–1860 G. Conrad
1860–1861 1. S. Ságody, deputy mayor
           2. A. Kerékjártó, deputy mayor
           3. L. Rottenbiller
1861–1864 J. Krászonyi
1864–1867 L. Rottenbiller
1867–1868 M. Szentkirályi
1868–1873 (folluwing the resignation of M. Szentkirályi:)
A. Gyöngyösi (Gamperl), formerly deputy
mayor

The Prefects of Budapest, 1873–1945

1873–1897 K. Ráth
1897–1906 J. Márkus
1906–1912 K. Fülepp
1912–1913 F. Heltai
1913–1918 I. Bárczy (pro tem until 1918)
1925–1932 F. Ripka
1932–1934 A. Huszár
1934   F. Borvendég
1934–1937 J. Sipőcz
1937–1942 J. Karafiáth
1942–1944 T. Homonnay
1944   Keledi Tibor
1944–1945 Gy. Mohai

The Mayors of Budapest, 1873–1950

1873–1896 K. Kamermayer
1896–1897 J. Márkus
1897–1906 J. Halmos
1906–1918 I. Bárczy
1918–1920 T. Bódy
1920–1934 J. Sipőcz
1934–1944 K. Szendy
1944–1945 Á. Farkas
1945   1. J. Csorba
           2. Z. Vas
1945–1947 J. Kővágó
1947–1949 J. Bognár
1949–1950 K. Pongrácz

The Chairmen of the Executive Committee of the Budapest City Council (City Council Chairmen), 1950–1990

1950–1958 K. Pongrácz
1958–1963 J. Veres
1963–1970 I. Sarlós
1970–1971 L. Kelemen, pro tem
1971–1986 Z. Szépvölgyi
1987–1988 P. Iványi
1989–1990 J. Bielek

The Lord Mayor of Budapest since 1990

1990–   G. Demszky

LIST OF ILLUSTRATIONS

128

59. The first Races in Pest. By Johann Prestel and Alexander Clarot, 1827. The History Gallery of the Hungarian National Museum
60. Equestrian painting of Count István Széchenyi. Watercolour by Károly Sterio and Manó Andrássy, 1857. The Hungarian Academy of Sciences
61. *The Town Hall Market on the Dreadful Day of March 15, 1838 in Pest.* Colour aquatint by Domokos Perlaszka and Carl Schwindt. The Municipal Gallery of the Budapest History Museum
62. *Herbaté* [Herb Tea] in a *salon* in Pest. Lithograph, 1845. Ignác Nagy, *Magyar titkok* [Hungarian Secrets], Book VII. Pest: 1845. The National Széchényi Library
63. A room in the István Főherceg (Archduke Stephen) Hotel. Watercolour by Iván Forray, around 1840. The Budapest History Museum
64. *Hotel Angol királynő* (The English Queen). Watercolour by Rudolf Alt, around 1848. The Budapest History Museum
65. *Wind storm in Váci Street.* Engraving by Domokos Perlaszka, 1844. An 1844 supplement to the weekly magazine *Életképek* [Genre Pictures]. The Ervin Szabó Library of Budapest
66. *The foundation stone of the Chain Bridge.* By Miklós Barabás, 1859. The History Gallery of the Hungarian National Museum
67. A Danube merchant. Iron table ornament made in the Ganz Foundry. 1860s. Property of the author
68. The Pest railway station, a target, 1854. The Budapest History Museum
69. A Biedermeier composition. The glass box showing buildings and scenes in Pest, around 1850; a drinking glass and a cup and saucer show cityscapes of Pest; 6 tarot cards from the 1830s. The Budapest History Museum
70. The Weber family in 1848. Oil painting by Henrik Weber. The Municipal Gallery of the Budapest History Museum
71. Model for the monument to King Matthias I by István Ferenczy. Daguerreotype, 1846. The Hungarian National Gallery
72. Lipót Rottenbiller. Daguerreotype from around 1850. The Budapest History Museum
73. The Pilvax Café in 1848. Coloured pen and ink drawing by József Preiszer. The Budapest History Museum
74. A trade sign showing Alexander Ypsilantis. Around 1840. The Municipal Gallery of the Budapest History Museum
75. The capture of Buda Castle on May 21, 1849. Colour lithograph by Károly Klette. The Budapest History Museum
76. Inauguration ceremony of the Dohány Street Synagogue. By Alajos Fuchstaller, 1859. The History Gallery of the Hungarian National Museum
77. Young ladies after the ball. Oil painting by József Borsos, 1850. The Hungarian National Gallery
78. A bird's-eye view of Pest-Buda. By Rudolf Alt, 1857. The Budapest History Museum
79. Public festival in Vérmező Park on June 8, 1867. By János Jankó. The History Gallery of the Hungarian National Museum
80. "Just married". Cartoon. In: *Borsszem Jankó*, November 24, 1872. The Museum of Hungarian Literature
81. The last meeting of the Budapest city council in the Old Town Hall on February 8, 1900. Photograph. The Budapest History Museum
82. Plan for a navigable channel in Pest, by Ferenc Reitter, 1860s. The Budapest History Museum
83. Count Gyula Andrássy. Oil painting by Gyula Benczúr, 1880s. The Municipal Gallery of the Budapest History Museum
84. Baron Frigyes Podmaniczky. Photograph, around 1905
85. "Sacred order, may your kingdom come, in Pest too". Cartoon by János Jankó. In: *Borsszem Jankó*, July 20, 1873
86. Andrássy Boulevard, with the Opera House in the foreground and cafés around it. Photograph by Mór Erdélyi, around 1900. The Budapest History Museum
87. The writer Mór Jókai in his study in Bajza Street. Photograph by Mór Erdélyi, 1892. The Museum of Hungarian Literature
88. A drawing-room in the Erdődy-Hatvany house at 7 Táncics Mihály Street in the Castle District. Photograph, around 1900. The Budapest History Museum
89. A 400-korona share certificate issued in 1895 for the construction of the Vígszínház Theatre. The National Széchényi Library
90. The Large Ring with New York House. Photograph by Mór Erdélyi, 1896. The Hungarian National Museum
91. Interior of the Gerbeaud Café
92. The "Table of Scholars" in the Café Centrál. Photograph. The Hungarian National Museum
93. Scene in a Budapest café. Cartoon by János Jankó. In: *Borsszem Jankó*, July 20, 1890
94. The interior of the Opera, by Miklós Ybl and Róbert Scholtz, 1880s. The Budapest History Museum
95. Caricatures of some typical Pest figures from the 1860s and 1870s.
96. Ráthonyi and the Merry Widows. Colour postcard on the occasion of the Budapest première of Ferenc Lehár's operetta *The Merry Widow* in Király Theater, 1907. The National Museum for Theater History
97. Jacques Offenbach in Pest in 1861. Photograph. The National Széchényi Library
98. The historic Millenary procession at Margaret Bridge. Photograph, 1896. Photograph Collection of the Hungarian National Museum
99. The Millenary Exhibition Complex, by Artúr Heyer, 1896. The Municipal Gallery of the Budapest History Museum
100. The Museum of Applied Art, designed by Ödön Lechner. Watercolour by J. Bischof, around 1900. The Museum of Applied Art
101. The "Millenary" Underground Railway, seen in a cross section underneath Andrássy Boulevard. After a watercolour by Brüggemann. The Municipal Gallery of the Budapest History Museum
102. Procession passing through the Large Ring for the funeral of Lajos Kossuth. Photograph by György Klösz, 1894. Photograph Collection of the Hungarian National Museum
103. The Austrian-Hungarian Bank. Watercolour by Ignác Alpár, around 1900. The Budapest History Museum
104. The National Flag Monument on Szabadság Square. Photograph by Ernő Vadas, 1930s. The Budapest History Museum
105. Béla Bartók as a young man. Portrait by Róbert Berény, 1913. The Bartók Archives, Budapest
106. The workshop hall at the Láng Machine Works. By György Klösz, around 1900. The Budapest History Museum
107. Foreign delegates at the 7th World Congress for Women's Suffrage, 1913. Photograph. The Ervin Szabó Library of Budapest
108. The Freemasons' Symbolic Grand Lodge "Hungary", a townhouse in Podmaniczky Street. Photograph by Mór Erdélyi, around 1900. The Budapest History Museum
109. The Jewish market in Újvásár (New Market) Square. Photograph, around 1900. The Budapest History Museum
110. The interior of the Central Market Hall. Photograph, 1897. The Budapest History Museum
111. The Wekerle housing project, designed by Károly Kós and his colleagues, 1909-1912. The Budapest History Museum
112. Sándor Bródy. Photograph by Mór Erdélyi, around 1900. The Museum of Hungarian Literature
113. Ferenc Molnár and Jenő Heltai. Photograph, around 1910. The Museum of Hungarian Literature
114. Endre Ady in 1908. Photograph by Aladár Székely. The Hungarian National Museum
115. Dezső Kosztolányi. Photograph, around 1930. The Budapest History Museum
116. *The Opium Smoker's Dream.* Oil painting by Lajos Gulácsy, 1913-1918. Janus Pannonius Museum, Pécs
117. The inauguration of the National Benefaction Statue. 1915. The Museum of Military History
118. The last coronation of a Hungarian king. Coloured tempera on photograph, 1916. The Budapest History Museum
119. Festive decoration in front of the Western Railway Station for the Mayday celebration. Photograph, 1919. The Budapest History Museum
120. The Pest reporter. Apollo projectograph. Poster, 1912. The Budapest History Museum
121. *Börzekirály* [King of the Stock Exchange]. Prosa Films, Royal Apollo cinema. Poster by Imre Földes, 1915. The Budapest History Museum

On the cover:
Bird's eye view of Pest. Lithograph by Rudolf Alt, 1857

On the front and back frontispiece:
Pest and Buda in 1617. Colour engraving by Georg Hoefnagel

Half title page:
Óbuda's medieval seal. The Budapest History Museum
Buda's coat-of-arms in 1703. The Municipal Archives of Budapest
Pest's coat-of-arms in 1703. The Municipal Archives of Budapest
The coat-of-arms of unified Budapest, 1873. The Municipal Archives of Budapest

Title page:
A bird's-eye view of Budapest. Photograph by Béla Tóth

On page 80:
CITY OFFICIALS OF PEST
Johann Lenner von Lennersberg (oil painting by unknown painter), chief magistrate, 1715-1719. The Municipal Gallery of the Budapest History Museum
János Boráros (painting by János Donát), chief magistrate, 1790-1807. The Municipal Gallery of the Budapest History Museum
István Szilágyi (oil painter by unknown painter), button maker, member of the citizen body, 1826. The Municipal Gallery of the Budapest History Museum
Jakab Pisztory (painting by József Pesky, 1834), magistrate, 1834-1843. The Municipal Gallery of the Budapest History Museum
István Staffenberg (painting by Ignác Berger), spokesman, 1838. The Municipal Gallery of the Budapest History Museum
Mihály Farkas (painting by Miklós Barabás, 1851), head master of the carpenters' guild

CITY OFFICIALS OF BUDA
Ignác Kramerlauff (Kalmárffy) (oil painting by unknown painter), chief magistrate, 1790-1792, 1797-1825. The Municipal Gallery of the Budapest History Museum

Ferenc Balássy (oil painting by unknown painter), chief magistrate, 1795-1797, mayor 1800-1828
Ferenc Házmán (oil painting by unknown painter), mayor, 1867-1873

On page 81:
CITY LEADERS OF BUDAPEST
Károly Ráth, prefect, 1873-1897, oil painting by Mihály Kovács. The Municipal Gallery of the Budapest History Museum
Károly Kamermayer, mayor, 1873-1896. Oil painting by Alajos Györgyi Giergl. The Municipal Gallery of the Budapest History Museum
Károly Gerlóczy, deputy mayor, 1873-1897. Oil painting by Gyula Stetka. The Municipal Gallery of the Budapest History Museum
István Bárczy, mayor, 1906-1918, prefect, 1913-1919. Oil painting by Bertalan Karlovszky. The Municipal Gallery of the Budapest History Museum
Ferenc Heltai, prefect, 1912-1913. Oil painting by Pál Jávor. The Municipal Gallery of the Budapest History Museum
Tivadar Bódy, mayor, 1918-1920. Oil painting by Ede Balló. The Municipal Gallery of the Budapest History Museum
János Buzáth, deputy mayor, 1920-1930. Oil painting by Géza Kukán. The Municipal Gallery of the Budapest History Museum
Jenő Sipőtz, mayor, 1920-1934, prefect, 1934-1937. Oil painting by Bertalan Karlovszky. The Municipal Gallery of the Budapest History Museum
Ferenc Ripka, prefect, 1925-1932. Oil painting by Oszkár Glatz. The Municipal Gallery of the Budapest History Museum
Endre Liber, deputy mayor, 1930-1934. Oil painting by Ferenc Csont. The Municipal Gallery of the Budapest History Museum
Károly Szendy, deputy mayor, 1934, mayor, 1934-1944. Oil painting by Oszkár Glatz. The Municipal Gallery of the Budapest History Museum

ACKNOWLEDGEMENTS

Atelier Müller – László Müller: 135;
Gál, Csaba: 27, 28, 29, 45, 53, 67, 80, 85, 91, 93, 95;
Hász, András: 2;
Janus Pannonius Museum, Pécs – Zoltán Kőhegyi: 116;
Kaiser, Ottó: 137;
MTI – Sándor Kovács: 134;
The Bartók Archives, Budapest: 105;
The Budapest History Museum – Ágnes Bakos, Bence Tihanyi: half title page, 4, 8, 10, 11, 12, 14, 18, 19, 20, 21, 23, 24, 30, 32, 33, 34, 37, 38, 40, 41, 42, 43, 44, 46, 47, 48, 49, 52, 54, 56, 58, 61, 63, 64, 68, 69, 70, 72, 73, 74, 75, ps. 80-81, 78, 82, 83, 84, 86, 88, 94, 99, 101, 103, 104, 106, 108, 109, 110, 111, 115, 119, 120, 121, 122, 123, 125, 126, 127, 128, 132, 133;
The Ervin Szabó Library of Budapest – Olga Fábián: 39, 55, 57, 65, 107;
The Hungarian Academy of Sciences – Béla Gáspár Würt: 60;
The Hungarian National Gallery – Zsuzsa Bokor, Levente Szepsy Szücs: 26, 71, 77;
The Hungarian National Museum, History Gallery – Bence Képessy: front and back frontispiece, 22, 25, 31, 50, 51, 59, 66, 76, 79;
The Hungarian National Museum, Photography Collection – Árpád Farkas, László Jaksity: 90, 92, 98, 102, 114, 118, 124, 131;
The Hungarian National Museum, Poster Collection – László Jaksity: 130;
The Museum of Applied Art – Ágnes Kolozs: 100;
The Museum of Aquincum, The Budapest History Museum – Péter Komjáthy: 5, 6;
The Museum of Hungarian Literature – Csaba Gál: 87, 112, 113;
The Museum of Military History – Árpád Farkas: 117;
The National Museum for Theatre History – Tamás Katkó: 96, 97;
The National Széchényi Library: 9, 16, 62, 89;
The University Library Budapest – Csaba Gál: 17;
Tóth, Béla: title page, 7, 136;

Published in Hungary by
Corvina Books Ltd.
Budapest V. Vörösmarty tér 1.

ISBN 963 13 4474 6

Printed in Hungary

A.

B.

PEST.

Danubius fluu

A. Propugnaculum nouum. B. Arx et Palatium Regium. C. Templum
F. Genus Hominum apud Turcas Barbarum, ac temerarium, ad omn
plumis in ipsa capitis carne insertis quo truculentiores appareant. a
Communicauit Georgius H.